WINDMILL POINT

WINDMILL POINT

AN EPIC NOVEL OF THE CIVIL WAR

BY

JIM STEMPEL

WINDMILL POINT by Jim Stempel
Copyright © 2016 James Stempel

All rights reserved. No part of this book may be used or reproduced by any means without the written permission of the publisher except in the case of brief quotation embodied in critical articles and reviews.

ISBN-13: 978-1-942756-50-7(Paperback)
ISBN :-978-1-942756-51-4 (e-book)

BISAC Subject Headings:
HIS036050 HISTORY / United States/Civil War Period
BIO008000 BIOGRAPHY / MILITARY
FIC032000FICTION / War & Military

Cover Illustration by Christine Horner

Address all correspondence to:

Penmore Press LLC
920 N Javelina Pl
Tucson AZ 85748

CONTENTS

Forward
1. May 31st, Late Afternoon ... White
2. June 2nd, Early Morning ... Lee
3. June 2nd, Late Morning ... Grant
4. June 2nd, Afternoon ... Alexander
5. June 2nd, Evening ... Grant
6. June 2nd, Late Evening ... White
7. June 3rd, Early Morning ... White
8. June 3rd, First Light ... Alexander
9. June 3rd, Dawn ... White
10. June 3rd, Morning ... Lee
11. June 3rd, Morning ... Grant
12. June 3rd, Late Morning ... Alexander
13. June 3rd, Forenoon ... Grant
14. June 3rd, Afternoon ... White
15. June 3rd, Late Afternoon ... Lee
16. June 3rd, Evening ... Grant
17. June 3rd, Late Night ... White
18. June 4th, Dawn ... Alexander
19. June 4th, Midday ... Lee
20. June 5th, Midday ... White
21. June 5th, Late Afternoon ... Grant
22. June 6th, Morning ... Grant
23. June 6th, Forenoon ... White
24. June 6th, Afternoon ... Lee
25. June 6th, Late Afternoon ... Grant
26. June 6th, Evening ... Custer
27. June 7th, Morning ... Lee
28. June 7th, Forenoon ... Custer
29. June 7th, Early Afternoon ... Alexander
30. June 7th, Late Afternoon ... Grant
31. June 7th, Evening ... White
32. June 7th, Late Evening ... Lee

33. June 8th, Early Morning ... Hampton
34. June 8th, Early Evening ... White
35. June 9th, Late Evening ... Lee
36. June 10th, Evening ... Hampton
37. June 10th, Late Evening ... Custer
38. June 11th, First Light ... Hampton
39. June 11th, Dawn ... Custer
40. June 11th, Early Morning ... Hampton
41. June 11th, Mid Morning ... Custer
42. June 11th, Noon ... Custer
43. June 11th, Afternoon ... Hampton
44. June 11th, Evening ... Custer
45. June 11th, Late Evening ... Alexander
46. June 12th, First Light ... Grant
47. June 12th, Early Morning ... Custer
48. June 12th Mid Morning ... Lee
49. June 12th, Noon ... Grant
50. June 12th, Mid Afternoon ... Custer
51. June 12th, Early Evening ... Hampton
52. June 12th, Evening ... Grant
53. June 12th, Late Evening ... Custer
54. June 12th, Midnight ... White
55. June 13th, Dawn ... Alexander
56. June 13th, Early Morning ... Lee
57. June 13th, Afternoon ... Alexander
58. June 13th, Evening ... Lee
59. June 14th, Noon ... Hampton
60. June 14th, Afternoon ... Lee
61. June 14th, Evening ... White
62. June 15th, Morning ... Alexander
63. June 15th, Afternoon ... Grant
64. June 15th, Evening ... Alexander
65. Three Days Later, First Light ... Lee
Epilogue
Afterword

STATEMENTS

"We must destroy this army of Grant's before he gets to the James River. If he gets there it will become a siege, and then it will be a mere question of time."
—Robert E. Lee

"Grant's whole character was a mystery even to himself. He exhibited a combination of strength and weakness not paralleled by any of whom I have read in ancient or modern history."
—William T. Sherman

FORWARD

It is late May, 1864, and the American Civil War is now concluding the bloodiest month of its long and bloody history. In the east, the Army of the Potomac, the Federal government's principal weapon, has been slugging it out overland against Robert E. Lee's Army of Northern Virginia. Three substantial battles have been fought, and while the casualty lists have been ghastly, no significant strategic advantage has been gained or lost by either side.

Since the battle at Gettysburg, George Gordon Meade has been the commander of the Army of the Potomac; but in the early spring Ulysses S. Grant is appointed lieutenant general and given command of all United States forces. Grant immediately moves east and establishes his headquarters with the Army of the Potomac. His orders to George Meade are simply to follow, fight, and ultimately destroy Lee's army, but that has proved a task far easier said than done.

While Meade is still technically in command, increasingly Grant sets both the tone and direction for the Potomac army. This leads to an uncertain command structure in which neither man's role is clearly defined. Over time, Meade comes more often to simply follow Grant's initial directives, rather than following up on them; thus the complex details and directions, so necessary for an army's proper deployment, become unwittingly lost in the shuffle: a prescription for eventual disaster.

After each stalemated encounter, Grant—rather than disengaging and backing off, as has been the case with previous

Northern commanders—maneuvers his army south and east, always trying to turn Lee's right flank and beat his adversary on the road to the Confederate capital of Richmond. Lee, a master of defense, responds quickly to each of these new threats, and frustrates Grant at every turn. So the tense, bloody face-off continues.

Because Lee has never once relinquished the field to Grant, many Southern observers interpret the month's fighting as a string of decided Confederate victories. But Lee knows these "victories" are pyrrhic at best. In the last few weeks alone, Lee has lost sixteen of his best generals. His army is rapidly being bled to death, the losses to his officer corps and manpower virtually irreplaceable, while he knows Grant can call upon a seeming endless supply of men, matériel, and financial resources to employ against him. If the war continues in this pattern, the South may soon "win" itself into defeat. So as Grant maneuvers against Lee's forces, Lee is constantly on the lookout for a blunder on Grant's part that might provide an opportunity to strike his adversary a damaging or even lethal blow. He knows he cannot allow Grant to continually move south and eventually gain the James River. If that occurs, the war will devolve into nothing more than a siege of Richmond, and, given the immense material imbalance between the two adversaries, Lee knows a siege is something he can never hope to win.

But Lee is also aware of the fact that most of the Northern press have recently turned on Grant, appalled by his bludgeoning tactics and the bloody toll his campaign has exacted. The roads and hospitals leading north are overwhelmed with the dead, wounded, and dying, with no end to the conflict in sight. If Lee can just hold on, he knows the North may soon lose its stomach for the fight, and sue for peace.

In late May, Grant again sidles south and east, bypassing Lee's formidable position along the North Anna River. The Army of the Potomac crosses the Pamunkey River on quickly erected pontoon bridges and begins marching south. On his map of the region, Grant has spotted an inconsequential crossroads due east of Richmond where several roads come together—and one leads directly into the Confederate capital. Control of that crossroads is essential, and the name of that junction is Cold Harbor.

Events accelerate. Lee sends his cavalry to defend the Cold Harbor crossroads, and Grant responds with cavalry of his own. Under the command of Phil Sheridan, the Federal horsemen force the Rebels back, and Lee counterattacks with infantry. The Federal riders, sporting new seven-shot repeating Spencer rifles, hold onto the crossroads in a deadly confrontation as Federal infantry race to their support. The Confederate forces fall back just west of the junction and begin digging in. Federal infantry arrive and attack, but the Rebel works are solid and ably defended, and the Union troops are violently repulsed.

Grant firmly believes that Lee's army is weak and will break if pushed hard one more time. Lee, confident of his defensive position, hopes that with one more bloody defeat, the North will finally have had enough of war and call its troops home. Both armies concentrate on Cold Harbor, each side hopeful that the next, climactic battle may finally resolve the war in their favor.

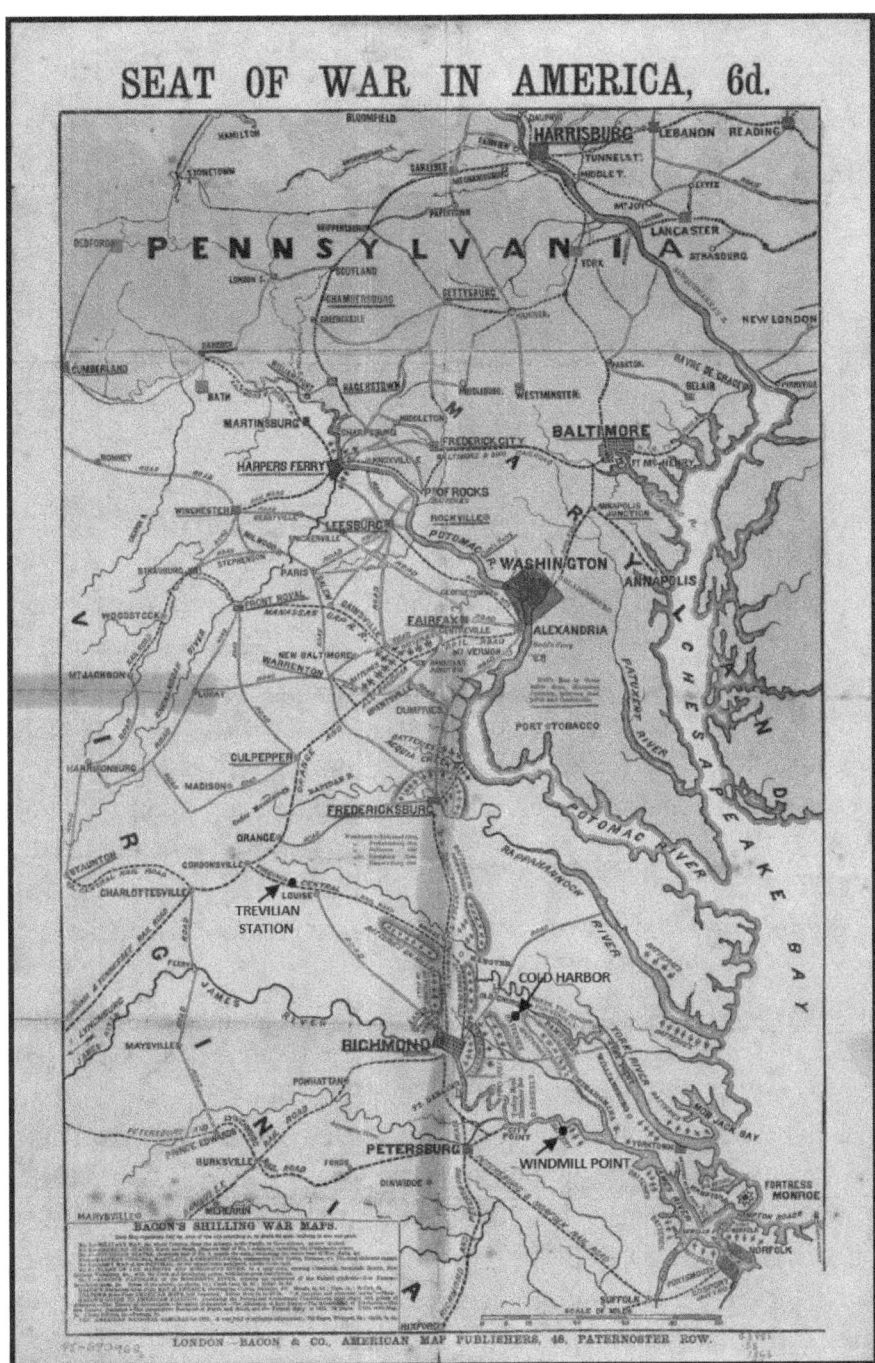

CHAPTER ONE

MAY 31ST—LATE AFTERNOON

WHITE

White waited patiently for the Rebel sharpshooter to reappear, one eye glued to his telescopic sight as the barrel of the rifle rested on a low branch. He, Sandborn, and Brown had all gone out well ahead of the picket line that afternoon, pushing back the Confederate skirmishers along the front as they did. The three of them moved slowly from tree to rock to bush in that deadly game of cat and mouse that often went on between the infantry lines. Earlier that day, their regiment had gone in hard against the Rebel position, and after a fierce and bloody time of it, the Confederates had finally backed off. That accomplished, he and the other sharpshooters had been deployed far ahead of the main line.

Wyman White took a deep breath, let it out slowly, and waited; he had his adversary's position fixed in his sight. He had seen the Reb fire before from just that location, and he was guessing that the Johnny would not move between shots. There was a sudden blur of movement, compact and professional; the Rebel popped up above the fallen tree trunk for just a moment, rifle in hand. Before the Reb could get off a single shot, Wyman squared the target and squeezed the trigger; almost half a mile away, the Rebel sharpshooter toppled backward from view, a bullet through his shoulder.

"Get 'im, Sarge?" Sandborn asked in a whisper.

"He's gone," Wyman answered softly, carefully positioning the rifle across his leg in order to reload.

"Whew! Hell, that's well on a half mile for sure," Sandborn observed, squinting through a few low branches, obviously impressed by the shot.

"That's nothing," Wyman replied, lovingly tapping the long barrel of the enormous gun. "I've gotten some very satisfactory shots in at close to a mile. *Those* Rebs never knew what hit 'em."

"Well, that one in particular was playing hell with us," Sandborn said. "Glad you got him, Sarge."

White shook his head slowly, letting out another long breath. "*He*'s gone, but there are plenty others out there, some a lot closer to us. You got to be careful, Sandborn. Be patient. Don't give 'em an edge. Not for a second."

"I *am* patient, Sarge. I'm as good a shot as anyone in the regiment."

"Lot of fellas can shoot," White replied. "You wouldn't be with us if you couldn't shoot, but it ain't just the shooting. It's being careful... patient, you might say. Now, move over that way some," Wyman said, pointing off to their left. "See what moves out there after I squeeze off another round. Maybe you can get the drop on one of 'em in close."

Sandborn moved away, sliding slowly between the bushes.

Wyman White was a twenty-three-year-old sergeant in the 2nd United States Sharpshooters, one of the most deadly and feared units in the Army of the Potomac. His grandfather had fought in the War for Independence, and his family could trace its roots all the way back to William White, who had stepped off the deck of the *Mayflower*. A Republican and a supporter of Abraham Lincoln, Wyman had enlisted to preserve the country that his ancestors had established and loved. He was a Union man all the way.

WINDMILL POINT

The U.S. Sharpshooters were the idea of General Hiram Berdan, a New Yorker who had raised two regiments in the fall of 1861. Wyman had been mustered into the 2nd regiment in November of that year. Clothed in distinctive forest-green uniforms with leather gaiters below the knee, the U.S. Sharpshooters were a hand-picked lot of only the biggest and burliest New Englanders. To join you had to pass a strict test of sharpshooting, putting ten shots into a ten-inch circle at a distance of two hundred yards, and there wasn't a man among them who was not considered a master with firearms. Armed with breech-loading Sharps rifles, the Sharpshooters generally fought in small groups of four or five, far out ahead of the army's main line, moving and covering one another while making use of all the natural cover and terrain. So rapid and accurate was their fire that the Rebels often confused a single regiment of Sharpshooters for an entire brigade of infantry.

Wyman reloaded the rifle, carefully dumping a good four inches of black powder down the barrel, followed by a tight flannel wad. It was an enormous gun, a thirty-pound telescopic cannon that could hurl a one-ounce lead bullet nearly a mile with precision. Only the cream of the sharpshooters were allowed to carry it, and while it was certainly an honor, the heavy, unwieldy weapon was also a burden to carry. And especially to reload. Once he had the wad firmly positioned, he wedged the bullet into the rifle's grooves by use of a false muzzle, and applied another percussion cap. With the gun loaded, he slowly crawled to a few feet from where he had last shot, and patiently waited for the next Rebel to reveal his location.

Now at war for almost three full years, Wyman White had seen action in almost every major battle in the East since Second Bull Run. On the second day at Gettysburg, the Sharpshooters had fought out in advance of the Federal line all morning, only to then be pushed back by the Rebel assaults to a knobby, rocky hill called Little Round Top. There, Wyman and many of the men had taken up positions behind the rocks on the western face of the hill and held off the Rebels all afternoon. The following day the Sharpshooters were moved to a position near the center of the Union line. In that location they endured a monstrous cannonade, and then took part in the repulse of what would later be known as Pickett's Charge. Over the month of May they had seen grim action at the Wilderness, Spotsylvania Court House, and again along the North Anna River. It had been a terrible month of marching and fighting like no other in memory, and the proud unit of sharpshooters had been slowly whittled down to but a precious few.

Wyman centered the scope on an area he considered to be most likely to harbor an enemy sharpshooter and let the air out slowly between his teeth. He thought of nothing, let his mind float, his whole body loose and relaxed, only his finger tense on the trigger. Then he heard the crack of a rifle and the sudden, dreadful thud of a ball striking flesh, and he knew without thinking that Sandborn had been hit.

"Sandborn!" Wyman hissed. "Sandborn!"

Wyman listened intently, heard only a thrashing sound, like feet dragging through dry leaves, perhaps twenty feet away. "Sandborn!"

Wyman White pushed his rifle aside and slithered quickly on his hands and knees to the edge of the bushes. "Sandborn!" he called again, but there was no reply. Wyman rolled under the trunk of a fallen tree, then spotted Sandborn's feet flopping near the edge of a small clearing, his upper torso shielded by the thick base of a large oak. Wyman jerked up to a crouch quickly and made a dash, diving the last few feet into the thick growth on the other side of the clearing as bullets hummed through the air and snapped at the dirt behind him.

White slid up next to Sandborn, heart thumping in his shirt. "Where you hit?" he asked, trying to get a look.

WINDMILL POINT

Sandborn rolled over, a bullet hole through his cheek, blood covering the ground and pooling in his hands. "Oohh," he cried, eyes rolling back in his head, blood pouring out from between his fingers. "I'm hit bad, Sarge. Bad! I fear I'm gonna die!"

Wyman studied the wound for a moment, thought it perhaps mortal, but had known men to survive worse. "You're gonna be fine, Sandborn," he insisted. He fished through his pocket, pulled out a handkerchief. "Stuff this here in it until we can get you back to the hospital," he said. "Least it will keep down the bleeding."

Sandborn took the handkerchief and applied it gingerly to the wound. "Oh God," he moaned. "You got to get me out of here, Sarge. Please. Oh God, please."

White frowned, looked around. "Yeah, I know. Where's Brown. You got any idea?"

Sandborn shook his head. Suddenly there was a rustle in the leaves, and Brown called over to them. "Sarge, you okay?"

"Sandborn's been hit," Wyman called back. "We got to get him outta here."

"Ahh, damn," Brown said. "I figured it was something like that. I'll just...."

Then there was another string of pops: bullets ripping through the leaves, snapping branches in half and sending splinters flying every which way. Wyman ducked instinctively, heard a sharp cry. Then he heard Brown topple into the dirt. "Oaahhh!"

"Brown! Brown! You hit too?" Wyman cried out.

"Oh, hell. In the damn knee. Ahhh ... damn!"

"Stay down! What did I tell you?" Wyman spat, as bullets snapped against the tree trunks all around them. "The Rebs are all over us now!"

"Damn, Sarge!" Brown cried. "I'm hurt. God damn, it hurts!"

"Stay down!" Wyman hugged the red Virginia dirt and crawled carefully through the underbrush. Thirty feet away he located Brown, writhing in pain. "Stay close to the ground," he instructed. "Raise your head up and they'll kill you for sure. Both of us probably."

"I can't walk, Sergeant," Brown told him, grimacing in pain. The wound was bleeding fiercely and it was apparent that Brown was quickly losing control.

Wyman pulled his belt from his trousers, and wrapped it around Brown's thigh. "I'm gonna pull this tight and try and stop all that bleeding," he said.

"Don't let me die here, Sarge," Brown implored, almost frantic.

"Try and stay calm," Wyman urged, tugging on the belt strap, yanking it tight. "You need some water?"

"Yeah. Oh yeah, please."

White tightened the belt until the bleeding subsided, then reached for Brown's canteen, yanked out the cork and dabbed some drops into the wounded man's mouth. "Go slow now," he cautioned. "Make it count for something. Don't go wasting it."

"What are we gonna do, Sarge?" Brown asked, his eyes wide with fear. Suddenly three more bullets snapped through the clearing, humming close, disappearing then into the trees behind.

Wyman thought for a moment. "Well," he said finally "I can't get neither of you out of here all by myself. Need help. Look here, if you two stay down you should be alright. The Rebels are just trying to pick us off. They won't be coming any closer."

"Okay, Sarge," Brown replied. "Just please don't leave me to die out here all alone."

"I won't!"

"I'll stay down, Sarge," Brown pledged. "I swear it!"

"Sandborn!" Wyman called. "Can you hear me?"

WINDMILL POINT

"Yes... yes," came the faint reply.

"I'm gonna leave my rifle here and go back for help. Brown's been hit too. Both of you need to keep yourselves down, for God's sake, and wait on me. You understand?"

"Yeah, Sarge."

Wyman stared at Brown for a moment. "You got plenty of water for now. You'll be fine for the time being. I'll go back to the main line and get some boys to come out with stretchers. Understand me?"

"Yeah," Brown replied, looking pale and fearful.

"Good." White grabbed a hold of Brown's Sharps rifle and looked it over. "This loaded?"

"Course."

He handed Brown the weapon. "Keep an eye out, then. As best you can, that is. Shoot once in awhile just to keep the Rebs honest, then try and roll a few feet away. I doubt any will come this way, but be ready just the same." Then he patted the wounded man on the shoulder, and slid back through the trees on his stomach.

The Rebels did their best to make it very hot and uncomfortable for him. Here and there they caught a glimpse of Wyman as he dashed across a small clearing, or bounded between trees, but thankfully they were always late and off target. He did his best to move in an erratic path, cutting down on the possibility that some smart Confederate might anticipate his route and bring him down with a well-placed shot. Once reasonably out of range, he leaped to his feet and jogged most of the way back to the main picket line. There he was able to gather up some men and stretchers, and they all headed back out into that deadly zone between the two armies.

It took some time to get to both of the wounded men, but Wyman knew it was much safer to go slow than to hurry foolishly. So it took the better part of two hours or more, but finally each was located and slowly pulled to safety without anyone else being hit. From there they were sent back directly to the field hospital, well behind the lines. But field hospitals tended to be grim places, and Wyman had no idea if either of them would live to see the end of the week, much less the end of the war.

That accomplished, White slid back into the woods alone, moving slowly on his stomach from tree-to-bush-to-tree. He followed the natural contours of the ground, slipping along the hidden slope or angle of any rise he could find, and eventually made his way back to the small, bloody clearing where his rifle still rested, just where he'd left it. Wyman White was one of the army's finest sharpshooters, and he was generally left alone to work as he saw fit.

Just as he had anticipated, the Johnnies had not come any closer, but were still infesting the woods hundreds of yards ahead. Wyman took up his rifle, slid a few feet away from the clearing to what he considered a well-concealed and serviceable location. There he rested the gun comfortably on a small grassy mound, watched through the scope, and waited. A few minutes later his patience was rewarded; there was a Confederate moving, off to his right, looking for a better position in a tree. He allowed the Reb to scamper up the branches and settle in amongst the leaves. Then Wyman took him down with a single, perfect shot.

White remained on line all that hot afternoon, doing good service with the enormous thirty-pound rifle, wreaking havoc along the Confederate skirmish line while well out of range of most of the opposing riflemen. As the sun set, the main picket line moved up, and he and the rest of the 2nd U.S. Sharpshooters were ordered to stand picket duty all that long night. The boys were tired, gruff, and hungry. It had been days now since they'd had a chance for a good sleep. Firing throughout the night was sporadic and ineffectual, both sides seemingly tired of the daily marching and fighting, and badly in need of some rest. An odd, exhausted quiet settled over the field. The night passed fitfully.

Dawn came, a red glow through the trees with a low-hanging mist. A few shots were fired at what appeared to be movements off to the west, but nothing came of it—just some tired men doing foolish, tired things. As the sun rose into the trees behind the line, a fresh regiment was sent out to replace them, and the Sharpshooters were finally allowed to move off to the rear.

There they cooked their coffee and enjoyed what few rations they had hidden away in their sacks—the first food they'd had in almost a day. Unfortunately, many of the men had very little to eat, as the army was once again on the move, and as a result the supply train had remained well behind the front lines. The men were all tired and groggy, and while the food initially did them some good, many, like Wyman, were soon consumed by an almost irresistible urge to sleep. The body could take just so much, orders or no. Wyman tossed his haversack onto the ground, rested his head, and in only seconds was sound asleep—but not for long.

Within the hour they were ordered up again and out to the picket line for further duty. The men grumbled a good bit, but soon they had all their gear in tow, and were headed back through the low underbrush and stubby trees. There they joined the existing pickets, and all that day they pushed the Rebels back a good distance, feeling ahead—Wyman assumed—for the whereabouts and strength of the Rebel army. Like two boxers stumbling about in the dark, while on the move both armies had lost contact with one another. In warfare, uncertainty was often a prescription for disaster.

Near sundown, Wyman received word to fall back to the ammunition train and box-up his long-distance rifle. The whole corps had received orders to move out, he was told, and the enormous gun was simply too large to carry on the march. So he would take up his Sharps rifle until the corps arrived at its new destination—wherever that might be—and begin dueling with the enemy sharpshooters again.

The U. S. Sharpshooters were a part of General Hancock's 2nd Corps, now considered the hardest hitting unit in the Army of the Potomac, and they'd all seen more than their fair share of action since General Grant had come east to take command. While a long night's march after days of uninterrupted duty did not sit well with most of them, there was little grumbling, for almost to a man they felt that the war would soon be pressed to a favorable conclusion. Grant had Lee on the run, everyone knew, and one more good push might just end it all.

The march began as darkness descended. No one knew where they were headed. They began pouring down the narrow, tree-lined roads, and it wasn't long before the dust had risen so thickly along the trail that it coated their uniforms and filled their nostrils. It was dry, miserable, suffocating work. The night was moonless, dark as pitch, and more than once the long column stumbled to a halt in the God-forsaken darkness, as units tripped over one another or lost their way in the tangle of confused country lanes that led south. Artillery horses stumbled blindly off the roads and limbers overturned, spilling their riders and ammunition onto the roadway.

Wyman White marched with his usual measured gait, having learned long ago to more or less sleep on his feet and trust his body to somehow get him wherever the regiment was headed. *Odd what the body could do,* he'd often thought. It was not so much sleep really, as a sort of unconscious reverie, a sense of deep and abiding peace that washed over him which made the long night marches at least tolerable. In that he wasn't alone. The whole regiment seemed to move in a mindless trance, and it wasn't until they were suddenly halted that every soldier invariably stumbled headfirst over the man in front of him. Then most of them awoke, and for the first time in hours became aware of their hunger, thirst, and general state of misery. But then the column would lunge forward into the darkness again, and the entire regiment would descend once more into its senseless, dreamlike stupor.

The sun rose round and red along the eastern horizon, and still the column trudged wearily on. It was June 2nd, and it promised to be another miserably hot day. The corps marched, with no stop for rest, water or breakfast. The men struggled, the dust and heat causing many of them to drop out along the way. Some, Wyman knew, would fall off into the trees, never to be heard from again. Still others collapsed and died on the road from simple exhaustion.

Wyman kept moving, his feet seeming to have a mind all their own. By the angle of the sun he could tell they were headed more or less south, but then the regiment struck a new road that led off to the west. Around 9:30 that morning they came to an open area along the road, and there they were directed off to the left. Soon after, they were allowed to fall out in the fields alongside the road. Many collapsed where they stood and immediately fell into a deep, exhausted sleep. Others searched for kindling, lit their fires, and enjoyed what few rations still remained in their haversacks.

Wyman took a long drink from his canteen, and munched thoughtfully on one of the few pieces of hardtack he had left. While he still had a few pieces of ham and bacon he could fry, he was too tired to kindle a fire. He was simply glad to be done with the long, hot march—to be finally resting. Truth was, he was glad to be alive.

Just ahead, musketry rattled the air, and the sound of artillery shook the ground. The war was not far away. In time, word came down the line that Sheridan's cavalry had fought and taken the crossroads ahead two days before, and that two corps of infantry had hit the Rebels hard just yesterday. Not far away Wyman White could see the terrible debris of battle strewn every which way across open fields: haversacks, shoes, rifles, and many corpses. Already the smell of death—stark, rank, and unmistakable—was on the breeze.

Soon, orders came for the men to rest on their arms for the remainder of the day: eat and sleep while they could. Who could say what it meant?

Wyman felt exhausted beyond all measure, and finally, with the opportunity for some real rest, his body relaxed entirely. He searched for a small piece of shade under some nearby scrub, and dropped his haversack. Corporal Joe Thompson joined him, positioning his head in the small scrap of shade that Wyman did not occupy.

"Help yourself, Joe," Wyman told him, settling down upon his sack.

"Thanks, Sarge," Thompson replied, stretching his legs out straight.

Wyman White felt his eyes begin to close then a thought suddenly rose up in his thoughts. He leaned up on one elbow. "Do you have any idea where we have marched to, Joe?" he asked. "Where on God's green earth we are?"

Thompson lifted a weary arm and pointed off to the east. "As I have it, this is the same ground the army fought over two years ago under McClellan," he answered. "That crossroads yonder is named Cold Harbor. Ain't much to look at, Sarge. Ever heard of it?"

"Yes, I have, and no, it ain't," Wyman replied, but he was too weary to consider the situation further. White rested his head back on his haversack, closed his eyes, and in seconds—as artillery thundered in the distance and the long column of blue soldiers poured from the woods behind him—was sound asleep.

CHAPTER TWO

JUNE 2ND—EARLY MORNING

LEE

R. E. Lee sat alone in the cool morning mist, sipping coffee from a tin as wisps of fog swirled like dancers above the two large millponds that led through the trees to Powhite Swamp, listening contentedly to the sound of his headquarters in action. He had risen early, intent on riding north to Mechanicsville, but soon realized that today coffee and food first was a necessity. Robert E. Lee had been out of the saddle for over ten days now, sick with an intestinal problem to the point that he could scarcely command his army. Fortunately, his loyal and efficient adjutant general, Walter Taylor, had been able to operate around his commander's illness and keep the Army of Northern Virginia moving while uninformed of its commander's condition. The degree of Lee's incapacitation had not leaked very far from his headquarters, and now—if not entirely recovered—he was at least back on his feet.

Yesterday the Army of Northern Virginia had returned to Gaines's Mill where they had fought and won more than two years before. Unfortunately, Doctor Gaines's beautiful home and mill had been torched during Sheridan's recent raid on Richmond, and were now nothing more than smoldering embers across the road, as was, sadly, much of the area east of Richmond these days. Lee wanted to be near the front so that he could better direct the action though still too weak to ride, so they had set up their headquarters' tents on the north side of Cold Harbor Road, not far at all from the hillside where they had smashed McClellan's army back in '62. For Lee, that remained a fond memory. But fond memories, he knew, would do precious little to alter the grim reality that faced him now. Lee was a realist, first and foremost, and the situation that confronted him that morning was far less than encouraging.

Ulysses Grant and his massive Army of the Potomac appeared to be sidling south again, intent on gaining the crossroads at Cold Harbor. To Lee two things had become painfully clear. He could not allow Grant to advance past the junction at Cold Harbor; that would give the enemy a straight route into Richmond while simultaneously allowing him to get firmly astride the right flank the Confederate Army. If Grant were allowed to cross the James River, the war, Lee firmly believed, would be reduced to little more than a grim mathematical formula against which the spirit, audacity, and almost endless resolve of Confederate forces would be entirely trumped by arithmetic alone. It would be checkmate.

He would have to mount another stout defense just as he had during all that May, first in the Wilderness, then again at Spotsylvania Court House, and finally along the North Anna River north of Richmond. His plan was to force Grant to maneuver out in the open where his long columns might be vulnerable. Lee's last real hope was to strike Grant's army while on the move, to induce a mistake, and then swoop down and gobble-up a portion of the Army of the Potomac, thus evening the odds a bit. If he could do that then ... well ... perhaps ....

"How are you, General? More coffee?"

Lee looked up, saw Taylor standing at his arm. "Why, yes, Colonel, if you don't mind. I can't tell you how much I appreciate your service. You have proved a godsend to me and this army."

WINDMILL POINT

Taylor smiled. "Think nothing of it, General. Believe me, it is my pleasure entirely. Some breakfast? You should eat before starting out."

"Yes, I think you are right," Lee replied. "Tell me, has Traveler been saddled?"

"I have already seen to it, sir."

"Very good. I will join you all in just a moment. Then I want to ride out to inspect General Breckinridge's lines. It is imperative that Breckinridge connect with Hoke's division in order to bolster our far right. Has he been guided to the correct position?"

"Major McClellan rode out last night to take care of it, sir."

Lee nodded. "Very well, then."

"I'll prepare a spot for you at the table, sir," Taylor went on hopefully.

"Yes, fine, I'll be right along."

Robert E. Lee was well aware of the fact that across the South and in many European capitals he was considered the leading military man in the world. The son of the famous Revolutionary War hero, "Light Horse Harry" Lee, he had graduated second in the class of 1829 from West Point, without a single demerit to his name. But his father had foolishly dribbled the family's money away, and young Robert had been raised by his mother in a meager home in Alexandria. Despite marrying into one of the most prominent families in all of Virginia, Lee could never forget his humble origins, and the fear of failure haunted him like an uncomfortable ghost.

During the Mexican War he had served on Winfield Scott's staff. After his handling of John Brown's infamous raid on Harper's Ferry in 1859, Lee was considered one of the leading officers in the Federal Army. The Lincoln administration had offered him full command of the Union Army at the beginning of the Civil War, but the thought of raising his sword against his native Virginia had been simply impossible. So he had resigned his commission instead and offered his services to the Confederacy; since the spring of 1862 Robert E. Lee had been in firm command of the Army of Northern Virginia.

Lee finished the last of his coffee and stood slowly, careful not to rise too quickly for fear of losing his balance. He was still tired and weak, but was pleased to hear that young Major McClellan had ridden out the evening before. Yes, that was good news. So many recent mistakes had been made by his officer corps that Lee now felt that he had to follow-up many of his orders personally, for fear his army would become unhinged at this most critical of times. He had to strike Grant's army during those few opportunities when it was out from behind its defenses and vulnerable. Time and space between both the respective armies and the James River was narrowing by the hour, and he could afford no additional foul-ups.

Illness and confusion seemed to be plaguing his senior lieutenants. Over the past week or so, even his most trusted subordinates had bungled numerous chances to strike a decisive blow. Ewell was so ill that Lee had had to relieve him of command, while A.P. Hill had missed an opportunity to wreck one of Grant's corps along the North Anna. Just the day before, Lee had planned a decisive attack at Cold Harbor, designed to catch the Federal infantry as it came up in detail, and drive them back in confusion into the woods one unit at a time, but Richard Anderson's attack had fizzled almost before it had begun. Why, Lee could not say. Now Grant was firmly in control of the crossroads, his infantry dug in across a long and widening front, and opportunities to even the odds were rapidly slipping away.

Lee walked slowly down the lane and joined the other officers, ate lightly, then slid gingerly into the saddle. At least his horse, Traveler, seemed well and happy to see him, and it was a joy to feel the strength slowly returning to his own body. The men, he hoped, would be pleased to see him out and about once more. The troops, he knew, drew energy from him, just as he drew energy from them.

The ride to Mechanicsville was only a few miles, and the day—while promising to be a hot one—was still reasonably mild in those cool early hours of the morning. The day before, Grant had hurled two full corps at Lee's lines outside of Cold Harbor, only to see them severely repulsed. The repulse had been complete, but Lee, after a long month of seemingly endless fighting and maneuvering, now knew enough of Grant to be sure that he would soon be back for more. Grant had turned a war of maneuvering into a war of endless hammer blows—a war the Northern commander was sure to win unless he was forced into a mistake. It was Lee's plan to create that blunder.

So Lee's strategy now was simply to hunker down behind the best defenses his men could manage to erect, and force Grant to attack him behind those trenches. Then when the Federals once again tired of hurling themselves against Confederate earthworks and moved off in yet another attempt to maneuver the Army of Northern Virginia into a more accommodating position, he hoped to pounce on any mistakes they might make. That was essential. Only that might even the odds.

Lee quickly located Hoke's division, but there was no sign of Breckinridge anywhere nearby, and inquiries proved inconclusive. After some searching, he finally located the former Vice President of the United States—now a Confederate general—far away from his assigned position, eating a leisurely breakfast with his staff. Lee's anger boiled below the surface, but he held it firmly in check. If ever there was a time for calm, it was now. They all stood to attention as he approached. Lee returned their salutes.

"At ease, gentlemen," Lee said, nodding politely.

"Good morning, General," Breckinridge replied, offering him a campstool. "Would you join us for some breakfast, sir, or at least some coffee. At least, that's what we still call it," he added, nodding toward his cup. Breckinridge pointed toward a lieutenant on his staff, and the boy raced off to fill a tin cup with fresh coffee.

"No, though I thank you, General," Lee replied. He smiled weakly. "I had hoped to find your division further down the line this morning, sir, on General Hoke's flank."

"Yes, sir," Breckinridge answered. "We've just been following your good Major McClellan."

Lee glanced at McClellan, and sensed immediately that the young major was lost. Lee pointed back down the road. "Your position is down that way a few miles or so, General," he said. "There is a gap in our line there, and it is imperative you move quickly, once you've finished your breakfast."

The smile disappeared from Breckinridge's face—he grasped the situation immediately. "I will order the boys up at once, General."

Lee held up his hands. "No. The men have already cooked their rations. Let them go ahead and eat, then hasten on down the road. You will find General Hoke waiting for you. He has my instructions."

Breckinridge turned to his lieutenant once more. "Alert everyone that we will be moving immediately after breakfast."

The boy ran off again.

Lee was pleased, knowing that Breckinridge would move quickly. The Kentuckian was one of the few political generals who understood the nature of war, and had adapted well to the field of battle. He could be counted on. Lee began to relax, leaning back on the stool. "Have you heard anything new of the enemy?" he asked, trying not to appear overanxious.

"Only that Hancock's whole corps disappeared last night from the Yankee lines on our far left, General."

Lee hesitated—this was important news. He thought it over. "Then Grant is shifting his strength for another attack on our

WINDMILL POINT

right, near Cold Harbor," he said. He glanced involuntarily toward the south, expecting to hear the sound of guns rise up at any moment. "Once you are finished here, General," he said, "you must move with all dispatch. You may find Hancock there already, once you arrive."

The Kentuckian's eyes narrowed. "We will be on the road in five minutes, sir."

Lee nodded approvingly. "Grant will come at us hard, General. We must be prepared. There can be no gaps in our lines. He will find them and exploit what he finds. We cannot be the ones who make mistakes."

Breckinridge tossed the last of his coffee into the grass. "Finish up, gentlemen," he said anxiously. "Then we move out."

Here was the thing. After a month of fighting, Lee's army was now to weak to go nose-to-nose with Grant's in the open field, so he knew he had to remain on the defensive. Thus he had packed his forces into a tight position outside of Richmond, with Totopotomoy Creek and the impassable swamps that surround it anchoring his left, and his right stretching down toward the Chickahominy River. With his army plugged tightly between the two streams, like a cork in a bottle, Grant would be unable to maneuver on either of his flanks, but would be forced to come straight at him across open country. Lee's army had never failed in the defense of such a position. But the Chickahominy—which protected his right flank—also ran directly behind his army, and if by some mistake the Federals were able to find and exploit a gap or a break in his line, then the whole position might implode, and his army wind up pinned in confusion against the banks of the river. Disaster could be the only outcome of such a scenario. It would mean the utter destruction of the Army of Northern Virginia, and, quite possibly, the end of the Confederacy; it was imperative that there be no mistakes, no breaks, and, above all, no foolish gaps.

Lee turned slowly. "Colonel Taylor!"

"Sir?"

"Please go to General Hill and inform him that I wish for him to send both Mahone and Wilcox to form on General Breckinridge's right, occupying all the ground clear down to the river. There must be no area where the enemy might slip by us uncontested. There can be no gaps. None at all."

"I understand, sir," Taylor replied.

Lee crossed his legs. "Has Hoke sent any word of Hancock arriving on his front yet?"

"Not that I have heard, sir," Taylor answered.

"Please inquire, if you would, Colonel," Lee asked. "I need to know where Hancock has gone. He is their best, and I would wager that Grant has shifted him to lead their next assault. So we must locate General Hancock."

"Of course, General," Taylor replied.

Around them now the troops were finishing their rations and packing quickly to resume the march. Sergeants were shouting orders, fires were being doused. The clank and clatter of soldiers on the move filled the small meadow. Lee watched absently as the men gathered their things. They were thin and scraggly and barefoot, and most of them had not had a change of clothes or a square meal in months, yet they were the best fighting force in the world. Many of the military observers who had traveled across the Atlantic Ocean from Europe to follow his army could not believe their eyes when they first beheld them, but all that changed when they saw them fight. Then they understood.

Lee watched approvingly as the troops began forming for the march, but he was still worried that Grant would strike before Breckinridge was in position. Grant was the latest of a long line of Federal commanders, and Lee had battled him furiously throughout the entire month of May. Both armies had suffered grievously, and Lee had lost many fine men and officers. Likewise, Grant's loss of veteran soldiers and officers had been nothing less than appalling, and now the Northern newspapers were howling. Both commanders had their own problems, and while Grant could make good on many of his losses with fresh troops, Lee thought that the bloodbath could not go on much longer without a public rebellion in the North, and a loss of confidence in the war effort. So for Lee it was a matter of digging in, hanging on, and not allowing Grant to gain the James. If he could accomplish just that, the Federal war effort might die from sheer exhaustion in the red Virginia dirt somewhere between Cold Harbor and the River James. He thought for a moment, then glanced again toward Taylor.

"You know, Colonel," he said, thinking it through as he spoke, "if General Grant has weakened his own right to reinforce his left, then there might be an opportunity there for us to do some damage up that way."

Taylor smiled eagerly. "I was thinking the same thing, General."

"Yes. Deliver a message to General Early for me, then."

"Yes, sir."

"Tell him to strike this way if he senses an opportunity. He just might be able to get astride Grant's right flank and drive the Federal line south toward Cold Harbor. You see—do to him just what he is trying to do to us, but from the opposite direction. With a little push, we might even be able to stampede the Federals and trap them against the river, just as we did at Chancellorsville. We must always be looking for opportunities to damage them."

Taylor saluted and headed off.

Lee watched as the troops quickly filed from the meadow and formed into their regiments on the road. Then, slowly, they started off toward Cold Harbor, dust rising in the air behind them like a heavy brown mist. Most of them were gaunt and weary, but they were all still ready to fight. He had never been more proud of his men. Lee watched them set off, then remounted Traveler and began the ride back to his headquarters. He half expected to hear the sound of heavy musketry rise up from the south as he rode, but that never came, and by the time he returned to his tents at Gaines's Mill he was able to finally relax.

In a few hours his line would be solid—that, at least, was a relief. But that line was very thin, stretching almost six miles from north to south, and he did not have a single brigade left in reserve to plug any gap or break, should one occur. If the line broke anywhere, the war might be over in a matter of hours. But Lee had no choice. He had anchored his flanks on the natural features of the land, and the space between Totopotomoy Creek and the Chickahominy River required every last ragged man he had if it was to be to properly defended. So today the men would have to dig in and fight like demons again. Everything depended on it.

CHAPTER THREE

JUNE 2ND—LATE MORNING

GRANT

U.S. Grant pulled another cigar from his coat pocket, lit the tip carefully, and took a long puff. Then he let the smoke slide slowly from between his lips. "No," he said finally. "Not today."

All heads turned toward him.

Ulysses Grant frowned, then glanced back down the road. He shook his head. "Hancock's troops are still coming up," he explained. "They've been on the road for almost fourteen hours now, and they're obviously in no condition to fight. Look at them," he continued, pointing toward the exhausted troops as they plodded past the staff officers in the swirling dust. "It will take more than a few hours for them to eat, rest, and be ready to assault the Rebel works. No, this afternoon will never do."

The generals and their staffs had all ridden to Cold Harbor early in the morning expecting to see an assault by three Federal corps against the Confederate lines. Hancock's corps was supposed to spearhead the attack, but at 4:30 that morning —when the assault had been scheduled to step-off—Hancock and his men were still nowhere to be found. Riders finally located them far back in the woods and well behind schedule. Poor maps, bad roads, and a moonless night had created havoc for the long night march, turning what was supposed to be a six-mile trek into a nightmare. Regiments went stumbling into one another in the darkness, causing long backups. Artillery limbers became wedged between narrow trees, while riders were toppled senseless by overhanging branches. Many men got lost in the woods, while others were trampled by artillery horses. Finally, a wrong turn added almost ten miles to the trip. The lead elements did not come trudging into Cold Harbor until almost 9 o'clock that morning—dry mouthed, dust covered, and bone weary—and the rear of the long column was still nowhere in sight.

Initially, the assault had been rescheduled for later that afternoon, but now it was almost noon and many of Hancock's men were still out struggling in the dust and heat of the day. Even had they been fresh, Grant knew, it would take hours just to get them all into line; and today they would not be coming in fresh.

At dawn that day they had moved his headquarters to Bethesda Church in order to be more or less in the center of the extended Union line. While the tents were being pitched and the headquarters readied, some of the staff officers carried the pews out of the small church and placed them on the ground in the shade of the trees. A large supply of New York newspapers had just arrived, and most of the party dug in to see what was being said about the campaign. Normally Grant devoured the papers, but today his thoughts were entirely lost in the details of the looming battle, and he had little time for anything else. After greeting a delegation from the Christian Commission—surgeons and nurses with wagons full of medical supplies—he mounted his horse, Egypt, and rode with General Meade out toward the front.

Ulysses Grant turned in the saddle and watched as a small cloud of dust hung almost motionless above the road, like some alien, vital presence. He frowned again and stared out past the front lines. Beyond him the blue troops stretched across an open plain, now trampled and barren, strewn with broken caissons, dead horses and the lost and discarded debris of war. Bordering the open plain, there stretched acre upon acre of pine forest, some of it on fire from the incessant artillery duels that had been booming all morning. Above the treetops, tumbling funnels of black smoke arched high into a grey sky. The feel of the place was hot and arid—almost like a desert—yet the smell was close, moldy, and fetid, the stench of death already lurking in every depression and crevice. The area surely had the sense of hell about it.

Cold Harbor. The name came, not from the refreshing possibilities of some cool water cove, but rather an old English expression for a stagecoach stop that offered shelter but no heat or warm food, hence a "cold harbor" for all travelers. The stagecoach stop was now long gone but the name had hung on. Desolate, dry, smoky, and now rank with days-old corpses, this Cold Harbor seemed almost like the crossroads of the underworld.

"General, I do not believe that giving the Rebels another twenty-four hours to improve their works is a good idea."

Grant turned, saw Horatio Wright, commander of the Union 6th Corps. The task of assaulting the Confederate position would fall to the commands of Wright, Hancock, and Smith, and while Wright's point was well taken, there was little Grant could do about it now. He took another puff from his cigar, thought it over, then replied, "I see no alternative. The men are too exhausted for any sort of attack today. If we try, the assault will undoubtedly fail and then we will have accomplished nothing except wasting more of our finest troops."

"Yes, General," Wright continued. "But the Rebels have become quite proficient in the art of trenching and throwing up all sorts of defenses. They have already been at it for the better part of a day. Twenty-four hours more...?"

"No," Grant replied emphatically. "Lee is weak here. We almost broke him here yesterday. In the morning our whole line will advance and occupy his entire six-mile front. If he has shifted troops, or if there is a weakness in his line anywhere, we will find and exploit it. Tomorrow he will break somewhere. Then it will only be a matter of exploiting whatever breaks we uncover. Tomorrow we will break him."

Wright frowned, then looked away—he was obviously not convinced. But he offered no further arguments, and Grant let the matter drop. "Tomorrow," he repeated for emphasis, "we will break him. Right here at Cold Harbor."

Ulysses Simpson Grant had been summoned east in the early spring by President Lincoln. Promoted to lieutenant general—the first to hold that rank in the field since George Washington—Grant had been placed in command of the entire Federal war effort. His star had risen with the capture of Forts Henry and Donelson in '62 and later Vicksburg in '63, and Lincoln saw him as someone who would fight. Since the principal weapon employed by the Confederacy in the quest for its independence was Robert E. Lee's Army of Northern Virginia, Grant packed his bags and moved into the field, accompanying the Army of the Potomac in its pursuit of Lee. George Meade—the hero of Gettysburg—was still the commander of the army. While Grant had no intention of relieving that able officer, he had taken strong steps to impose his will on the chain of command. So, while Meade remained the titular head of the army, it was Ulysses Grant who now pulled the strings.

Grant had met with President Lincoln early in the spring, and the orders he had received were both simple and specific—fight. So in May—when the weather had warmed and the roads were finally dried enough to support his enormous army and miles of supply trains—he had pushed the army across the Rapidan River into Virginia's Wilderness country west of

WINDMILL POINT

Fredericksburg. That movement had plunged the Army of the Potomac into a bloody month of horrific fighting. Already his army had suffered almost 45,000 casualties, and while he had pushed the Army of Northern Virginia a good bit south, Lee was still directly in front of him, blocking his path toward Richmond. Many of the Northern newspapers—which just a few weeks ago had been trumpeting his praises—were now seriously questioning his abilities. But his orders came directly from Lincoln, after all, so he simply tried to ignore the papers while keeping his army fighting and moving.

George Meade tucked away his field glasses and turned. "I'm fearful Wright has a point," he said, scowling out at the Confederate works across the open plain.

Overhead the clouds were thickening and a light, misty rain began to fall, pelting the dusty ground.

Grant nodded patiently. "Yes, I agree he has a point," he said, "but it doesn't change a thing. Hancock got lost. His men are exhausted. They will not be ready to advance any time soon, and now even the rains are coming. We must wait until tomorrow to attack. It's not what any of us wanted, but I'm afraid it's the best we can manage, given the circumstances."

Meade folded his arms across his chest and looked away. There was nothing left to say.

Later that afternoon the light rain began to fall harder. The powdery roads soon turned to a muddy soup, making passage all but impossible. Grant returned to his tent and penned a simple order:

> In view of the want of preparation for an attack this evening, the heat, and the want of energy among the men from their movements last night, I think it advisable to postpone assault until early tomorrow morning. All changes of position already ordered should be completed today and a good night's rest

given the men preparatory to an assault at, say, 4:30 in the morning. Corps commanders will employ the interim in making examination of the ground in their fronts and perfecting their arrangements for the assault.

He read it twice, signed it, and sent the order off to George Meade for implementation. Then he lit another cigar, leaned back in his camp chair, and watched the dreary scene outside his tent as the rain turned the red, Virginia clay into small rivulets and streams.

In the Federal works, the men pulled coats and blankets up over their heads and tried to get some rest despite the rain. Some played cards or wrote letters home, but the drizzle made everything difficult. Some few tried to cook their rations, but most of the fires turned smoky and burned out. Many of the men simply lay still and listened to the clatter of axes and shovels that rose up from the Confederate works across the way. Those preparations went on non-stop all afternoon. Some of the men tried not to listen, because they knew what it meant; the Rebels would be ready come morning. For those that understood, it was a depressing sound.

CHAPTER FOUR

JUNE 2ND—AFTERNOON

ALEXANDER

Porter Alexander walked the Confederate battle line slowly, pausing here and there to take in the lay of the land and the contours of the gently undulating ground. He studied each fold of earth, every stand of trees, but, most of all, the open spaces. Edward Porter Alexander was a West Point engineer, and over the years he'd become extremely proficient at the expert placement of artillery. By and large the land in front of him was flat, dotted here and there with scraps of briars and small stands of trees. Here the opposing lines were too close for long range dueling, but the open spaces and broken tree lines were quite favorable for sweeping cross-fires and smooth-bore ricochet volleys that could have devastating effects on approaching infantry. He made a few mental notes, then moved on.

In particular, Alexander favored positions where his guns could sit hidden away behind a small hill or in a shallow defile at the end of a long line of works. Those sorts of arrangements always worked nicely. If properly placed, the guns and crews would remain entirely unobserved by the enemy until their own infantry was far advanced, and thus much too late for them to avoid the various artillery traps he had prepared. Then his guns would open a terrible enfilading fire as they approached, raking the Federal battle lines from flank to flank with charges of canister or spherical shot at close range. With his guns and gunners hidden away from the Yankee lines, his batteries could deliver lethal volleys while remaining virtually immune to counter battery fire—the best of all worlds. General Edward Porter Alexander knew just what he was looking for, and as he walked the Confederate battle lines outside of Cold Harbor that rainy afternoon, he certainly liked what he saw.

Alexander paused atop a small rise and yanked the collar of his coat up tight against his neck. The rain was coming down harder now, turning the powdery dirt around the trenches into a slippery muck. All day long they had been waiting for the Yankees to attack again, but now it appeared the assault would be held off until the rains cleared, or perhaps even the following morning. He took a long look at the Federal position through his field glasses, but could see no obvious sign of anything imminent. Of course, they had all learned over the course of the last few weeks that Grant would not back away; Alexander knew it was only a matter of time before the Federals assaulted again. But time now worked in his favor, and Alexander planned on making the most of it. If he had his way, when the Yankees finally came at them again they would charge straight into the jaws of an artillery hell.

He slipped the glasses back into their case, and went on calmly about his business. All around him the men were busy digging-in, using shovels, bayonets, even their tin cups to fashion deeper, ever more effective earthworks. After months of defensive warfare, they had all become skillful in the design of trenches. Now they were constructing a labyrinth of zigzagging, overlapping entrenchments that were the most formidable he'd ever seen, yet all were neatly tucked into the natural features of the terrain. Creeks, swamp lands, small wood lots, even outgrowths of brambles and weeds had all been fitted nicely into an overall design that ran from Totopotomoy Creek in the north, clear down to the Chickahominy River in the south—almost six miles.

Far behind the front lines, crews of pioneers had felled whole swathes of timber to provide head logs and sturdy cover for the trenches. Those in turn had been covered with dirt, leaves, and branches. Directly in front of the works, miles of wild ash and pine had been cut, shaved and fitted to form a layer of abatis—sharp points and branches that would obstruct and ensnare any approaching infantry, virtually pinning them in front of the muzzles of the Confederate guns. Trenches had been dug using the natural flow of the land to funnel the enemy toward interconnected honeycombs of enfilading gun emplacements. Every conceivable approach had been ingeniously incorporated into the scheme, yet, because of its use of natural features, the magnitude of the defensive structure remained virtually hidden to the Yankees just across the clearing. To Alexander's trained eye, it appeared the position was fast becoming impregnable.

"General," one of his battery commanders called, "right here?"

He walked over and studied the position. "Yes, right," Alexander replied finally. "Angled out toward those trees over there. You cannot see beyond the branches from here, but when the Yankees advance there will probably be plenty of them out that way, too. So you must shoot at long angles, and the chances are you will cause damage well beyond your immediate front. Do you understand? Then when they come in close, shift over to canister and fire it into the ground right in front of them so that it will ricochet up and create havoc in their ranks. If General Grant is going to keep coming after us, we must make him pay dearly for his efforts. It is the only way."

"Yes, sir."

This was the third long and dreary year of war for Porter Alexander. When it had all started, back in '61, no one had even dreamed it would go on for so long, yet even now there seemed no end in sight. Born in Washington, Georgia, Alexander had graduated from West Point with the class of 1857. He had served in the army all of his career, first as a professor of engineering at West Point, and later on an expedition to Utah to quell a Mormon revolt. When Civil War came he felt compelled to side with Georgia, and Alexander resigned his commission. At Bull Run he served on General Beauregard's staff, and soon thereafter was appointed chief of ordinance for the Army of Northern Virginia. Later he was promoted to chief of artillery for Longstreet's corps, and in that capacity had arranged much of the cannonade that preceded Picket's Charge during that fateful third day at Gettysburg. But as he walked the muddy plain around Cold Harbor, that July afternoon in southern Pennsylvania seemed so lost in time it could easily have transpired in some other lifetime. Indeed, in some odd way the war seemed to have gone on for most of his adult life.

General Lee had given Alexander orders to keep a steady, harassing fire on the Yanks all day long, so he used the guns that he had facing them directly to pound away at their artillery emplacements, along with any infantry units that happened to show their faces. In those spaces between the opposing lines that were broad enough, he ran his batteries quickly out in front of the works, unlimbered, and blasted away at the Federal entrenchments just to cause them misery and slow down and confound their preparations. There was no glory in any of this, of course; the war had devolved into a gruesome study in death, and over time Porter Alexander had become one of its brightest students.

Alexander placed the last of his batteries one at a time, explaining in detail the advantages and disadvantages of each position to his various commanders, then slipped back later just to make sure the weapons had been positioned properly. They could afford no mistakes. Then he went to the rear and checked

WINDMILL POINT

on his ammunition train, ordering plenty of short-range shot to be distributed to the guns at the front. That accomplished, he walked the line one last time before returning to his headquarters for dinner.

The rain was falling steadily now, and Cold Harbor had quickly taken on the mournful look of a barren and depressing landscape. Here were acre upon acre of mud, smoke, and corpses, all of it stretching clear to the horizon, now under a grey canopy of low tumbling clouds. He pulled the collar tighter around his neck, shook the water from his cap, and made his way back to his tent. There his servant was preparing a meal of potatoes, a few recently scavenged eggs, and part of a small chicken—a sumptuous feast these days when compared to what most of the troops had for rations. Outside, the men kept working in the rain, tired and muddy, their efforts at least keeping their minds off their empty stomachs. There was no telling just how long the army would be able to keep fighting with so little food or rest. One day at a time. That's how they all got by now. One day at a time.

Porter Alexander sat on a short stool and sipped what remained of a foul cup of coffee. He dared not complain, knew he had it far better than most. For just a moment his thoughts drifted toward home, and he thought of his wife and family.

He recalled fondly the winter of 1863. After the battle at Fredericksburg he had marched his artillery battalion down to the North Anna River and found a fine place to winter near Ruther Glen. An abundant pine thicket provided cover for the horses and more than enough material for the men to construct cabins and to burn fires throughout the long, cold months. No more than a half mile away he took quarters in the Wortham home, where he was soon joined by his wife, Bettie, and their little fourteen-month-old daughter, Bessie. Both had come up on the train from Richmond. General Pendleton was camped nearby, and he came down one cold afternoon to baptize little Bess; Porter Alexander recalled the day with great fondness.

Alexander also remembered hunting and fishing in the woods nearby, the house abundant with love, merriment, and all variety of foods. Little Bess grew like a wildflower and had the full run of the Wortham's large backyard, and she was just then beginning to talk. They were the best three months of his life. After the Confederacy's stunning victory at Fredericksburg, everyone felt that the South would soon prevail, and that within months they might all be home again. He smiled at the recollection, struggling to remember even more of those days, but the rain cast a sudden pall over his fond memories, and he soon turned his mind to less comforting things. As supper simmered in the pot nearby he thought of the infantrymen out in the gathering dusk, scooping dirt from the bottom of their trenches. In the darkness they seemed almost like gravediggers, and for Porter Alexander there seemed a great sense of sadness in the activity.

Suddenly the rumble of artillery came to him through the low-hanging clouds, distant and low. He cocked his head, gauging that it was coming from up north—General Jubal Early had probably gone in against the right flank of the Yankee line. He had heard Lee give the orders, suggesting Early try and secure Hancock's abandoned works, then launch an assault that might turn the Federal right flank. The sound of war grew like distant thunder. Who knew what it might mean, he wondered absently? Maybe Early would drive them clear into the Chickahominy River. Pleasant thought. But then maybe he wouldn't. Best be ready anyway.

By now everyone realized that Grant was different than the rest. This was no Pope, Burnside or McClellan—previous Federal commanders who had seemed to do little more than dabble at war. Grant clearly had come to fight, and all the South knew by now that he would never back away. No, Grant would have to be beaten, and beaten badly.

But the Federal effort had already cost Grant's army dearly, and Alexander knew the North would not sit idly by forever as its sons were devoured daily as fodder for Grant's seemingly insatiable war machine. All May the Confederates had beaten back Grant's massive assaults and he had yet to drive them from a single field of battle. And those contests had been fought on fields where often they had had precious little in the way of time to organize or perfect their defenses. Here at Cold Harbor, on the other hand, they had been granted almost two full days to develop a formidable network of entrenchments unlike anything they had ever before constructed. Now, every man in line felt confident they would be able to stop the Yanks dead in their tracks.

Alexander removed his cap, slapped the water away across his knee, then gazed out into the falling rain. No, the bloodbath simply could not go on much longer. Both armies were now fought-out, to the point that one or the other must soon prevail. Alexander was an engineer and mathematician, and after three long years he had come to finally understand the physics of war. One day either Grant would break them or they would stop him dead in his tracks for good. It was as simple as that. In the morning, he guessed that the Yankees would come storming after them again, perhaps as many as three full corps—almost 50,000 men—marching across that narrow space between the lines, in search of that final victory that had eluded them all spring. The Rebels, of course, would be waiting for them in their trenches, rifles and artillery primed and ready. Porter Alexander took one last sip of the awful coffee, spit it into the grass at his feet and thought, *perhaps tomorrow will be the day. Yes, maybe tomorrow we will stop General Grant dead in his tracks, finally put an end to all this madness, and I will go home and see little Bessie again.*

CHAPTER FIVE

JUNE 2ND—EVENING

GRANT

Grant listened patiently as his aide, Horace Porter, explained what he had learned of the most recent action on the Federal Army's right flank. Grant slowly drummed his fingers on the top of his desk, digesting every detail. "Who was it?" Grant asked finally.

"Early's Corps, as I have it, with some reinforcements from Harry Heth. It was Early who led the attack," Porter responded. "We've taken a number of prisoners, and that's all we've seen so far. Heth and Early."

The Rebels had hit his extreme right flank up north, but from all of the reports he'd received so far the situation seemed to be under control. Both Burnside's and Warren's corps had been engaged, but according to Burnside, the Rebels had been, if not entirely repulsed, at least contained, and he need not fear any further problems from that quarter. Lee, of course, was moving and shifting, trying to anticipate Grant's next move, while Grant was trying to fathom his opponent's intentions. After a month of steady marching and engagements, he had come to realize that discerning the intentions of Robert E. Lee was not an easy thing to do.

"Does anyone report any other movement along their line anywhere?" Grant asked.

"None," Porter replied. "The Rebels are reported to be working on their earthworks, and that's all."

Grant nodded, and stopped drumming the desk. "Lee's probably just searching to see what strength we left up north," Grant said. "He's looking for an opening: probing. The pickets must keep a keen eye tonight, and notify us of anything that looks or sounds suspicious. Tell Burnside I want regular reports on his situation."

Porter saluted and turned away.

Late in the afternoon, headquarters was shifted again some two miles south to be closer to the main attack at Cold Harbor, which was scheduled for 4:30 the following morning. Grant's thinking was simple. Lee was deployed along a six-mile front, with water on both of his flanks, so the Rebel line could not be turned. Thus one of Lee's flanks would have to be crushed. Then, with his flank destroyed, the remainder of the Confederate line could be turned and stampeded back toward Richmond. Grant's entire army was now deployed to match Lee's six-mile front: Hancock's Corps on the extreme left followed in order by Wright, then Smith, Warren, and finally Burnside on the far right. In the morning they would all go forward, the three corps' on the far left delivering the critical blow, while Warren and Burnside demonstrated aggressively. If Lee had left a gap or an opening, or if he was weak somewhere, they would find that spot and exploit it. There would be no place to hide.

The truth of the matter was, of course, that Grant knew he had precious little in the way of options. His hands were virtually tied. If he attempted to cross the James River without a fight at Cold Harbor, he would open himself to being attacked once his force was divided by the river, and he knew Lee would not pass up the opportunity to strike. Moreover, the people in the North were rapidly becoming war-weary, and another jog south with no interim success would surely be looked upon as just another prolongation of a war that had no apparent end in sight. The war expenses had reached almost four million dollars a day. The government was already deep in debt; those sorts of expenses could not go on indefinitely. Soon, too, the heat would be upon them, and operating in the sickly Virginia low country during the hot summer months would take a severe toll on his army from disease. Two years before, campaigning in the same country, McClellan's army had suffered far more from "Chickahominy fever" than it had from Rebel bullets, and Grant knew that he could expect nothing less. What had begun in early May as a wide-open campaign with countless strategic possibilities had now been narrowed down to a tight, six-mile front with little in the way of choices and even less room for maneuver.

So in the morning he would send three full corps in on Lee's right flank, and hopefully smash it wide open. With the river running in the Confederate's rear, he might be able to destroy the Army of Northern Virginia on the banks of the Chickahominy, and take Richmond by nightfall. That was his hope. In many ways it was not only his best play, it was his only play.

Yet, if somehow Lee was able to hold firm again, then Grant might have to move south toward the James River with an eye toward crossing over and coming up on Richmond from the south. He had already wired General Halleck in Washington on the 30th, asking him to ship all the available pontoon-bridging to City Point on the river, to be ready for just such an eventuality. While a movement in that direction looked good in theory, Grant knew that in practice it would be fraught with problems and potential hazards. First the Chickahominy would have to be crossed, then the James, but all of the bridges on both rivers east of their current position had already been destroyed. Lee might swoop in and try to destroy parts of Grant's army while they were separated by the rivers, perhaps even splitting the Union forces in half. Indeed, Lee had come close to doing just that on the Peninsula in '62 against McClellan, and Grant was not anxious to provide him a similar opportunity.

Or, Lee might march for the Bermuda Hundred, a stretch of land between the Appomattox and James Rivers where General Ben Butler's Federal army had been bottled up by the Confederate general Beauregard since landing. Lee would, after all, have all of the advantages of interior lines and better roads, and would be able to move far more rapidly than Grant could respond. If the Confederates marched quickly, Lee could conceivably crush Butler and then fall upon the lead elements of Grant's army as they made their way across to the southern shore of the James—an unmitigated disaster for the Federal cause, and one that just might destroy the war effort for good. So, for the time being, he would forget about moving south and rely instead on the attack scheduled for Cold Harbor in the morning. Much would ride on it.

The evening meal was a pleasant one. Grant was beginning to feel strong again, confident that Lee's weaknesses would be found and rapidly exploited come morning, and his appetite responded accordingly. There was beef with gravy, hard bread, and another barrel of fresh oysters, just shipped in from the Chesapeake Bay. All of it was washed down with coffee and glasses of ice water—General Wright had discovered an ample ice-house not far from his headquarters—and the dinner conversation was reassuring. Outside, the rain continued falling, gently drumming the tent's roof. Despite the glum weather everyone voiced their opinion that tomorrow's attack would succeed where so many previous ones had not, and that the war was now winding down to what appeared a triumphant finale.

Grant's staff worked well into the night. Several divisions still had to be shuffled around for the pending assault, and it was decided to wake all the men around midnight and issue them a full two day's rations. As always, there were seemingly a million small details that had to be worked through. That accomplished, he finally bid everyone good night and laid down in the hopes of catching at least a few hours' sleep. The massive assault—the largest ever planned by the Army of the Potomac—would go off at first light. As Grant closed his eyes he could not help but think of all the men lying out in the cool, dismal rain that night. He hoped that they would all be well rested come morning. He prayed that they would be up to the task, and that maybe, God willing, this would be the last assault he would ever have to order.

CHAPTER SIX

JUNE 2ND—LATE EVENING

WHITE

Wyman White finished hammering the last peg of his tent into the soggy ground, tossed the rock aside, and started across the muddy field toward the fire. While the drizzle had come on steadily all evening, a few fires had been strategically placed under drooping canopies of branches back in the trees. Relentlessly fed a diet of dry pine, several had managed to burn hot and bright, even through the drumming rain. He could feel the reach of the fire a good fifty feet away, and the heat felt good on his face. Wyman found a seat under a tree and held up his hands, letting the warmth work its magic, first on his fingers, then his palms, and finally up his arms. His tattered uniform was thoroughly soaked, but with a little luck and patience it would soon be dry from the heat of the fire. He smiled. For the first time in days he was beginning to feel alive again.

Numerous pots of coffee were boiling on the glowing coals. Skillets stuffed with frying bacon, salt pork, and ham filled the small clearing with a delicious aroma. His stomach grumbled loudly, and Wyman White suddenly realized that he had hardly eaten in well over twenty-four hours. He had slept for the better part of the day, now felt somewhat rested for the first time in weeks, and it was a wonderful feeling. He looked at the man to his right but didn't recognize him. It didn't matter.

"Say, brother," Wyman asked, "would you mind saving this spot for me? I'm gonna go fetch my pan and sack."

The man nodded, smiled briefly, a toothy sort of grin. He understood. "Get what you need, Sarge," he replied. "I'll do my best for you."

In mid-afternoon the U. S. Sharpshooters had been moved back behind the lines to division headquarters. From there they were to be detailed out as needed, some off to be skirmishers, others used as sharpshooters along or between the lines. But all the officers were busily preparing for an assault, and over the course of the long afternoon seemed to have forgotten entirely about the sharpshooters. So Wyman had taken the opportunity to rest, and slept the day away in as deep a sleep as he could ever recall. Over the last few weeks he had pushed his body well beyond exhaustion, so when the opportunity for rest finally came along, he simply tumbled down upon the wet ground and, in moments, was consumed by sleep. When he finally awoke the sky was dark, rain was falling, and the infantry was already moving off toward the front. So he pitched his tent, tossed his things inside and then started off toward the warmth and light of the fire.

Wyman found his sack and made his way back quickly to the group huddled around the campfire. He greased his pan, carefully unwrapped his bacon, and set a handful of strips on the coals. A few days ago he had been sent off to the 9th Corps, not far from Hanover Junction, for a long day of sharpshooting. He had been detailed out with a fellow from a Michigan outfit, a full-blooded Indian who spoke little English but was an excellent shot. They had been deployed together atop a high ridge. Wyman wanted to work his way down through a cornfield to the cover of some thick brush below, but the corn

WINDMILL POINT

was short and he had been fearful he would be an easy target on the move.

The Michigan boy told him, "Make self corn. Do as I do," and started stuffing corn stalks into his shirt, clothes, and equipment until he looked like a human cornfield. Wyman promptly did likewise, and they both made their way down through the cornfield without the Rebels ever spotting them. They had a fine day shooting, and later he had stumbled upon a stout-looking pig on a farm nearby and shot it dead. He and the Michigan fellow then butchered the animal in the field and carried off as much as they could manage for their respective regiments. Well salted, the bacon would last a few days, and the smell of it frying in the pan now was almost intoxicating. His stomach churned in anticipation.

The man seated off to his right pulled a pot of coffee from the fire and poured himself a steaming cupful. Then he nodded toward Wyman. "I got plenty here, Sarge," he said. "No sense wasting any. Care for a fresh cup?"

White's eyes lit up, and he yanked the tin cup from his sack.

"Oh, that would be very kind of you, brother," he said, watching the dark liquid as it disappeared into his tin. He took a long sip, swished it around appreciatively in his mouth, then swallowed it slowly. It was fine, rich, Yankee coffee, and it was perfectly delicious. Wyman felt the heat pass down into his stomach then begin a slow crawl toward his limbs, and the experience warmed his mood considerably. Many of the soldiers gathered around him began to chat, stretch out, even chuckle here and there, showing the first real signs of life he'd seen in weeks.

In a few minutes the bacon was ready. First he carefully poured some of the hot grease onto a few biscuits of hardtack to soften them. Then he slipped the strips gingerly from the pan onto the biscuits. "Coosh," the soldiers all called it, and Wyman didn't know why, but he called it coosh, too. He devoured all of it lovingly. He ate slowly, a discipline he'd perfected since joining the army, savoring every last morsel. Then he licked the last of the bacon grease from his fingers, and washed it all down with another hot cup of steaming coffee, the closest Wyman figured a boy might ever get to heaven while campaigning in the Virginia woods. For just a moment his spirits soared.

On the far side of the trees the infantry was up and moving again in preparation for the morning assault. The attack was to begin at first light, someone said—that had become Grant's way—and he could see the troops just beyond the fall of the firelight, moving in the darkness like shadows or ghosts in the night. Many of them, he knew, would depart this mortal world for the spiritual realm come dawn if the assault went off as planned.

He slipped away from the warmth of the fire and slowly ambled down toward the front. Wyman's regiment, the 2nd U.S. Sharpshooters, was attached to the 3rd Division of Hancock's 2nd Corps, and the division was commanded by General Birney. The other two divisions of the 2nd Corps were moving off into position as he watched: Barlow's on the far left, Gibbon's on the right. His own division was being held just to the rear, in reserve, to be sent forward once the Rebel line was broken in the morning. White strolled down toward Gibbon's boys, and soon ran across the lines of the 19th Massachusetts regiment. Wet, tired, and joyless, they seemed a depressed and miserable lot. Wyman could hardly blame them.

As he walked along the line of seated troopers a fresh breeze came up, then a spirited wind in great rushes from the west. Wyman pulled his coat tight around his shoulders. The temperature dropped noticeably, and suddenly the rain turned into a shower of hail, tapping dully on the artillery limbers and cannons parked nearby. The hail quickly covered the mud like snow in December, and soon turned an unpleasant scene into a miserable one. Men sat in the darkness trying to write their last letters home, reading bibles, or staring glumly off into space. Suddenly, they were covered in a cold layer of white, while the sweet aroma of swamp magnolias hung almost ironically over the trenches. Then the hail stopped just as quickly as it had started, and a mist began pooling in all the low elevations. Yet the men seemed to notice none of it. It was enough to almost break his heart.

Wyman knelt along the edge of a trench amongst the troops. Never before had he seen men so demoralized before an attack. A few of them acknowledged his presence, nodded his way, but had nothing to say. No one spoke.

Near midnight, two day's rations of coffee, hardtack, and sugar were issued to all of the men. The troops accepted the rations without comment, stuffed them away into their haversacks then returned to the trenches. The bully enthusiasm displayed by many of the officers was not mirrored by the boys who were huddled there in the cold. The mist continued to build in a cool, white layer, blanketing them all in the woven likeness of what appeared to Wyman a funeral shroud, and it was a troubling image.

Further down the trench Wyman noticed that many of the men were working on their overcoats. He thought this an odd enterprise for such a late hour, and he walked closer to see what they were up to. Here he noticed the boys sewing their coats, and he slid down into the trench to see what it was all about. Then he stopped short. For the troops—all the way down the long line—were carefully sewing small scraps of paper onto the backs of their coats upon which they'd scribbled their names and hometowns. The utility of it struck him immediately.

Here, it seemed, the dead were preparing for the dawn of their own demise. Not one of them, it was clear, expected to survive the morning's attack. Never before in three long years of war had he seen anything like it. No words or commands had initiated the strange sacrament. The men simply knew. Tonight was their last on earth, thus they were preparing for death as best they knew how.

Long gone were the heady days of shouts, cheers, and patriotic speeches that had stirred them all during the early days of the war. They had seen far too much death and horror to be moved by windy slogans anymore, and Grant's campaign had crushed out the last romantic ideas of war anyone might still have harbored. By the summer of 1864, for Wyman White, heroism had become a cheapened term, much overused by journalists, who often got their stories second, or even third hand. While in the New York papers heroes might still appear a dime a dozen, Wyman White knew better. Indeed, so tired had he become of the term's overuse that Wyman had virtually dropped it from his vocabulary, and used it now under only the most extraordinary of circumstances.

Now they simply marched and fought, the conflict having descended into a savage struggle of wills. At "the bloody angle" at Spotsylvania Court House only weeks before he had seen men literally tear one another apart with their bare hands. But in the end those conflicting wills had been forged by the power of ideas. For the Northern boys this meant the good of a free and democratic Union, along with the obvious evil represented by the institution of slavery. The Army of the Potomac was an army born and impelled by ideas that men considered worth dying for, and never was that more apparent than in the wet, muddy trenches late that night at Cold Harbor.

Yet it seemed there was more to it than even that. For there in the dark, miserable trenches, for Wyman White, flesh and idea seemed to have suddenly merged into something entirely indistinguishable, freedom animated in the exhausted bodies of these sad, desperate men. It was surely an odd notion, yet Wyman had never seen anything more clearly before in his life. These seemed not just soldiers anymore, but the willing architects of a whole new world, the human embodiment of an

WINDMILL POINT

idea whose time no longer could be denied, and he was proud just to be numbered among them.

Nothing had to be said. Every last man understood the task at hand, and would go to his death in the morning to serve that higher purpose. They would die for what was right; it was as simple as that. This too was clear: while they might die unknown, their deeds would never be forgotten. For the men arrayed before him now had in some sense become freedom's instruments, and through that freedom, Wyman was sure, their efforts would surely live on.

So Wyman White sat along the top of the muddy trench, and silently shared in the sorrow of the moment. He could not leave them now—no, not now. In a strange, sad, yet wonderful way they had all become brothers in a far greater mission. So he stayed with them silently through the cold night, shared every dismal breath, every imagined regret, each and every pang of remorse—painful recollections of sons, lovers, wives, and friends who would never be seen again. It was a time of almost indescribable sadness. No matter how many months or years the war might drag on, Wyman knew he would never forget this one night at Cold Harbor—a night when freedom seemed to shine through the eyes of the dead, and liberty reached out and held them all lovingly in her arms. In time he grew weary and laid his head down in the mud to sleep. He would stay with them to the end. Heroes, he knew, deserved nothing less.

CHAPTER SEVEN

JUNE 3RD—EARLY MORNING

WHITE

Wyman awoke with a sudden jerk, and realized that the hour for the great assault was upon them. All around the trenches regiments were forming in the darkness, the clank and jangle of canteens, bayonets and haversacks punctuating the early morning hour. Officers slid down the long battle lines, quietly encouraging the troops as they passed. Men folded away their pictures, bibles, and letters, and silently took their positions. Hardly a word was spoken. Every man understood; it was time.

Wyman White grabbed his cap and stuffed it back on his head. Then he wished everyone good luck and started for the rear where his division was being assembled in reserve. The rain had stopped, but the morning was still dark and misty. The smell of wild azaleas and magnolias hung low and heavy over the lines, a fragrance, he knew, that had seeped so powerfully into his recollections of Cold Harbor that it could never be pried apart.

Then gradually the darkness began to fade. Looking up toward the heavens he could still see a few stars blinking through the mist, but soon those began to disappear as the morning sunlight slowly caressed the fields around him. As daylight increased, the Rebel pickets suddenly began firing, a staccato popping all along the front, red dots stabbing the mist, but their shots flew wild and seemed to have little effect. Several pieces of Confederate artillery were then swung into action, but those shells also ranged well overhead and bothered no one. Behind the Federal earthworks cannon crews immediately jumped to their guns, and in moments the Rebel shells were answered, shot for shot, the artillery pieces bucking and thundering and spitting out death like enraged beasts of war. Wyman could see the shells bursting high over the Confederate artillery positions like great, scarlet roses blossoming in the dawn, a stunning sight at that early hour. Both sides dueled ineffectively for a few minutes more. Then everything returned to the same, pregnant stillness as before. For a moment or two, smoke danced sluggishly around the silent guns before spiraling aloft, finally disappearing altogether in the air above.

Wyman picked up his Sharps rifle and took a seat with the rest of the sharpshooters. They were waiting for fresh orders, but it was apparent the assault was about to move forward, and for the time being, at least, all else had been forgotten. So there was little to do but sit and watch.

"Where was you at, Sarge?" Joe Thompson asked him.

"Off a ways," Wyman replied.

"Didn't see you all night," Thompson went on. "Feared you might have been hit by a Rebel ball. Glad to see you okay."

Wyman nodded. "Yeah, I'm okay. Thanks for thinking of me, though, Joe."

"It's no problem, Sarge. Ain't too many of us left anymore. I'm thinking we got to look out for one another."

"Well, that's about right," Wyman agreed. He shuffled his feet and thought for a moment. "You heard anything of Sandborn or Brown?" Wyman asked.

Thompson shook his head. "Not a thing," he replied. "They's back somewhere up near Hanover Junction in the field hospital, is my guess. I heard they got hit, but, shoot, I didn't have no time to pay them a visit. Who's got time anymore? March and fight. March and fight. Know what I mean?"

Wyman nodded, spit in the grass between his boots. "Ain't that the truth," he said.

Thompson pointed out toward the front. "What you think's gonna happen here this morning, Sarge? Whole thing looks right frightful to me."

"Think we're about to have one whale of a fight," Wyman answered.

Joe Thompson frowned miserably. "The damned Rebels were working on their entrenchments for the whole day yesterday, Wyman. I could hear them clear as a bell. That don't bode well, you ask me. Not at all."

"Well, the whole corps is going in," Wyman said. "I suppose we'll just have to wait and see."

Daylight grew and finally filled the plain between the lines with an amber glow. Wyman spotted two lines of Federal infantry ahead in the clearing. Both lines were lying on their stomachs, one far out ahead of the other. About six hundred yards beyond them he could clearly see the Rebel earthworks for the first time now, brown and somber, seemingly unmanned. Then, almost as if a magician had waved a wand, a long row of slouch hats appeared along the top of the parapets, and small puffs of smoke began to dot the horizon.

"Look there!" Thompson said, his body tensing. "That don't look good to me, Sarge. You see them Rebs? They're ready for us!"

Wyman nodded, spit again. "We'll just have to see, Joe."

Almost immediately two batteries of Union artillery went to work, hurling shells high over the Confederate position again. The puffs of smoke from the Confederate side gradually trailed away. A few hundred yards west of the blue infantry, Rebel pickets jumped from their rifle pits, and began racing back to the main line of fortifications. There they turned and unleashed a few shots at the blue artillerymen, but Wyman saw only one man struck down, and his wound appeared only superficial. The artillery continued to roar until an officer came running back from the front, motioning for the guns to cease firing. The infantry was about to move off.

A few hundred feet away Wyman spotted General Hancock on his horse with the rest of his staff. Hancock gave the signal to advance, and at once all the brigades leaped to their feet, let out a tremendous roar, and started forward. Wyman thought it an impressive sight, and his heart began to race, the long lines of blue infantry stretching off to the north and south for as far as the eye could see.

Marching at a somber, measured cadence, with flags flying majestically overhead, the massive assault appeared virtually irresistible. Straight ahead the men marched into the mist toward a small swamp. There the low ground caused the long lines to naturally divide, part of Barlow's division going off to the left, the other off to the right. The blue lines had closed to within almost two hundred yards of the Rebel works across wide-open ground, yet there had hardly been a shot fired by the Confederates in opposition. Wyman was beginning to think the attack unstoppable, that the Rebels had abandoned their works and were perhaps running for their lives as the great blue assault lines swept toward them. But he was wrong.

Suddenly a sheet of flame exploded across the entire Rebel front, an explosion of such extraordinary magnitude that the sharpshooters simply gasped in common astonishment. Thunderous, well directed, and horrifically delivered, the initial Confederate blast appeared not so much an orchestration of military firepower as a volcanic explosion. A virtual wall of flame and smoke consumed the assaulting lines of blue infantry to such a terrifying extent that in mere seconds the assault disappeared entirely from view.

Wyman White leaped to his feet and stared at the enormous cloud of smoke that had buried the Federal infantry, which then came roiling back across the field toward them all, like a vast, tumbling curtain. He had never before witnessed anything so awful. "Oh my God, Joe!" was all that he could think to say. "Oh my God!"

CHAPTER EIGHT

JUNE 3RD—FIRST LIGHT

ALEXANDER

Alexander heard the order to load, then, in rapid succession, to aim and fire. The order was given in a professional tone, the words calm in tenor, almost passionless. The result was anything but. A thunderous storm of shot, canister, bullets, grape, and shell exploded from every gun along the lengthy Confederate battle line, in one of the most awesome displays of fury Porter Alexander had ever witnessed. Flames lit the sky and the ground shook under his feet. The roar was utterly deafening. Alexander could not hear the officer standing next to him, though he was screaming at the top of his lungs.

Alexander had been one of the architects of the Rebel position on Marye's Heights overlooking Fredericksburg, Virginia in the winter of '62. That had been a position so formidable that after preparing the artillery pits he told General Longstreet that a chicken couldn't find room to scratch on the open fields covered by their guns and not be raked with lead. When the Federal general, Ambrose Burnside, had finally sent his men up the hill to their deaths, the blue formations were simply shot to pieces all that long afternoon, and not a single Yankee soldier ever made his way to the stone wall at the top. For the Union, Fredericksburg had proved an unmitigated disaster. The Confederate position on Marye's Heights had been virtually unassailable, the storm of fire lethal beyond imagination. Yet the eruption along the line at Fredericksburg that day paled in comparison to the avalanche of death he had just witnessed unleashed at Cold Harbor.

The open fields approaching the Rebel works were covered from every conceivable angle. At Cold Harbor there were crossfires within crossfires, and enfilading fire that not only struck every square inch of ground, but also struck every square inch from numerous directions. The result was simply appalling.

Alexander had been up early inspecting the artillery placements, but the dawn had come on grey and murky. They had not gotten a good look at the Yankees as they advanced, only heard the shouts and cheers go up, and knew well enough what those meant. All night long they had labored to construct a new line of works behind the old one in the narrow area the Yankees had broken through two days before. The new line was a sort of bow or horseshoe shape, set directly behind the old, in a design that would subject any assailant who entered the bow to a withering fire from all angles; the deeper the penetration, the more enfilading the fire. Now the Yanks were on their way, and there was nothing left to do but load again and wait.

"General, do you see anything?"

Alexander turned, saw a captain by one of the guns. "Not yet, but rest assured, they are on their way!" he replied. He glanced up at the clearing sky. "First light!" he yelled. "I'm afraid this is General Grant's favorite hour. Stand by your guns, Captain. They'll be in your sights soon enough!"

Then they saw the Yankees come up through the mist, long battle lines three deep in places. Alexander watched as they came on—flags flying, marching smartly in formation—storming up and over the old, evacuated trenches, then stumbling headfirst into the horseshoe with no real idea of what was waiting for them. It was to prove an unwelcome surprise.

WINDMILL POINT

Here the guns had been double, even triple-shotted with canister. With such a concentration of artillery, and at such close range, his crews could hardly miss. Wood lots, small stands of trees, sturdy oaks and narrow saplings, clumps of brambles and weeds along with regiment upon regiment of Yankee soldiers were all blown away in a sudden, savage rage of howling lead. Guns bucked, smoke swirled, and riflemen fired again and again, leaving the ground ripped, burnt, and bloody beyond imagination. The poor Yanks appeared suddenly out of the mist, and within seconds had been blown back into it again.

After the initial avalanche of fire, the Confederates settled down to a steady fusillade, firing at anything that moved or appeared to move on the ground along their front. The Yankees tried to return the fire as best they could, but they appeared to be pinned down on open ground, and the storm of Rebel missiles made movement virtually impossible. Grant had thrown everything he had at them, and the initial clash was like two titans colliding. Down in the works infantrymen were firing so rapidly that Alexander feared their guns would foul, or that they would use up their allotment of ammunition before the Yankees finally struck the line. His batteries were firing and bucking and reloading as fast as they could manage. The roar of battle was the most deafening Alexander had ever heard.

He moved rapidly from battery to battery, checking the ammunition chests on the limbers, and ordering up fresh ammunition all across the front. He had to write small notes to communicate with the battery crews, as the deafening thunder of the guns was making speech all but impossible. Gun smoke boiled over the earthworks and mingled with the last of the morning mist. Despite the increasing sunlight, visibility in the area between the lines was close to zero. After a while they seemed to be firing at little more than shadows. One of his captains held up a note to him, which read—"Where are the Yankees?"

Alexander read it, smiled briefly, then rolled his shoulders. For the time being, at least, they were nowhere to be found.

CHAPTER NINE

JUNE 3RD—DAWN

WHITE

White stood, watching in horror as the great assault unraveled before his eyes, Joe Thompson by his side. Both men were appalled by what they saw. From north to south the boom and crash of guns shook the earth like a chorus of thunder, and smoke billowed over the treetops in rippling torrents. In that one awful moment it seemed to Wyman White as though the whole world might well be coming to an end, such was the magnitude of sound and death and misery.

The infantry had not been moving forward for more than ten minutes when the Rebels opened on them with everything they had. In only seconds the scene was entirely obscured by smoke. After a few minutes, however, that blanket of smoke began to rise just slightly, leaving behind small pockets of visibility here and there, and while it was hardly the grand view he had witnessed before, it was enough for him to begin piecing things together. Directly ahead, the attack appeared to have come unhinged; some men were trying to flee the murderous Rebel volleys as the lines behind them continued to press forward. The ranks were thus colliding, falling, tripping, stumbling everywhere. Wyman could clearly see that many of the men were on the ground. Whether they were dead, wounded, or just taking cover was impossible to tell.

Joe Thompson rubbed his face nervously. "This here looks awful!" he hollered in order to be heard, scratching his boot heel in the dirt nervously.

Wyman White knew it was true, but understood as well that the infantry had just stepped off barely ten minutes before. "It ain't over yet, Joe!" he yelled back, still hoping for the best. "This army's got a heck of a lot of fight left in it. The day has just begun! You wait and see!"

Thompson stared out at the carnage and cringed. "I seen plenty enough fighting to know what I'm looking at, Sarge!" Thompson screamed back. "So have you. The longer they stay out there the worse it's gonna get. That's my opinion!"

"No. We're gonna break 'em!" Wyman insisted, but a hollow, sickening feeling was beginning to invade his stomach.

"No, we ain't, Sarge!" Joe objected. "Least not here! Maybe someplace up the line, but not here. Not today. And you know it!" Thompson dropped his head; he could not watch anymore.

Wyman frowned, and looked back into the tumbling smoke. Directly ahead the red nips, puckers, and flashes of Confederate guns were blazing away so relentlessly that they occasioned a sort of pulsating, crimson glow, not unlike a vibrant sunset all across the western horizon. Indeed, from where Wyman stood it appeared the Federal infantry was not advancing against a mortal foe at all so much as marching directly toward the glowing gates of hell. Even for a seasoned veteran like Wyman White, it was an unnerving spectacle.

"This is one hell of a piece of business, if you ask me!" Joe Thompson yelled, not so much astonished anymore as angry.

"Well, yes, it does appear ugly from here!" Wyman agreed finally, watching the horizon flash scarlet.

Along the Union entrenchments officers were moving about impatiently now, trying to fathom just what had happened. Field glasses in hand, they were squinting and pointing and gesturing this way and that, trying to make sense of the chaos

WINDMILL POINT

and carnage through mystifying twirls of smoke. It seemed a bewildering task. So many men, officers, and flags were already down that the attack had lost all coherence and resembled little more than a vast, bloody jumble.

General Hancock sat his horse like a statue not fifty yards away, staring glumly into the swirling melee. Hancock, Wyman knew, was not one to panic.

Wyman White had nothing but respect for Winfield Hancock—thought him perhaps the finest officer in the entire army, after Grant. Hancock had been seriously wounded on the third day at Gettysburg during the repulse of Picket's now famous charge, not far from where Wyman had been positioned that afternoon. The general had returned to the army prematurely, still suffering from the effects of his wounds, but Hancock was made of stern stuff and nothing was going to keep him away. Not many understood such commitment and fortitude, but Wyman did. He admired Hancock as much for his character as he did for his skill as an officer. Whether the wounds, years, and constant pain had affected his judgment or not Wyman could not say, but something had clearly gone wrong that morning at Cold Harbor.

Just then the smoke lifted for a moment, and it only took one quick glance to see that the assault was being utterly shot to pieces. As the ranks of blue infantry continued their advance they were being methodically mowed down line by line, just as wheat falls before the scythe. Wyman watched in horror as row upon row of men pitched backward, then toppled to the ground in unison like hundreds of falling dominoes. Whole regiments went down together, flags tumbling, never to come back up again. The ground in front of the Rebel entrenchments was cluttered with bodies, many of them writhing in pain. The dead were beyond counting, the wounded too far away to help. In many places bodies lay in assembled ranks, just as they had marched off only minutes before, all cut down in the same flash of a moment. In others they were piled on top of one another in heaps and stacks like wood stacked for winter burning. The slaughter was simply appalling. Wyman had never seen anything like it.

Joe Thompson took a deep breath and turned away, unwilling to witness the gruesome spectacle. "I hope they don't have any ideas of sending us out there too, Sarge!" he screamed. "There ain't a square inch of livable ground out there. Hell, our boys aren't being killed, they're being *murdered*."

Wyman folded his arms across his chest, a sudden sense of depression consuming him. "I don't know, Joe!" he hollered back. "I really don't know what to say!" He turned toward division headquarters but saw no sign of any imminent movement. All the officers seemed either confused or stunned, struck dumb by the scene before them. No one said a word.

Three times that morning the blue infantry reformed and tried the Rebel works and three times they were blown to bits. From what Wyman saw they never got closer than a few yards from the Confederate entrenchments, and those that managed to get that close paid for their valor with their lives.

The worst of it was over in no more than twenty minutes. After that the few blue infantrymen who were still alive tried simply to burrow into the ground and avoid the barrage of bullets that greeted every movement. To move or crawl drew an immediate hail of bullets. To stand meant instant death. What was left of the assault was utterly pinned down between the lines, but there didn't appear to be much of it left.

Never had Wyman seen men display more raw courage. Many of the boys he had stayed with the night before, he knew, now lay dead or wounded on the ground before him. It was simply ghastly. They had gone across the field with their names pinned to the back of their coats, knowing all the while they would probably not return. It was surely one of the bravest things he had ever seen. And it had all been for nothing.

CHAPTER TEN

JUNE 3RD—MORNING

LEE

Robert E. Lee found a seat on a short stump behind the lines, where he waited, listening intently for the sound of the guns. Lee had risen early, nervous about the strength of his line, then slipped quietly from his tent into the silent, dewy morning. At first there was only a sense of peace, a deep and profound silence that seemed to stretch out and hold the entire world in its grasp. Strange, in the midst of this awful war, he thought, to stumble upon such a tranquil moment. The ground was wet, the air still thick with mist. There were no sounds to speak of. Nothing moved.

For a moment he was reminded of his youth in Alexandria, of days when he would rise early only to discover the fog hanging low and heavy just beyond his window in the city streets that led down to the Potomac River. Then he would gladly tumble back into bed again, and sleep for another hour or so under a tangled heap of warm covers. When his mother finally called up the stairs, the fog would often have burned away and the sky stood clear and blue in the heavens beyond his window, like a blissful invitation to a fine new day. It was a pleasant memory, and he hovered there for just a moment before turning away.

Robert E. Lee walked along the edge of the tents, vaguely watching the mist as it spiraled over Doctor Gaines's millponds across the road, and his thoughts turned to Grant. Lee was sure the Union general would attack at first light, just as he had done so many times during the month of May. It was a practical move, of course. Should Grant score a breakthrough he would have all day to press whatever advantage he'd gained, and Lee knew only too well that in war a few precious hours of daylight could often spell the difference between victory and defeat.

Lee had lost Stonewall Jackson from just such a misstep in '63, Jackson riding out beyond his lines at Chancellorsville to press an attack forward into the darkness that with just a few more hours of light might have crushed the Army of the Potomac against the banks of the Rappahannock River and ended the war that very night. But in the murky no-man's-land between the lines, his own troops could not identify Jackson or his party, and a North Carolina regiment cut him down. Jackson lost his arm, but everyone still thought he would live. Sadly, it was not to be, and a few days later Stonewall Jackson was dead. With that the South lost one of her legends, and Lee his most trusted lieutenant. Now Lee himself was tired and ill, and his finest officers often sick and confused. At times he wondered just how long they could all go on against Grant's overwhelming numbers.

Near the base of a large maple he discovered a pile of wood, and he sat on the largest and most inviting stump. When he looked up he spotted Taylor right behind him.

"Good to see you up, General," Taylor said, radiating energy as usual. "I have coffee boiling already. May I bring you a cup?"

Lee smiled, appreciated the young man more than ever now. "That would be wonderful, Colonel. Thank you. Have you heard anything from the front yet?"

WINDMILL POINT

Taylor smiled, sniffed the air. "Not a thing, sir," he replied. "But it may be somewhat early for our good General Grant. Soon, though, I suspect we will hear his usual greeting."

Lee frowned. "Yes, I'm sure you're right."

"And then, he will receive ours in response, General."

Lee nodded.

Taylor smiled broadly. "Let me get you that coffee, sir."

The officer disappeared into the darkness and Lee was left alone again with his thoughts. He had fretted all night that his line was too long, and that as a result, somewhere there had to be a weakness that he was not aware of. But there was really no way to shorten the line and still guard his flanks, so it stretched a good six miles and required almost every last man he had to defend it. Yet the river ran behind him, and if Grant found a weakness....

"Here we are, sir, piping hot for such a chilly morning."

Lee reached for the cup, took it gladly, and enjoyed a long sip. He said nothing, let the heat spread its magic slowly throughout his body. Lee was beginning to feel better now, could feel the strength beginning to return to his legs. For a while yesterday he had almost felt like his old self again. But he was still very weak, and he was beginning to think the army needed someone else, someone younger perhaps, to see this war for independence through to the end. Yes, a younger man was needed, with the strength and stamina to fight Grant off, maintain the army, and carry the hopes of the fledgling Confederacy on his back. Often now he thought that it would not be so terribly difficult to turn the job over to someone else. Maybe then he could go back to Richmond and simply... rest. But, of course, there was no one else.

Lee finished his coffee, and handed the cup back to Taylor. "Are we certain that Breckinridge is now in position on Hoke's flank, Colonel? That is a very critical area. Those people broke us there the other day. Grant is no fool. Don't think he won't be back. We cannot afford any miscues today."

"He is where you ordered him, sir," Taylor answered. "I checked myself last evening."

"You did? Oh, very well then. And have the...?"

Lee stopped in mid-sentence, a low rumble, like rolling thunder, suddenly booming up from the east. Both men shifted slightly and cocked their heads to better hear. The sound grew and grew, the ground beginning to vibrate under their feet. Within minutes the whole earth seemed to be roaring and shaking with the terrible music of war.

Lee stared at his adjutant. "That would be General Grant."

"And our welcoming committee in response." Taylor pulled his watch from his pocket and flipped it open. "Right on time as usual, General. I have 4:46."

Lee closed his eyes, listened for a few seconds. "The whole front is alive," he said. "Grant has come in with everything he has."

"Yes, and so I guess we will simply have to repulse everything he has, General. The boys are prepared."

Lee nodded slowly, but was not so sure. He took a deep breath and listened intently as the furious rumbles rolled and oscillated across the treetops, trying in vain to make some sense of the extraordinary symphony of violence.

Daylight began peeking through the mist now, and Lee could just make out the other staff officers standing out by their tents, ears turned toward the mayhem. Whether any of it meant victory or defeat was impossible to say at that early hour, but he knew that if a breakthrough occurred his troops would come washing back like a broken, panicked wave through the woods, and he would have to try and stem the tide himself. He had no reserves to plug any gap, so the only option left would be to try and rally the men. Lee's heart began to beat faster.

WINDMILL POINT

Up the road about fifty yards, a shell crashed into some high branches and sent them toppling onto the road below. Then another landed in Doctor Gaines's front yard, pitching a giant wedge of dirt and grass up toward the front steps.

Lee folded his arms across his chest slowly, cleared his throat. "The Yankee artillery is losing the range," he noted. "Do you see? The front must be very much obscured with smoke. They can't see at all, so now they've lost the proper elevation. Those people don't usually shoot high. Their artillery is good. Very good."

Taylor looked at him queerly. "What does it mean, General?"

"Hard to say exactly," Lee replied softly, trying to visualize it all in his mind's eye. "But I'm guessing our lines are holding. That would explain such a concentration of smoke."

"Yes, sir. I understand."

They sat together without saying another word for almost a half hour, listening only to the great rumble off to the east. Then, slowly, there came breaks and gaps in the thunder, moments of lesser intensity, followed in turn by brief periods of what might almost be called calm.

Lee shook his head, stood suddenly. "General Grant's initial assault has quite possibly been repulsed," he said. "I need reports from the field. I want to know the conditions all along the line. The fighting was very brief. Perhaps it was nothing more than a feint, you see, something to confuse us. I need some information... now."

"I will send the couriers, sir," Taylor responded, leaping to his feet. He left immediately to attend to the task.

Robert E. Lee strolled slowly back toward his tent, nodded politely to several officers as he passed, then sat on his camp chair and waited. Here near Doctor Gaines's house, at least, there were no signs of a Federal breakthrough, no streams of Confederate soldiers swarming through the woods in chaos toward the rear. That was something surely to be thankful for. He crossed his legs, and sipped from a second cup of coffee.

Maybe twenty minutes later two riders came bounding down the road and reined to a stop in the muck nearby. Taylor jogged down a short hill to converse with them both, then turned and came back to report as the riders disappeared up the road again.

Lee turned slowly, patiently awaiting the news.

Taylor was smiling, could not contain himself. "The first report was from General Hoke, sir. The second from Wilcox."

"Go on."

"Well, sir," Taylor continued, catching his breath, "Hoke reports that the Yankees have been entirely repulsed all across his front. He says the ground over which the Yanks advanced is literally *covered* with the bodies of their dead and wounded. And, sir, General Hoke reports that he has not lost a *single* man! Not *one*! The rout was complete!"

Lee did not blink. "And Wilcox?"

"Wilcox was not even *engaged*, General. He reports the Federal advance never even made it to his lines!"

Lee nodded, seeing another rider approaching on the road. He pointed. "Tell him to come up here if you would, Colonel. I would like to hear directly from this man."

Taylor turned, waved the courier forward. The rider, a captain, sweating and covered in mud, dismounted with a quick twirl. He handed his reins to an orderly and scampered up the hill. There the captain stopped in front of Taylor and saluted. He was breathing hard. "Sir," he gushed, trying to catch his breath, "sir, General Hill begs to report that the Yankees have been severely repulsed all across his front. The Yankees are now lying in vast heaps just beyond his works. It is that way all along his entire front, sir."

Lee returned the officer's salute. "Thank you, Captain," he said. "Please get yourself a drink of water or some coffee before returning to your command. You deserve it. Your report has been very much appreciated. Please tell General Hill to keep us informed."

The captain smiled, shook his head. "Yes, sir. Thank you, sir!"

The reports came in steadily for the next half hour, each remarkably similar, all touting significant success. The Yanks had been thrashed. There had been a slight breakthrough on Breckinridge's front—Lee had known that Grant would hit that area hard—but that small setback had been easily contained, then quickly reversed.

Lee listened to all the reports carefully, slowly piecing the event together just as one assembles a jigsaw puzzle, piece by jagged piece. By 7 o'clock that morning the picture appeared to be complete. There were no additional reports of renewed fighting, so it was natural to assume that Grant's initial assault had not been a demonstration or feint after all. No, Grant had come at him with a major force and had been thoroughly whipped in minutes only. It sounded almost too good to be true. Could it really have been that simple? He stood and called for Traveler. He would have to go see for himself.

CHAPTER ELEVEN

JUNE 3RD—MORNING

GRANT

U.S. Grant had ridden with his staff to a central location behind the lines in the early hours, so that they might judge for themselves the effect of the great assault. All commanders had been notified of his movement, and instructed to file prompt reports once the attack was underway. In that manner, any breakthroughs could be properly reinforced, and Lee's line collapsed as soon as possible. They all had some coffee and eggs before departing, and spirits were high. Now everything was set. The whole army would be moving forward at first light to engage Lee's entire six-mile front. There was great anticipation among the staff, the sense that this might truly be the final assault. The smell of victory seemed to hang in the air.

The telegraph tent—the most important accommodation, and the first to go up—was only a few feet away, and the staff waited in the open while the other tents were being erected. The morning air was cool and wet, but no one seemed to mind. Grant sat close to General Andrew Humphreys, his new Chief-of-Staff of Operations. Humphreys was a commanding figure and a fine soldier who had the respect of the entire army. Grant also considered him sane and sensible, not at all prone to the violent bursts of temper that often affected George Meade. Things were bound to go wrong in war, and when problems occurred he much preferred to think, rather than shout, his way through them. While Meade was a fine soldier, his fits of temper often cast a pall over his own headquarters staff, making effective communication next to impossible.

Humphreys was wired to all the corps' headquarters via the telegraph, an innovation that had vastly improved coordination between the far-flung wings of the army. Now Grant had up to date information from all parts of the battlefield, and could respond sensibly within minutes. Only a year or so ago they had been bound to horse-mounted couriers who often took twenty minutes or more to deliver a single report—and that only if they got through. Now the messages were almost instantaneous. The telegraph had altered the face of war.

In short order the tents were pitched, and everyone made themselves comfortable. More pots of coffee were set to boiling, and the first, faint trace of light began to gently streak the eastern horizon. Grant checked his watch. It was just past 4:30. Soon, he thought. Ten minutes later the heavens exploded with the most violent cannonading he had ever heard—the assault, he reasoned, must have struck the Confederate lines.

For a long while, as the tenor of battle rose to an ominous pitch, the telegraph remained silent. Officers shuffled back and forth, or stared at the ground, or quietly sipped their coffee. Others smiled while chatting amiably, pretending that all was well. Grant sat by himself and said nothing as minutes that seemed like hours slowly ticked away. Then there was a sudden clatter in the telegraph tent, and everyone stopped what they were doing. No one moved.

Humphreys stood, walked slowly to the telegraph and took the message. He read it slowly, methodically, then strolled back toward Grant and sat at his field desk. He held up the paper. "It's from Smith," Humphreys said, referring to "Baldy" Smith, an officer Grant had recently transferred east from the Western theater. Baldy Smith was one of Grant's favorites.

George Meade folded his arms behind his back. "And?"

Grant leaned forward just slightly.

"It doesn't sound favorable," Humphreys continued, handing the message over to Grant. "He reports that two of his three divisions are cut-up and pinned down. He is facing heavy enfilading fire on both of his flanks. He says he cannot advance any further unless the fire on his flanks is subdued. And he cannot subdue it."

Grant leaned back, crossed his legs. "Well, that's not so bad," he said. "Wright should be coming up on his left very soon and Warren on his right. They should be able to relieve the pressure on both of his flanks almost immediately. Then they should all go in together..." He stopped, looked over at Meade. "They all need to go in together. I thought that had been taken care of?"

Meade grew slightly red in the face. "Yes, of course. I gave the orders yesterday. All corps commanders were to coordinate their assaults."

Grant turned back to Humphreys. "Once the other two corps come up on his flanks, Smith will advance with them. He knows his business. I think we're okay."

Humphreys stared at him blankly for a moment then looked away.

Just after 6 o'clock the telegraph began to tap again. Meade sprang from his seat and marched off to the tent. "It's from Wright!" he called back over his shoulder. Meade took the message, read it carefully then dropped both arms to his sides. "My God!' was all he said.

Grant re-crossed his legs, and took a long puff on his cigar. His pulse quickened.

George Meade handed the message to Humphreys who digested every last detail deliberately before speaking. Then he looked directly at Grant. "Wright reports that he too is taking

WINDMILL POINT

enfilading fire on his flanks. *He* cannot advance unless the corps on *his* flanks do likewise."

Grant stared down at the grass between his boots. "So Smith waits on Wright while Wright waits for Smith. Where is Hancock? What about Warren and Burnside? Where is everyone?"

Meade, now clearly demoralized, looked up into the sky for a moment. "All right, all right," he said finally. Meade walked back over to the telegrapher. "Tell Wright I want him to move forward immediately, independent of whatever Smith does. Then tell Smith that Wright has orders to attack at once, and he is ordered to attack as well, regardless of Wright. They must *move*, damn it! Now!" The orders were promptly relayed, but over the slow, unfolding minutes nothing seemed to happen. Then messages came in from both Burnside and Warren indicating some initial success. Buoyed by the reports, Grant ordered the assault pressed in all quarters, but in time it was discerned that both Warren's and Burnside's success's were more imagined than real. Reports from Hancock came in both confused and conflicting. Other messages were received that contradicted previous reports, at times, even themselves. The assault was rapidly devolving into a confused jumble. From their tent behind the lines it was impossible to tell what was actually taking place on the field. Ulysses Grant quickly realized that he might as well have been on the moon for all the good the telegraphed reports were doing him.

But one thing was clear. The heavy sound of battle from the front had dropped off significantly; that could only mean that the fighting had for some reason subsided. Meade sent urgent orders out to all corps commanders to advance again and again, but nothing seemed to come of those orders.

At 6:30 Meade, along with his entire staff, mounted-up and left for the field. Grant, frustrated by all the confusion, sent Cyrus Comstock, one of his own aides, off to see Baldy Smith in the hope that Smith's problems could be clarified, and that he could resume his movement forward. Then Grant sat down and waited for additional reports, but those soon trailed off to but a trickle. Oddly, not one of those was even the slightest bit optimistic. To Grant the whole thing made no sense. There was no reason the attack should not move forward smoothly. There was no reason the great assault should not have been successful.

Just after 7:00 o'clock Grant received a note from Meade that did not sound promising at all. The general indicated he would be glad to have Grant's opinion "as to the continuance of the attacks."

Grant read the message aloud twice to Humphreys and fought to contain his anger. Meade, he had come to believe, was simply scared to press an attack. Any attack. Not scared for his own safety—Meade was no coward—but fearful for the loss of his troops.

But death was an integral part of war, and when it came to that, Grant seemed to understand one thing far better than anyone else: the misery and death would not end until the war was won, and the war would only be won by pushing the thing to a vigorous conclusion. In the end far more men would suffer and perish by the use of timid, inconsequential tactics that just prolonged the hostilities, than would ever be lost in one, thunderous assault that might sweep the Confederacy into oblivion. The anger boiled in his chest. Why could they not understand? The press called him a "butcher" now, but the end of the war lay in Richmond, and Lee and his whole army stood in his way. Grant was not trying to destroy his own army. He was trying to *win* the war. Grant stood, paced back and forth for a moment. Then he tossed his hands in the air plaintively and glared at Humphreys. "Do I have to teach him how to fight this war?"

"Sir?" Humphreys replied.

WINDMILL POINT

"Yes, I mean George Meade, and you know it! Is that really necessary?"

His chief-of-staff merely returned his gaze, said nothing at all.

Grant puffed on his cigar furiously. "Does he think I don't see the long lines of coffins heading north every day?" he demanded. "Do they all think that? Well, I see them!"

Humphreys cleared his throat. "To attack is a part of war, General," he replied calmly. "We all understand that. To attack senselessly, imprudently, is not."

Grant stared at him for a moment. "Do you think that is what has been done here today?"

"No, General. The assault made perfect sense this morning. But now the situation may have changed." Humphreys picked up his pen, smiled. "Now, how would you have me respond to General Meade?"

Grant took a long pull on his cigar, blew the smoke out slowly. He began to calm down. "Okay, fine," he said. "Tell him this: When it becomes obvious they will not succeed, break off the attacks. But when one does succeed push it vigorously, and if necessary, pile in troops."

Humphreys finished writing then motioned for a courier. "Take this to General Meade," he said. "Quickly."

The courier raced from the tent and Grant returned to his seat. "There is no reason these attacks cannot still succeed this morning," he insisted, as much to himself as to his chief-of-staff. "Lee is *weak*. He must break *somewhere* if we press him *everywhere*! That is the plan."

"Yes, General," Humphreys replied.

But the enemy was not pressed that morning and the breakthrough he had been waiting for never materialized. By 11:00 o'clock the sound of the guns had trailed off to almost nothing. Order after order had been issued to all the corps commanders, but for some reason no one advanced. By then it was painfully obvious that something had gone terribly wrong.

Tired of waiting, of guessing, of reports that made no sense, Grant marched from the tent and called for his horse. If the great assault could still be pushed, then by God he would push it himself.

CHAPTER TWELVE

JUNE 3RD—LATE MORNING

ALEXANDER

Edward Porter Alexander stood for a long while and simply stared at the ground in front of his guns, overwhelmed by the scene.

Once the Yankee assault appeared to have withdrawn, he had made sure that all of his batteries were adequately supplied with fresh ammunition. He then returned to the front. At first it was not even clear just what had happened. So voluminous had the Confederate fire been, and so quickly had the Yanks disappeared back into the smoke and mist, that it was difficult to determine at first whether the Federals had attacked in strength and been repulsed, or had approached only weakly—a probe or reconnaissance in force—and then withdrawn. A few of his guns had barely opened before the whole thing simmered down and appeared over.

Once the sun rose and the smoke cleared, however, it became frighteningly apparent just what had occurred. All along the front—within 100 to 200 yards of the Confederate entrenchments—the ground was simply covered with the bodies of the wounded and dead. Here were heaps and rows and mounds of bodies in all manner of gruesome poses, blanketing the earth, acre upon bloody acre. In the small dips and narrow furrows of ground the dead lay on top of one another as if stacked, apparently having sought any sort of natural cover they could find before being struck down anyway. Not one of them moved, the slightest tremor now drawing at least a score of shots. Alexander assumed that some of the Yankees had to still be alive and were simply playing possum. He pitied those that were. For there would be neither help nor refuge for them out there on that pitiless ground, at least for the time being.

At Gettysburg he had taken his artillery out far in advance, in support of Picket on that third and fateful day, and Alexander had learned a frightful lesson that afternoon about the awful damage that could be inflicted by artillery on troops advancing across open ground. The Yankees had had almost a hundred guns in play against the Confederate infantry as they closed on Cemetery Ridge that terrible afternoon. When the Yank muskets had finally joined in, Picket's attack had no longer appeared a formation of troops at all, but had taken on the appalling specter of a cloud of dirt and smoke barreling across the open fields, like a storm on the Great Plains, trailing toppled flags and dying men in its wake. It was something he had never forgotten, and often he marveled at how even a single Confederate soldier had managed to live through that terrible July afternoon. Alexander could really not imagine a more thorough and relentless fusillade than the Yanks had laid down that day, but the carnage at Gettysburg on July 3rd, 1863, did not even come close to matching what he saw on the fields before him now.

Here at Cold Harbor it had all ended in less than twenty minutes. Indeed, so brief and ineffective had the Federal assault been that many Confederate officers did not even realize anything of substance had taken place. It was not until the smoke finally cleared and they had a chance to examine the ground that the almost unbelievable truth was discovered; the Yankees had suffered a staggering, awful, and lopsided defeat.

WINDMILL POINT

Porter Alexander was a professional artilleryman, so he took the opportunity to study the distribution of the dead and wounded on the field with utter detachment, analytically assessing the effect his batteries had had on the approaching ranks of infantry just as a professor of rhetoric might deliberate the structure of a sentence. He was most interested in which positions and configurations of guns had proved the most effective. The heaps of Yankee dead represented evidence, therefore, and nothing more, and the evidence this day offered compelling testimony to the almost unholy performance of his guns. The Yanks had been blown away by a veritable wall of lead. In the final analysis, their attack had been suicidal.

Yet, on the Confederate side, few men were even injured. Firing from well-constructed works with substantial head logs in most cases, the Rebels had hardly been grazed. To Alexander's mind, the affair appeared to be the most one-sided of the entire war. Now men joked with one another as they reloaded and fired, jocular as boys on a squirrel hunt.

His artillery continued a sporadic shelling while the infantry took aim at even the slightest movement. While the guns still rattled and thundered, it was becoming increasingly apparent that the major fighting for the day was over. Wherever possible, the Yanks had burrowed like prairie dogs into the dirt, digging with their cups, bayonets, even fingers, in order to escape the hellish fire that raked the open ground above them. Almost unwittingly, it seemed, the Confederacy appeared to have scored a major victory without even knowing what it had accomplished. Grant's attempt to break their lines and move against Richmond had been violently dashed by some twenty minutes of concentrated hell.

Later that morning Alexander encountered General Lee, out briefly to inspect the lines. The general appeared pleased with everything he saw, and nodded approvingly toward Alexander as he trotted by on Traveler. "General Alexander!" he called out.

"Good morning, General Lee," Alexander replied.

"You know your business, sir," Lee said with a smile. "I will never forget your advice on the positioning of our artillery at Fredericksburg. Indeed, you know your business very well, General Alexander, and today your batteries proved their mettle again."

"Thank you, General."

"God appears to have granted us a great victory today, General."

"Yes, it surely appears that way, General," Alexander replied. "God and our guns."

Lee smiled, saluted, and rode off.

For the rest of the morning, Alexander instructed his crews to maintain a harassing fire on the Federal lines in order to delay and restrict any plans they might be hatching, but nothing ever came together, and no sizeable force approached. Indeed, the opposite seemed to be the case. Substantial units of blue infantry appeared to be poised and ready to advance at times, only to remain inert and motionless instead. From Alexander's vantage point, the great Federal war machine seemed rudderless and broken. By late morning the sun was high, and the sultry summer heat had returned. On the fields before them the Yankee wounded cried for water and mercy. Neither was forthcoming. Confederate riflemen hung low in their pits, saving their strength and energy for the Yankees' next move. But, except for the few blue wounded who tried to crawl from the field back to the safety of their own lines—and lost their lives in the effort—to Porter Alexander the Yankees appeared to have lost all inclination toward movement. Grant's great assault had been utterly and brutally repulsed.

CHAPTER THIRTEEN

JUNE 3RD—FORENOON

GRANT

Grant rode hard, the irritation in his chest having blossomed into a gnawing sense of frustration. None of it made any sense, not the reports, the slackening of gunfire, or the glaring lack of progress all across the six-mile front. So he would find out for himself just what was going on—eliminate the layers of staff, all the carefully crafted messages, and the slow, awful pecking of the telegraph. What good were instant messages when they told you nothing? What use was a machine that spit out only confusion?

Ulysses Grant left his headquarters in a huff, called for his horse, and, with several staff members trailing behind like a flapping pennant, rode off for the front. He'd start at the top, then work his way down the chain of command if need be. The first stop was nearby at Hancock's headquarters. Grant intended to talk to each corps commander face-to-face so there would be no more confusion or evasion, no misinterpretations. Then he could look into their eyes and see for himself just how they stood and spoke—how their bodies betrayed their ideas and emotions, be that for better or worse. Then he would know. Then he could *do* something.

Grant looked forward to seeing Hancock, because he respected him as the hardest hitter in the Army of the Potomac.

Winfield Scott Hancock was nothing if not aggressive. Indeed, at times he actually had to be held back, given just a bit of rein slowly, like you give a young colt, so that he didn't go storming off and wreck himself and everything around him. Hancock was a fighter. He was not at all like Warren or Burnside, endlessly slow and rarely, if ever, where they were supposed to be when you needed them there. Hancock was fast and furious, and generally professional. If anything of the great assault could still be salvaged, Grant knew that Hancock would be the man to do it.

The sun was high now, the day warming. Grant took a sniff. The air felt close, his clothes already sticky. The flags drooped lamely on their poles as he approached the 2nd Corps headquarters and reined his horse to a stop. Here, in the open, the wet ground had already dried, and a light dust swirled for just a moment.

Several of Hancock's staff officers were standing about. They saluted smartly but there was a sense of gloom almost palpable in the air around them. Hancock was lying down, Grant was told, worn thin from his efforts of the last twenty-four hours, but the commanding general, they knew, was not to be put off, and one went off to fetch their commander. Grant pulled out his watch, took a look—it was 11:12.

Soon Hancock appeared, obviously exhausted and in considerable pain—the wound he had suffered at Gettysburg had yet to heal properly—and he leaned against a camp chair for support. He was a large, robust, handsome man, but today he did not look well. Hancock saluted.

Grant returned the salute and smiled briefly, trying to force his own hopes back into one of his most trusted subordinates. "How are you, General?" Grant asked.

"I am fine, sir," Hancock replied, tottering noticeably against the chair as he spoke.

WINDMILL POINT

"I would like to renew the assault as soon as possible," Grant told him, coming straight to the point. "Can your corps lead the way?"

Grant's question was met by nothing more than stony silence. Hancock's staff appeared sullen, the general himself staring at the ground. Finally he looked back up at Grant. "Did you say, 'renew the assault,' sir?" Hancock asked.

"Yes."

Hancock sighed. "General Grant," he said, "my corps was very roughly handled this morning. We are still trying to tabulate the casualties. That will take, I am told,... quite a while. We were hit *hard*."

Grant hesitated for a moment, knowing that Hancock was not one to exaggerate. He took a puff on his cigar, then looked again at the eyes of the staff officers as they gazed up at him. One seemed half defiant, the other half dead. Then they looked quickly away, and Grant was starting to feel uncomfortable. He let the smoke drift out of his mouth slowly. "How hard?"

"Very *hard*," Hancock repeated emotionally. "Both Gibbon and Barlow suffered extensive casualties. At least thirty, perhaps even fifty percent. Some regiments are simply ... gone. We hit the Rebels hard, broke them here and there, but we could not hold on. Now both divisions are dug in along their respective fronts, but for all practical purposes they are pinned down."

"Don't you still have Birney in reserve?"

"Yes."

"Well, if you send in your reserve, surely the other...."

Hancock folded his arms across his chest, anger clearly flashing in his eyes. He glared at Grant. "The position on my front cannot be taken," he stated emphatically.

Grant was stunned by the assertion but tried not to show it. "You're sure?"

"I'm sure."

"Very well then," Grant replied, as surprised as he had ever been in his life. But he kept his voice calm, fought hard not to tip his emotions. "See to your corps then, General," he said. Then he pulled his hat down low over his eyes, and, yanking the reins hard, Grant turned and rode off.

Ulysses Grant was beginning to feel beleaguered, confusion rapidly mushrooming into self-doubt. He was not one to spend much time second-guessing himself. Grant left that to the Washington brass, the politicians and journalists who were more than happy, it seemed, to make up for any deficiency, real or imagined, that he brought to that particular task. In war, he'd come to realize, a sensible course, well-taken and adhered to, was generally far more productive than the most brilliant of schemes, endlessly retooled and reshuffled. "Brilliancy" was a term McClellan had often used to describe his own initiatives, but all of McClellan's brilliant maneuvers had gotten him nowhere. If Grant blundered somewhere along the way, then he'd fix it and move on. No sense in looking back.

But the assault earlier that morning should not have been a blunder. Five corps striking the Rebel line simultaneously should have broken them somewhere. But it hadn't. And now one of his finest officers had glared at him as though he, Grant, was an incompetent amateur. The fighting had trailed off to almost nothing, and for some strange reason his army would not move. Could it really have been botched that badly?

Grant turned and rode north, Porter and Rawlins following closely behind, not one of them offering even a word of advice. They finally located Horatio Wright, and Wright was at least slightly more optimistic than Hancock had been. Wright agreed that a breach in the enemy's works was a possibility if he moved his whole corps forward. Grant became suddenly optimistic. Here at least was something to work with.

"What is your situation now?" Grant wanted to know.

WINDMILL POINT

"We're dug in across the entire front. My boys are under constant fire," Wright replied.

"Can you move forward?"

"I think so. Yes, possibly," Wright said.

Grant was encouraged, was beginning to feel at least somewhat reassured. "When can you begin?" he asked.

"Well," Wright replied, thinking it over, "I can move within the hour, I suppose." he answered.

"Fine," Grant told him, "Let's get...."

"But then of course," Wright interrupted, "nothing will come of it unless Smith and Hancock advance with me. If I go in alone, the Rebels will chop my lads to pieces. I can't do that again. This morning was nothing but a slaughter pen. Have you seen the front, General? Have you seen what it's like out there?"

Grant hesitated for a moment, surprised by the remark. "Not yet," he admitted. "I'm trying to piece something together. I want to *move*."

"Yes, fine," Wright said. "Tell me, General, what do Smith and Hancock say?"

Grant shrugged. "I haven't talked to Smith yet," he answered. "Hancock seems to think the Rebel position on his front cannot be taken. His troops were heavily engaged this morning. He says they are quite cut up."

"Well, so are *we*," Wright replied. Then he shook his head forlornly. "I can't possibly go in if Hancock won't cover my left. My boys will just be slaughtered... *again*."

Grant felt the last word like a slap in the face, knew it had been meant for him. He took a deep breath, struggling to hold off the anger that was fast rising in his chest. "Fine, all right," he said. "If I can get everyone to go in at once," he asked, "do you think you can take the Rebel works on your front?"

Horatio Wright rolled his eyes up toward the heavens. "Breach them,... perhaps. Take them? I doubt it. The Rebels are dug in, General Grant, and their artillery covers the field from every angle. This is a hell of a place to fight if you ask me, sir. One hell of a place."

"I see," Grant said.

So there was nothing to do but continue his trek north to see Smith, Burnside, and Warren and hope that something could be patched together. He found each in their headquarters tents, none of them pushing their men forward as previously ordered, all of them cool to his visit. Burnside was originally somewhat optimistic, but Warren—who was an extremely cautious commander in Grant's opinion—disagreed with Burnside entirely. Smith—who had refused to even communicate with Meade for the better part of the morning—was doubtful now that any assault, no matter how amply composed, could be successful against the formidable Confederate entrenchments.

If, to a man, his commanders were not reasonably assured of success, then any more orders to advance were simply a waste of time, and Grant knew it. So he returned to his own headquarters as thoroughly despondent as he had ever been during the course of the war, and at 12:30 wrote a note to General Meade. It read:

> The opinion of the corps commanders not being sanguine of success in case an assault is ordered, you may direct a suspension of farther advance for the present. Hold our most advanced positions, and strengthen them....

Then he stopped, put the pen down, and thought of something that only hours ago would have been beyond contemplation. If his army had suffered some sort of defeat—and increasingly it was looking as if it had—then Lee might actually be encouraged to go over to the offensive, come out of his entrenchments, and come after *him*. Many a Federal commander had had his career cut unnaturally short by taking

WINDMILL POINT

Lee lightly in the past. Could the hunter suddenly become the hunted? He thought for a moment, then picked up his pen and continued.

> Wright and Hancock should be ready to assault in case the enemy should break through General Smith's lines, and all should be ready to resist an assault.

At 1:30 that afternoon Meade distributed a circular based on Grant's instructions.

Grant received a copy and looked it over carefully. It read:

> Orders. For the present all further operations will be suspended. Corps commanders will entrench the positions they now hold, including their advance positions, and will cause reconnaissances to be made with a view to holding against the enemy's works by regular approaches.

Ulysses Grant finished reading the circular then tossed it aside in disgust. He slowly ran a hand back through his hair, feeling suddenly lost; as if he were drowning in something he couldn't quite comprehend. *This must be what quicksand feels like*, he thought. Then he slumped low in his chair, and felt a headache coming on. So he took a long sip of water and rubbed his temples gently with the tips of his fingers. The morning seemed to have turned into a nightmare, none of it making any sense. Unfortunately, one thing was now abundantly clear: for some unfathomable reason he appeared to have lost control of his army.

CHAPTER FOURTEEN

JUNE 3RD—AFTERNOON

WHITE

Wyman dove into the open trench, grabbed hold of a shovel, then quickly let the other man pass by. The soldier was nearly exhausted, covered in dirt. "Thanks, Sarge," the man said, smiling weakly.

"You had it, friend?" Wyman asked him, acknowledging the man's obvious efforts with a quick smile.

The soldier stopped, tried to wipe the sweat from his forehead with the back of a filthy hand. "For now, mate," he answered, breathing heavily. "But I'll be back. Just need some water and a short blow. We're getting closer now."

For hours they had been cutting trenches across the field of battle, ranging far out from the Federal works in a desperate race to get to the wounded. No cease-fire had yet been ordered, and the sun was high and hot, but nothing was going to stop them. The heart wrenching cries of the wounded were motivation enough.

No orders had been given, no authority needed, to begin the effort. They had all seen the assault, the terrible blasts from the Confederate works, the grizzly acres of dead and wounded that now littered the field. Men were digging frantically to get to their friends and relatives, or the officers they admired and had marched off to war with. They were digging because it was the right thing to do, because had it been any one of them out there on that blasted field they would expect someone at least to try and do the same. So now the dirt was flying, the trenches were moving forward, and they were inching closer by the hour.

Wyman could hear the cries of the wounded not too terribly far away: sad, desperate, unnerving. He tried not to listen, worked instead on the dirt right in front of his face. It was easier that way, one shovelful at a time, tossed back and over the head. That way he would get to the wounded as fast as he could, no time taken to worry or grieve, no time taken to think about what he had seen earlier that day or what was happening to those wounded men now caught out there in the open. It wasn't the assault that was eating at him; he had seen men die before. At Second Bull Run, Chancellorsville, and Gettysburg the fields had been almost as littered with bodies, their cries equally as piteous. Just weeks ago in the Wilderness he had lain awake on his rifle all night, and endured the cries of the wounded who could not escape the unforgiving wildfires that swept through the woods and dry thickets. The ground in the Wilderness could not be burrowed through as could that at Cold Harbor, so rather than take up the shovel, friends had taken up the rifle and drawn deadly aim on their own brothers and comrades, ending their lives in an instant with a bullet to spare them the agony of flames. All night long the dreadful pops rang out, men crying like babies as they squeezed the trigger. It was a terrible thing to ask a man to do, yet he had learned long ago that war was nothing if not a frightful business. But that at least was war. What had happened earlier that morning at Cold Harbor was a different story altogether.

Earlier that day the army had simply stopped fighting. There had been no plot, treachery, organization, or ringleaders. The reaction had been entirely spontaneous and considerably widespread. There had not even been the slightest talk of disobedience in the ranks that morning, and all the officers had taken their usual places. Then the awful assault had gone forward. All the men had seen what had happened, of course, and that was all it took.

Now no one was moving any more, despite all the orders coming down from Meade to attack; just as a fire dies when the last log finally burns out, so too had the army's will been extinguished by the result of that morning's ghastly assault. Cold Harbor appeared to be the last straw in a long month of horrific fighting, an involuntary point of no return that the army had crossed, and from which there appeared to be no return. The men had seen enough, and it was as simple as that. Orders had become meaningless. The troops would not fight any more.

From corps headquarters on down to the captains in the field, orders to attack were being issued but they were all being ignored. Most officers would no longer lead, and where they tried, the men would no longer follow. It was almost as if the spirit of the Army of the Potomac had been crushed under the heavy boot of that last, dreadful charge. There had been no vote, conspiracy, or even the slightest discussion. It had just happened. And now the army lay in and about its entrenchments at Cold Harbor, licking its wounds like a great wounded beast. Who could say when, or even if, it would stir to fight again?

Wyman had seen it all with his own eyes: Staff officers riding down the line by the score, delivering orders all along the front. In most cases no one so much as budged. Here and there the officers would order the men up and into lines of battle, all the while cursing loudly at the stupidity of the orders they'd been issued, as the troops slowly filed into position. But then when the order to advance was finally given, not a man moved, and the officers did nothing but shake their heads and thank God for the wisdom of their own men.

WINDMILL POINT

Whether it meant the end of the army, the war, or even the country, Wyman White could not say for sure. But he knew it was a moment like no other he'd ever witnessed, and that the future of the nation now hung in the balance. If the army would not fight anymore, then the war was surely lost, and the South would soon have its independence. Beyond that, he really had no idea what to make of it, nor clear opinion as to what to do next.

So, for the time being, Wyman White just dug away as hard as he could, animated by the needs of the wounded, and the fear that all the death, misery, and effort of the last three years might all have been for naught. It was all he could think to do. By late afternoon the trenches began to snake and bend all across the plain, giving the area between the lines the rough, haphazard appearance of an enormous burrow instinctively engineered by prairie dogs. Above ground death was almost instantaneous, but the Rebel rifles had no range below grade. So men struggled forward in the trenches, dirt flew by the shovelful, and the methodical clank of shovel on rock filled the air. When one of the boys digging ahead finally tired, his shovel was simply exchanged with someone waiting in the rear, and in that manner the work continued without a hitch throughout the long, hot afternoon. Details were sent back for water and blankets, and ropes dragged forward to wrap around the wounded in the hope of pulling them to safety. It seemed that almost every man was willing to pitch in.

Around 5 o'clock a few attempts were made to secure some of the wounded, but these proved futile and in some cases even fatal. The Rebels had the entire area in their sights, and their sharpshooters drew quick, steady beads on anything that moved. To range above the trenches in the light of day was to ask for an almost instantaneous death.

Once the trench came within striking range of the wounded, a soldier from Pennsylvania came clamoring up from the rear.

He was a man no more than perhaps twenty-three years old, dragging blankets and ropes behind, sweat pouring from his face. The fellow asked Wyman to help him recover his brother-in-law, who, he calculated, lay probably not too far distant from the end of the trench. The Pennsylvania boy had tied ropes to both ends of a blanket with the intention of wrapping his brother-in-law up once he'd found him, and then slowly pulling him back into the trench. Wyman, one of the finest sharpshooters in the army himself, did not fancy the odds for such an endeavor as being terribly high.

"You'd best wait till dark," Wyman told the man. "I know it's a few hours, but I believe it's the only way to get him out alive. You go up there now and the chances are you'll die right along with your brother-in-law. The Rebs got good rifles and they know how to shoot. They aim to kill anything that moves, Pilgrim."

Just then a man down the line inadvertently held his shovel aloft for a few seconds and a Rebel bullet blasted it right out of his hands. "Woow! Jesus Almighty!" the man screamed, diving down to the bottom of the trench.

Wyman shook his head. "See what I mean?"

But the Pennsylvania fellow would have none of it. "Hell," he cried, "he'll be dead by *dark*. You expect me to go home and tell my sister I did nothing but sit here and wait for him to *die*? Damn, Sarge, they're all gonna die if we don't get out there soon. All of 'em been lying all day in that awful sun, damned Rebs shooting away at 'em. They ain't none of 'em got any water." The Pennsylvania boy rolled his eyes then tossed his hands in the air. "Try now and maybe he dies," he said, "or wait till nightfall and bring him back dead for sure, as I see it. Don't seem like much of a choice to me, friend."

"Go ahead then, brother," Wyman told him. "But you'd best be awful careful. Move slow and stay behind the dead. Once you've found your brother-in-law, yank on the line, and me and some of the boys will pull him on in. You be careful now."

"Pull slow!" the soldier insisted. "Fast and they'll shoot him for sure."

"I understand," Wyman assured him.

So the man scurried up over the edge of the trench and was quickly gone. He was off for a while, searching through the bodies. From time to time they could hear him moving, cursing, and they could hear the bullets plunking off the ground, or burying themselves into other men's bodies. Occasionally someone would let out a gasp or a whimper when one of the bullets struck, and Wyman knew then that another poor soul had probably departed this pitiful earth.

It took the better part of a half hour, but then he finally saw the Pennsylvania man again. He scrambled back to the top of the trench, and told them to begin pulling. Wyman and two other men began pulling slowly, but the brother-in-law soon became snagged, and the Pennsylvania boy had to go back out again. This time it didn't take long. A few shots rang out, and the lines all went limp. Wyman had a sense of where the Pennsylvania boy had gone down, and he took a quick look—not more than a second above ground—and he spotted him far off at the end of the ropes. Then he quickly ducked and not more than a second or two later a bullet hummed right above where his head had been and splashed into the piled dirt nearby. But it was poor shooting, he thought—the Reb had pulled the trigger way too late.

Then Wyman turned back to the boys in the trench. "That Pennsylvania fellow is dead," he told them, and that was all he had to say. He didn't want to tell them the rest. He didn't want to talk about the hundreds upon hundreds of bloating, stinking bodies that lay strewn across the open fields, or about the corpses that had been torn to shreds by the Confederate canister, or the hands, arms, legs, and heads that littered the field just as leaves fill the woods in autumn. Wyman didn't care to talk about that.

The Pennsylvania boy was dead. He had died to save his kin and there was surely bravery and honor in that, but that didn't make him any less dead. Better had he waited till dark. Then there would have at least been a chance. They tried to pull on the ropes to pull the brother-in-law back in, but the ropes were snagged. No, it would have to wait till dark.

The boys in the trench shared a canteen, then took up the shovels again. They angled their digging far out amongst the bodies, hoping to have more than one route for rescues. Come darkness they would at least have a fighting chance of removing those few who were still alive, laying them on blankets, and pulling them slowly back to the trench, hopefully unseen in the darkness by the Confederate marksmen. But the cries were weakening now, fading by the hour. The sun was very hot. Soon, Wyman knew, there would be no cries at all.

Close to 6 o'clock that evening most of the boys crawled back to take a short break and eat their dinner rations, but Wyman stayed on in the trench. He would eat later, once the wounded were in, once he'd had a chance to make sense of what was going on all around him. He had been through a lot that month, but nothing that came close to what he was experiencing now, and he was beginning to feel somewhat unnerved by it all.

Now he sat at the end of a trench, very near exhaustion, the sad cries of the wounded rising up to him on a gentle breeze. Many, he knew, would die before he would be able to get to them. The rancid stench of death was growing by the hour, and he had no idea if the army would ever stir to fight again. The sad truth of it was that at that desperate hour it seemed as though he had come to a great deal more than just the end of another long trench. For Wyman White, it felt as though he'd come very near the end of the line.

CHAPTER FIFTEEN

JUNE 3RD—LATE AFTERNOON

LEE

R. E. Lee crossed his hands slowly behind his back, and waited patiently for Jefferson Davis to dismount. The President of the Confederacy had ridden out from Richmond upon receiving word of the great battle, and was anxious to hear from Lee firsthand his impressions of the fighting. While Robert E. Lee still felt physically weak, the positive news from the front was beginning to lift his spirits, and he looked forward to chatting with the President.

Lee had been receiving official visits from Richmond for much of the afternoon. A few hours earlier Postmaster General Regan, along with two local judges, had made the trip out. Lee welcomed them all, and patiently explained the situation on the field before turning to more important matters.

Once he had their ear, he described the army's lack of supplies and urged them all to return to Richmond and impress upon the commissary-general the dire necessity of sending out all the food and medical supplies that could be scraped together. To counter the outbreak of scurvy amongst his troops, the men would require potatoes, onions, and any sort of vegetables that were stashed away in the warehouses in Richmond. He took them on a quick tour of the hospital, a graphic demonstration of the fact that the lack of proper food was responsible for many more Confederate casualties than were Federal bullets. The situation was becoming desperate. Lee's worst fear, he pointed out, would be to watch his army simply melt away from illness and malnutrition. Then Grant might just brush them aside and march into Richmond unopposed, taking the Confederate capital, not by storm, but by default.

The officials left pleased by what they had seen, and vowed to impose on whatever authority necessary to get his men the food and supplies they required. Lee saw them off, and not long thereafter the President, accompanied by Josiah Gorgas, the Confederacy's Chief of Ordinance, arrived on horseback. Davis was a West Pointer himself, an outstanding soldier in his own right, and Lee held him in the highest regard. Davis could be gruff, and at times imperious, but with Lee he had always been friendly and straightforward. Their relationship was one of mutual respect. The President dismounted and smiled broadly.

Lee saluted. "Good afternoon, Your Excellency. Welcome to Gaines's Mill."

Davis returned the salute crisply. "Thank you, General. I can assure you, it is a pleasure to be here today."

"I trust your ride out from Richmond was a pleasant one."

"Under the circumstances, General Lee," the president replied, "it could not have been more so. We heard the guns booming away in Richmond all morning. The windowpanes in my office were actually rattling from the tremors. The whole city is on edge, I don't mind telling you. Fortunately, I received your message around one this afternoon, General, and later Colonel Johnston filled me in on all the details. As soon as I heard the good news I decided to come out and have a look for myself. The Yankees came on twenty-six deep all across our front, Johnston told me, and suffered thousands upon thousands of casualties in less than a quarter of an hour:

amazing, just amazing. Once I heard that, I sent a note off to Josiah, and called for my horse."

"Well, the casualty counts are not yet confirmed, Your Excellency," Lee explained. I fear it will be some time...."

Davis smiled, waved Lee's objections aside. "Yes, I understand, General," he replied. "The report sounded too good to be true, I must admit. Yet as we rode up through Mechanicsville we could see out beyond your lines for ourselves, and it appeared the Yanks were lying very thick across the entire front. I'm told that it is that way up and down the line. It appears they have suffered a terrible defeat."

"Yes, it does seem that they have suffered considerably," Lee agreed. "Most of them went down very early in the day, and the worst of the fighting seemed to have ended abruptly this morning, it is true."

Davis handed his reins to an orderly and dusted himself off. "I observed your position as we rode out, General, entrenched in places up to three lines deep." The President put his hands on his hips, chuckled to himself. "Remember when all those journalists in Richmond referred to you disparagingly as the 'King of Spades' for having your men dig entrenchments back in the spring of '62?" he asked. "I wonder what those journalists might be thinking now?"

Lee bowed slightly, recalled the situation clearly. Entrenchments were not fitting for true Southern soldiers to fight from behind, they had written. Then they went on to insist that Lee himself obviously lacked the necessary dash and audacity requisite in a Confederate officer. What fools! At the time there was nothing for him to do but sit quietly and take it. Fortunately, journalists do not fight wars, and soon he had proved to everyone's satisfaction just what sort of dash and audacity he had, by running McClellan and his army from the outskirts of Richmond back to the James in only seven days of heavy fighting and maneuvering.

Now, a full two years later, they could see for themselves the advantages good entrenchments provided. Indeed, it was their works alone that had saved the Confederate Army at Cold Harbor, and had proved the undoing of Grant's. Dash, élan, audacity... by the spring of '64 no one was fool enough to write such gibberish anymore.

Suddenly Taylor was at his side, whispering quickly in his ear that today, of all days, was the President's birthday. Lee knew that Davis's health and spirits had recently deteriorated considerably with the sudden and tragic loss of his young son, coupled with Grant's unrelenting campaign across Virginia toward the Confederate capital. Lee nodded, motioned toward the front. "I am given to understand that today is your birthday, Your Excellency," he said. "Perhaps our efforts here this morning at Cold Harbor will serve as a humble, but fitting, present."

Davis broke into an immediate grin. "I could think of none finer, or more fitting, General Lee," he replied. "Your success here today is simply inspiring. Yes, absolutely inspiring. I have not felt so good in months."

Lee returned the smile, knowing as well as anyone the pain of failure and loss. "I only hope it will continue to serve you well, Your Excellency," he said.

"Your victories always serve me well, General" Davis went on. "Unfortunately, you are one of the few of our general officers capable of consistently providing me these moments of euphoric relief."

"Thank you, sir," Lee replied. "I'm sure our fortunes in other theaters will soon improve. But, of course, the real fight is *here*. If we can defeat General Grant's army, then we can still win the war. I do not believe that opportunity exists anywhere else."

"No, you're absolutely correct, General," Davis agreed. "We must stop General Grant and his vast army here at the gates of Richmond. If we can do *that*, then the spirit for war among the

WINDMILL POINT

Northern people may quickly dissolve. And you have done an extraordinary job, General Lee, of doing just that—over a month of hard fighting without a single defeat. And now *this*. Amazing."

Lee bowed slightly again. "Yes, it is true he has not broken us," he agreed, "but I'm afraid Grant is far different from previous Federal commanders, Your Excellency. He should not be taken lightly."

"Yes, well, McClellan was very timid, Hooker arrogant, and Meade, I suppose we could say, ineffective."

Lee nodded. "But more than even that," he said, "Grant will not go away. Losses do not seem to faze him, and that is, I believe, because he understands one critical thing that all their other generals did not...."

"Go on, General."

"... that he outnumbers us by a considerable margin, and that in terms of matériel and logistics we are no match for the North. So when he fights and loses, Your Excellency, in a very real sense he still *wins*, because Grant can make up his losses, while we cannot. In the end, Your Excellency, if Grant stays after us, we might just perish, not from our losses on the field of battle, but as a result of our victories."

"That is true, General," the President agreed. "But he cannot suffer such staggering losses forever. His army is not a machine —although he may try and use it as if it were one—but a collection of *men*. And those men have fathers and mothers, wives, sisters, and lovers. The human cost of General Grant's campaign against us this last month was appalling, and don't think for a moment they don't understand that up in the North. They do! The Yankee papers have been howling over Grant's almost incomprehensible losses. The long, long lists of casualties have shocked everyone. And that was before this defeat today, this savage calamity they have just suffered here at Cold Harbor. The North will not allow their sons to perish in a sea of blood like this forever, General. The Army of the Potomac has reporters with them from many of the Northern papers. When word of this gets out..."

"What you say is true of the sentiment in the North, but all that will take some time to generate results," said Lee. "In the meantime, if Grant comes at us again today or tomorrow, I will still need more men to hold him off. Is there anyone you can send?"

Davis thought for a moment. "I can detach Ransom's brigade from General Beauregard," he replied finally. "Beauregard has the Federals bottled up, and should be able to spare a brigade or two for the time being. And perhaps some additional artillery."

Lee bowed. "And food, Your Excellency."

Davis grimaced. "We have food! Maybe not all we need, but we have *food*. So help me, General, I will get your men fresh rations if I have to load them into wagons and drive them out here myself.

Lee smiled. "Thank you."

Davis nodded, thought it over. "We must *beat* Grant again soon," he said. "One more time! If he assaults tomorrow as he did today, and suffers another staggering defeat tomorrow as he did today... well, I think the war will end."

"Perhaps," Lee replied.

Davis stared at him curiously. "I have heard reports, General, certain stories or rumors from the front, let us call them, that the Yankees refused to budge this afternoon. I've heard that Grant's army, or at least some parts of his army, may have actually—for lack of a better term—*mutinied*."

Lee hesitated. "Yes, I too have heard those reports."

"And?"

"Yes, some do sound reliable," Lee replied. He shrugged. "But there is precious little we can do now except wait and see. But you must remember, Your Excellency, the boys we are

WINDMILL POINT

fighting, well, they are not cowards. Fredericksburg, Spotsylvania... and here again today at Cold Harbor ... they fought even when the cards were stacked dramatically against them. They may have been misused, but they are hardly cowards. It would be a severe mistake to doubt their willingness to fight."

Davis smiled thinly. "I know that, General. I did not mean to imply that they were cowards. But even brave men have their limits, and the boys across the way may have reached their limit today. Have you ever heard of them acting like this before?"

"Never," Lee admitted.

"So we must beat them badly one more time, General," Davis said emphatically. "I sense we are very close to that important, final victory. Very close. One more good whipping and the North may strike their tents and call their boys home for good, no matter what Abraham Lincoln says, or General Grant orders. So you shall have whatever troops can be spared, and all the food our wagons can carry."

"Thank you, sir," Lee replied, then showed Davis toward his tent.

Late that afternoon President Davis departed. Ransom's troops arrived, and Lee immediately had them stationed down at Bolton's Bridge on the Chickahominy to checkmate any moves Grant might envision in that direction. While the lines along the front at Cold Harbor still erupted from time to time with nervous outbreaks of artillery and musketry, it seemed obvious that Grant had no further offensive intentions in mind for that day. The Army of the Potomac had been soundly whipped. That much was clear.

Lee, exhausted to the bone, yet elated by the day's events, plowed through a stack of paperwork after dinner, then prepared to get some much needed rest. Before turning in he realized he had not written a single report concerning the day's activities since dashing off a dispatch to the President before noon. So he picked up his pen, collected his thoughts, then jotted a brief note to the Secretary of War:

> Our loss today has been small, and our success, under the blessing of God, all that we could expect.

He would have liked to have written something far more comprehensive, something that would give full credit to all the men who had struggled and performed so well today, but that would have to wait. Robert E. Lee was simply too weary and worn. So for the time being the short message would have to do. He held it under the lamp, read it over once again, and handed it over to Taylor. Then he found his cot, unbuttoned his coat, and blew out the lamp.

CHAPTER SIXTEEN

JUNE 3RD—EVENING

GRANT

U. S. Grant walked deliberately to his chair and took a seat in the closing darkness, as his staff gradually gathered round. Grant looked carefully into their faces, tried to gauge each man's mood, and supposed in the end that they all still appeared at least reasonably confident. Good, he thought. He would need all the help he could get. He lit a cigar, took a long puff and tried to think of what he could possibly say to make this horrible thing right. Could words do that?

The reports had been trickling in all afternoon, staggering estimates of the army's dead, wounded, and missing. The messages were uniform only in their desperation: grim numbers generally coupled with a hopeless analysis of this or that corps commander's situation. And those were the officers who reported. Many, for some reason, had ceased to respond at all. A conservative estimate of their losses suggested that as many as 7,000 men had gone down in less than twenty minutes that morning. Perhaps more had fallen. Perhaps many more.

Over the course of the last few hours he'd finally been able to piece most of it together. While instructions had been issued the previous day ordering the corps commanders to synchronize their attacks, for some inexplicable reason the assault had gone forward piecemeal. The individual corps had moved ahead at their own pace, with little or no coordination between them. Thus the Rebels had been able to shift their firepower to strike them in turn, each separate assault drawing enfilading fire from all across the field. Worse still, no preliminary reconnaissance of the Confederate position had even been attempted, no understanding developed of the ground the assaulting troops would have to traverse, or what awaited them once they reached the other side. The basic rudiments of soldiering had been entirely absent from the planning and execution of the attack, and many, many men had paid for those failures with their lives.

The slaughter had been unprecedented. At no other time during the war had so many men been cut down in such a short period of time. Not at Gettysburg, Shiloh, Antietam, or even Fredericksburg had such carnage reigned. His men had essentially wandered head first into a firing squad, and their execution had been terrible. In only fifteen, maybe twenty minutes, the worst of it was over.

Late in the afternoon Grant had ridden out to take a brief look for himself. By then he'd figured out the bulk of the failure, but even then he was shocked by what he saw. Like a great blue carpet, his men lay dead and dismembered for almost as far as the eye could take in, and all of it for naught. Not a thing had been gained. It was one thing to ask men to die for a cause they believed in, quite another to ask them to die for nothing. The sight was more than unnerving, and he had turned away and ridden back to his tent in stony silence.

Grant let the smoke slip between his lips, watched for a moment as it circled slowly, then wafted up and out the flap of the tent. Then he cleared his throat, and all the low banter around him ceased. These were his men, hand-picked and hard-boiled. They believed in their mission, and they believed in him, and today, he knew, he had let them down.

Ulysses Grant was the commander of all Federal forces, the great Lieutenant General, the first to hold that rank in the field

WINDMILL POINT

since George Washington himself. He was the one who had ordered the attack, and the only man ultimately responsible for whatever nightmare Cold Harbor had turned into. This disaster was his alone, and now he would have to try and explain it, somehow make sense out of this almost incomprehensible slaughter. But, of course, there really was no sense to it. The morning's assault had been a great, bloody blunder, and now somewhere between seven and ten thousand men lay blasted to hell because of the compounded errors. He wished with all his heart that he could take it back, redo the whole day as if it had never happened at all. But that was impossible.

They were all looking at him patiently, waiting....

In the end, he realized, there was really nothing he could do but tell the truth and hope they would understand. He was just a soldier like them, no better or worse, only a fighter, and this morning he had done nothing more than try to fight. But this one had been botched. Badly.

"I regret," Grant started, the words sounding very distant, as if they were not coming out of his own mouth at all, "this assault more than any I have ever ordered."

The tent grew deathly silent, every eye glued to Grant. Cigar smoke swirled gently overhead. Far off there came a rattle of musketry, then that faded away and an uneasy, unnatural stillness returned.

"I... regarded it as a stern necessity," Grant continued stiffly, "and believed that it would bring compensating results." He took a long puff, thought a while longer, shrugged. "But... as it proved, no advantages have been gained sufficient to justify the heavy losses suffered." There, he'd done it ... said it ... had somehow gotten the words out.

No one said a word. Here and there an eye blinked, or a man cleared his throat, but their attention remained entirely focused, and they seemed to understand that this was neither easy nor natural for him.

Finally, Comstock spoke up. "We have gained some footholds, General."

Grant shook his head. "No," he replied, but barely above a whisper. "The early assault at Vicksburg, you see," he continued, trying to explain himself, "while it was not successful, brought compensating results."

The men began to nod, shift on their seats, relax.

So he went on to explain the advantages gained from the assault he had ordered at Vicksburg, not so that they would understand his thinking regarding assaults, but so that they might in some sense grasp his intentions. He had been asked by the President of the United States to lead the country in war, and to do that he had to take the fight to the enemy. A natural and inevitable consequence of aggressive warfare was death. But death was only acceptable if it brought justifiable gains; death for nothing was almost a crime. And today nothing had been gained.

When he had finished he simply stopped talking and looked them all in the eye. Then finally, when it seemed there was nothing left to say, Grant nodded once, and moved ahead with the business at hand. It was the first, and he hoped the last, apology he would ever have to make. But it was one that he knew had been owed.

Later that night he sat alone by the fire in front of his tent. Along the western horizon the sky flashed from time to time and the air rumbled, but nothing of substance ever came of it. Both sides were simply restive and uneasy, sleeping on their guns, the slightest movement drawing an avalanche of fire. In time he found a decent branch and began to whittle—an old nervous habit that always helped pass the time.

Often, he knew, more could be gleaned of an army's disposition by the sounds at night than by all the official reports stacked together. A confident, aggressive army had a tone and swagger all its own, easy to distinguish, clear to the ear.

WINDMILL POINT

Responses were sharp and immediate, the men's chatter light-hearted and optimistic. An army that was ready to fight had a certain, well... feel.

Meade had instructed all of the artillery to open up across the front at midnight. The guns were to continue blasting away at the Confederate lines until dawn, in the hopes of driving back some of the advanced Rebel positions. Grant had decided to stay up and listen for the first few rounds, with the hope that they might reveal something of his army's morale. A heavy, stunning cannonade would be a very good sign.

Grant had heard the rumors that had been flying around the headquarters tents all afternoon, of whole units refusing to advance. As well, he had seen for himself the glazed, demoralized looks in the eyes of the corps commanders earlier that day, looks that were far from optimistic. Men were apparently refusing to fight. Orders were being deliberately disobeyed. His army was clearly wounded, but just how badly wounded remained to be seen.

The chips at his feet gradually grew into a small pile. Grant had reduced the branch in his hands to the size of a toothpick, so he tossed it aside and grabbed up another. Then he wiped the blade on his trousers, started whittling again, and tried to think the problem through.

Here was the thing: Many European officers and officials routinely visited his camp as observers for their own countries, and while they understood the weapons and tactics employed in the American conflict perfectly well, they seemed to grasp nothing at all of the men who actually did the fighting. Decked out in flamboyant uniforms, plumed hats, and generally adorned with rows of ribbons and medals, these visitors were often shocked and amused by the simple, unassuming dress most Federal officers preferred. Born to aristocracy, the foreign observers naturally misinterpreted the absence of pomp as a sign of poor breeding, the lack of ostentation as a lack of class.

Never once did it seem to occur to them that in a culture where excellence—no longer the prestige of family or lineage—had taken precedence, military affectation had simply lost its allure. In the field, men dressed for comfort and simplicity, their actions being far more important than their appearance. Grant himself was perhaps the simplest, most homespun example of this lack of style, often being mistaken for a disheveled private while on campaign, but the issue he was thinking about went far beyond mere dress.

In Europe, armies were often comprised of nothing more than professional mercenaries, armed thugs whose only allegiance was to the highest bidder. While these troops were generally well trained, in Grant's mind they were no match for the finest American soldiers. Because the best American troops were not professionals at all but simple *volunteers*—shopkeepers, lawyers, teachers, carpenters, farmers. Here were men of intelligence and learning, grace and character, men who with but a little training could quickly outperform even the best professional soldiers. And the reason was simple. They believed in what they were fighting for—had in many cases willingly walked away from homes, jobs, and families to endure the frightful hardships of war. And why? For a *cause*. European observers understood only the power of wealth and gunpowder. What eluded them entirely, it seemed to Grant, was the extraordinary power of *ideas*.

The Army of the Potomac was just such a force, a great assemblage of like-minded citizens, marching not for glory or booty or land, but to set the slaves free and to restore the Union. They had all come from the same towns and cities, generals and privates alike. Grant knew of many privates in his service who had more knowledge and refinement than any number of generals he'd met from the continent. Many were men who, only months before, had been working as professors or lawyers, and now marched in the ranks with a rifle. In that sense they were all the same, and Grant was no different. He was one of them, in many ways still as much a shopkeeper as a Lieutenant General. Yes, it was true that many of those original volunteers had now served-out their enlistments, or had been killed our wounded in combat, and that their places had been taken by bounty men or conscripts, but the core of the army, thus its will and determination, was still volunteer.

In that sense the Army of the Potomac was not an army that could be prodded by the whip or motivated with threats. These were free men who marched of their own accord, in the process often accomplishing feats of stamina and valor that most European commanders could only envy. John Gibbon's famous Iron Brigade came to mind, a force of Mid-Western farm boys who had become perhaps the most feared and respected brigade in the army. At Gettysburg they had stood almost alone on McPherson's Ridge against overwhelming odds and held the Rebels off for an entire afternoon. When finally withdrawn late in the day, that same brigade had been fought almost to death, yet not a man had budged, and its stand that day had in all probability saved not only the army, but quite possibly the nation. No, these were not men who had to be prodded to march or fight. They only needed to be properly led, and pointed in the right direction. The great spirit of their convictions took over from there.

Grant stopped whittling for a moment, a disturbing notion suddenly blossoming in the back of his mind. He had always thought the army's spirit limitless and indefatigable, had never even once considered the possibility that it could be misemployed and possibly squandered, extinguished, just as a glass can suffocate a flame. He put the knife down, began to fret, thought... *Have I destroyed their spirit? What will I do if they will no longer march? What will the nation do if I have lost the army?*

Grant thought for a long while, came at it from every angle, but in the end the answer seemed simple. There was only one thing to do. He would have to see for himself: wait for the cannonade Meade had ordered, and then judge the damage inflicted on his army's will to fight. An avalanche of lead would speak for itself. Anything less would be cause for concern.

Grant rooted around, found another branch and began to whittle harder. The chips began to fly, the minutes ever so gradually ticking away. He smoked his cigar to the stub, tossed it away, pulled another from his side pocket. He lit it slowly, went on whittling.

Midnight finally came, then just as slowly slipped away. No sound came from the front. The minutes continued to run, but not a gun discharged. 12:15, then 12:30 passed, and still not a single artillery round was fired. Grant found yet another stick and began whittling away furiously.

After one o'clock had passed with no activity, he finally folded his knife away, stood, and marched deliberately into his tent, the horrific, almost thunderous sound of complete and total stillness pounding in his ears. Never had silence reverberated more clearly. Never before had nothing meant so much.

He closed the tent flap and slumped down in a chair. Then he threw his hat onto his cot and ran his hands back anxiously through his hair. His heart was racing. For the first time in many, many years he felt completely lost.

"My God," he whispered. Grant stared at the dirt between his feet, crossed and re-crossed his legs. "Ulysses, what have you *done*?" he asked the empty tent. He closed his eyes, dropped his head into his hands. "Oh my God, what have I done?"

He had lost his army; it was as simple as that. There was no longer any question. The throbbing silence told him everything he needed to know. All those boys, those shopkeepers and

WINDMILL POINT

lawyers, the men who would march anywhere and do almost anything they were asked to do—he had lost them all. What do you do, Ulysses, he wondered, when an army that moves and fights on the spirit of ideas alone, will no longer move or fight? Do you give them the bayonet? Do you apply the whip? No, of course not. But what then? Grant rubbed his face, thought, *You have crushed their spirit, Ulysses, the one **damn** thing that made it all possible in the first place. What will you do now?* His hands began to tremble.

Ulysses S. Grant reached for the bottle of whiskey he kept hidden away in his trunk and, fingers shaking, poured himself a quick drink. Just one. He knew it was dangerous, knew what the bottle had cost him years before in California when they had forced him to resign his commission. It had surely ruined his reputation, almost ruined his life, but he did not care anymore. He was shaking now, entirely lost, in need of a drink. Just one stiff drink.

The whiskey went down, hot and soothing. He felt it in his gut, the heat racing up the back of his neck. Grant rubbed the cool glass against his cheek, ran his fingers back through his hair again. He was beginning to sweat.

He closed his eyes, rocked back and forth slowly for a moment or two. "Oh, my God," he whispered again, praying no one outside would overhear. Then he reached for the bottle again.

CHAPTER SEVENTEEN

JUNE 3RD—LATE NIGHT

WHITE

White wrapped the rope around his wrist twice, looped it carefully around his elbow, then began to pull.

"*Slow*, Sarge," Thompson whispered, peering over the top of the trench.

"I got that down now, Joe," Wyman answered, fighting off the anger of exhaustion, trying hard to remain patient.

Since nightfall the front had been alive with frantic efforts to locate and bring in the wounded. As soon as it was judged dark enough, many had gone over the top, scurrying on their hands and knees, whispering, poking, searching off in the direction of those who had last been seen moving, or were still crying for help. The smallest and quickest were the first to go over, speed and agility being deemed far more important than strength on the open death trap between the lines.

Early on, a few of the wounded were pulled in, but it took a serious effort, and for those men out on the open fields it was an exercise in pure heroics. The Confederate sharpshooters were ready, any sound or movement quickly drawing intense fire from every angle. The red snap of the Rebel muzzles popped angrily in the distance for hours on end. Anyone outside of a trench took his life in his own hands, but the sense

WINDMILL POINT

of honor and loyalty was strong among the men, and nothing was going to stop them.

Wyman helped bring in many of the wounded, one a man not too far off from their own works. Joe Thompson went over the top about dusk, and crawled to where the man lay, a New Hampshire boy from a different regiment. Joe gave the man some water, fastened a blanket and rope around his waist, and they all pulled him to the safety of some bushes where he lay until dark. Then Joe went up again, made sure of the rope, and they pulled him back into the trench, Thompson crawling by the man's side all the way. The Rebs never saw them, and Joe came tumbling back into the trench safely. Wyman said nothing about it, just felt relieved.

Once they'd gotten the wounded boy down into the trench Wyman could see for himself that he was in very bad shape. He had a bloody hole in his right thigh, another in his shoulder, and had lost a great deal of blood. The fellow had evidently suffered enormously under the sun, skin now red and burnt, and caked blood covered his uniform. He was much too weak to talk.

They removed the boy carefully from the rope and blanket and laid him straightaway onto a stretcher. Then a few men hustled him off to the hospital, crouching low all the way. Wyman hoped for the best, but doubted the boy would survive. Later Joe went up again and followed the rope out to the Pennsylvania man who had been left behind earlier by his brother-in-law, but he was dead now too, and there was no use in pulling.

The work went on unabated well into the night, then continued into the wee hours of the following morning. Men crawled, scurried, and stumbled amongst the dead, desperate to find friends and comrades. The red flecks of Rebel musketry briefly illuminated the night as they worked, the wicked zinnngg of bullets slicing through the air or slamming into the body of some poor dead or wounded man with dreadful thunks all the while.

In Wyman's area alone they pulled in almost thirty men, but only two were strong enough to make it back to the field hospital, and they both died within the hour. The rest were so far gone they all expired, either as they were being dragged in, as they were being hustled through the long trenches, or while stretched out and waiting to be moved further to the rear. No amount of water or medical attention seemed to help. The long day under the unforgiving sun without water or care had doomed most of them to a miserable death. Wyman became dispirited watching them die.

After a few hours the hunt for the living gave over to a hunt for the dead, men now risking their own lives to simply retrieve the bodies of their friends for burial. It was a sad and desperate business. The awful stench alone was almost unbearable, and many of the boys who went out amongst the dead were in time overcome themselves, and had to be escorted to the rear on stretchers. Some of them were crying and half crazy from what they'd been through. Wyman shook his head and looked away.

Around 2 o'clock in the morning Wyman finally had had enough. Most of the men had quit by then, exhaustion eventually overcoming all their best intentions. So he crawled back through the trench and found the place near division headquarters where his regiment was spread out for the night. His tent was right where he had left it, his rations still wrapped away in his haversack.

But food was out of the question. The foul odor of death was still much too oppressive to even consider eating, and his tent seemed far too hot and claustrophobic for sleep. So he spread a blanket on the ground and tumbled down under the stars in the hope of at least a few hours' rest. In just minutes he was joined by Joe Thompson, tired and hot, but at least safe after his night's effort among the dead. Joe spotted Wyman right away and shook his head wearily as he drew near.

"Hey there, Sarge...."

"Hello, Joe," Wyman said, sitting up quickly. He nodded respectfully.

Thompson kneeled in the dirt next to Wyman's blanket. "Some kinda night we had out there tonight."

"Yes, that was sure a great deal of work out there," Wyman went on, "but I'm glad it's been done."

"Yes," Joe agreed.

"Yet there were not so many boys alive as I would have liked to have seen," Wyman remarked. He dropped his head and for a moment and felt almost overwhelmed by the ordeal. "I don't know."

Thompson nodded, seemed to understand. "No," he replied. "Not many at all."

Wyman sat very still, said nothing for a long while. Then he said, "You are a good man, Joe. The regiment is lucky to have you. I want to tell you that."

"Oh my... well, thank you, Sarge," Thompson answered. "Thank you a whole lot." Joe rolled his shoulders. "Had to be done, is all, I guess."

"Yes, that's right," Wyman conceded. "Still...."

Thompson went off and found his own blanket, then came back and stretched it out by Wyman's side. Then he lay down, rolled over on his back, and stared up into the stars. After what seemed a great deal of time Joe said, "It was a difficult day, Wyman."

"It was," Wyman agreed. Then he dropped back onto his blanket and stretched his legs out again. Between small swirls of clouds he could see a few stars blinking. The night was beginning to cool.

Joe rose up on one elbow and stared through the darkness toward Wyman. "Did you know I went up a ways and helped some of those Vermont fellas pull in quite a few of their own boys. It was not quite as hot up there, by the way. I guess the Rebs must have dozed off to sleep or something."

"Or *something*," Wyman replied angrily, but he was too tired now to dwell on how the Rebels seemed to take pleasure in shooting at wounded men, so he pushed the thought aside.

"Yes, well, anyway," Thompson continued, "like I said, we managed to bring in quite a few."

Wyman was pleased by that news and sat up directly. "Really?" he asked. "How many, Joe?"

"Close onto twenty would be my guess," Thompson answered, nodding forcefully.

Wyman felt a bit more hopeful. "Well, tell me, how are they, Joe? How are those boys?"

Thompson lay back down and stared up into the darkness. "Dead, Sarge. Every last one of them. "They're all dead now."

CHAPTER EIGHTEEN

JUNE 4TH—DAWN

ALEXANDER

Porter Alexander awoke with a sense of lazy ease, almost like an autumn Sunday in Savannah, or on one of those rare but wonderful days when he and his wife had the time to take a quiet stroll late in the afternoon along the battery in Charleston. Perhaps it was the distinct odor of magnolia that hung so heavily around his bivouac, or maybe it was simply the profound, almost boundless silence at daybreak that allowed for such a peaceful moment. But whatever the inspiration, Porter Alexander lay curled comfortably under a large oak until the first distinct rays of sunlight finally came sifting through the branches and struck him directly in the face. Then he yawned, sat up slowly, and rubbed the last trace of sleep from his eyes.

It was not until then that Alexander recalled with a sudden start that the army was wrapped around him almost like a great slumbering city—all of its guns, wagons, baggage, men, horses, ambulances, and ordinance stacked, deployed, and piled in the surrounding lanes, fields, and woods. The army, he thought, was really nothing if not an extraordinary collection of disparate motivations, all of them somehow molded to a single task by General Lee. An army fighting or on the move was an amazing thing to see. And as he contemplated that vast enterprise in a sort of drowsy reverie, he shuddered suddenly as three sequential thoughts exploded with alarming clarity in his mind: Cold Harbor,... War!... *Grant*! Porter Alexander stumbled to his feet. Alexander had meant to be up by first light. There had been no doubt in his mind that Grant would launch another assault as early as possible, so he had taken the precaution of having every gun under his command double-shotted with canister late the night before. If the Federals came booming in again at first light, he would be ready for them.

He had no intention of being caught unprepared—the sort of thing that had happened at Spotsylvania Court House, when Grant sent Hancock's entire corps rumbling in on the "V" shaped salient of the Confederate line early one morning. The blue legions had come bursting out of the fog, drizzle, and trees that dawn, rumbling right up and over the Confederate breastworks, and in a whirling, chaotic melee of guns, rocks, fists, and bayonets, had almost sheared Lee's army in half. Much of the artillery had been removed from the front earlier in anticipation of a rapid redeployment, and by pure luck Grant had caught them with their pants down. Only a bloody, almost Herculean effort had allowed the Confederates to avoid disaster that day, and it was a lesson Porter Alexander was not anxious to revisit.

Yet now the sun was already cresting the eastern horizon, and there was not even a hint of an advance from the other side —no troops or flags to be seen, no shots or shouted orders to be heard. He began to relax.

"Coffee, General?"

He whirled, spotted Charley, his cook and handyman, standing by the fire with a fresh pot in his hand. Both Charley and his driver, Abram, had been with him throughout most of the war, and the two formed the backbone of his camp.

"Well, you are right on the spot this morning, as always, Charley," Alexander replied with a grin.

Charley smiled, began pouring a tin full of steaming liquid.

WINDMILL POINT

"I believe I must have overslept, Charley," Alexander went on, taking the tin gladly. He tasted it gingerly. "Oh, yes, that's quite good. Anyway," he continued, "I could have sworn that the Yanks would have been up and after us early this morning. Would have bet a month's pay on it yesterday without thinking twice. I should not have overslept."

"No Yankees this morning, General," Charlie answered. "I looked myself, early."

"You did? Well, it's good to see that at least someone around here is on their toes."

"Yes, General."

Alexander sipped his chicory coffee and stared far out toward the battle lines. "This is quite interesting, you know," he said absently. "General Grant has always preferred to attack at 4:30 in the morning, Charley," Alexander pointed out. "It is one of his wonderful consistencies."

"Yes, General. That's a fact."

"So I doubt he will attack today at all if he has not yet done so. There certainly appears to be nothing in the offing."

"No, sir," Charley agreed.

"Perhaps we damaged him yesterday far more than I originally thought," Alexander suggested, thinking it over calmly. "I always thought it would take a whole lot to stop our good General Grant, Charley. He is quite persistent. I will most certainly admit that much. So perhaps we did some considerable harm to his army yesterday morning. That would be something worth thinking upon."

Charley nodded toward the front lines. "Whole lotta dead Yankees out there, General. Smelling something awful." Charley shook his head, pinched his nose.

Alexander laughed. "Yes, there are a lot of dead Yanks out there," he admitted. "Yet, in a way I had hoped he would try us again, Charley. One more licking like we gave them yesterday, and those boys over that way might just up and quit this war. Least, that is my hope."

"Whole lot of Yanks got kilt lickety-split yesterday morning, General," Charlie agreed. "Now they's smellin' up the whole world."

Alexander folded his arms across his chest. "They did that, Charley," he replied. "And if they come at our works again there will be a whole bunch more killed lickety-split again." He took a long sip from his tin, then scratched his head. "I wonder what General Grant is thinking about this morning?" Alexander pondered. "I would love to know what's on his mind."

Charley smiled. "Maybe about getting himself away from this here Cold Harbor place."

Alexander chuckled. "I can see you've been studying up on our good General Grant, Charley. You seem to know him as good as anyone, I reckon, and I believe you may just be right. But I hope not. No, I hope not. I hope he stays put and tries us again. That's what I hope. Cause he can't push us out of these works no matter how hard he tries. We're dug in way too good. The only thing he'll accomplish in the end by attacking us here is the ruin of his own army, Charley. So I hope he stays, and I hope he attacks us again. If he does, I believe the war will finally end in our favor. Right here."

The morning remained reasonably calm, so around 8:00 o'clock Porter Alexander decided to go draw his pay for the past month, and then take a tour of his lines. Word had come down by courier that Floyd King's battalion of artillery had just arrived and was being assigned to him, and further that he was also being placed in charge of all of Hoke's guns. It would take the better part of the day, he knew, to make sure they were all properly placed, and would require an arduous hike through every trench on his front.

Alexander found the paymaster not far from Lee's headquarters. There he signed the necessary document, and received his usual pay: $301 in crisp, new pink notes called "New Issue." The bills had all been recently printed in Richmond. They had then made their way through the signing room where some 400 pretty Confederate ladies applied the signatures of the proper officials, before the notes were finally boxed and shipped out to the army. Of course, $301 dollars in Confederate script was hardly worth more than $25 in gold these days, but he stashed it away carefully in a large envelope just the same. Then Alexander folded the envelope over several times, tucked it away in his breast pocket, and made ready for his rounds.

He began at the extreme left flank, sending Abram ahead with his horse to meet him again at the closest outlet on the far right. It was not a task he looked forward to. In fact, it was a job he dreaded. At Cold Harbor the trenches were some 2 to 3 feet deep with another 3 feet of dirt tossed on top along the edge facing the enemy. Only the shortest men could stand erect and not expose their heads or shoulders, and Alexander was not one of the shortest.

Moreover, the Yank sharpshooters quickly took note of any shallow areas, or spots where the trenches did not connect perfectly. It was there where a hat, head of hair, or set of shoulders might become accidentally exposed, so it was along these narrow intervals where the sharpshooters naturally trained their weapons. Then they lay in wait, watching for the slightest movement. Resting with their fingers curled tightly around the triggers, it required only a fraction of a second for them to wreak havoc. Thus any extended inspection of his lines would require that Alexander plod almost two miles while bent over nearly double, but that was by no means the worst of it.

To escape the intolerable sun during the heat of the day, the troops had strung their blankets up over the trench for a modest form of cover. To do this four men would stick the bayonet ends of their muskets into the ground, sling a blanket across the stock of the muskets, then fix the blanket firmly in the hammers of the guns at each corner. This would keep the blanket aloft about three feet above the bottom of the trench, and all four men—with all their equipment and possessions—would huddle together underneath. Almost the entire Army of Northern Virginia was arrayed in just this manner from the forenoon until almost sundown. To make his rounds Porter Alexander would have to get down on all fours and literally crawl under each blanket, then over all four men as they slept or lounged, group after group, mile after tiring mile. To conduct such an inspection was beyond simple exhaustion, for the men were often covered in lice and vermin and reeked horribly from days without even the rudiments of proper cleaning or sanitation. There was no water to drink beyond what he carried, and the heat below the blankets generally rose to intolerable levels. Add to that the filth, human sewage, corpses, and the sick men who could not move, and for Alexander each adventure into the trenches had become something akin to a nightmare. He comforted himself only with the thought that the job had to be done, and that at days' end he would at least be able to leave the trenches behind for the evening—something the front line troops almost never got the opportunity to do. Once safely out of the trenches he would go directly to a steam well behind the lines. There, finally out of sight and range of the Yankee guns, he would bathe thoroughly and wash his clothes before returning to camp for dinner.

After topping off his canteen, Alexander entered the trench at the extreme left of his position, and began working his way south. He clamored over men and equipment, stumbled twice upon dead bodies—it appeared both had recently been shot through the head—and more than once slipped or fell on sleeping soldiers. Often the men announced in advance his passing, but the troops ahead were so hot and fatigued they generally failed to move or respond at all. So he had to crawl on

WINDMILL POINT

all fours up and over a few thousand men, always watching diligently for any spare knife, gun, or bayonet that might have been set aside for protection, and that might accidentally discharge or slice his hand or knee as he passed.

There were small gaps at three locations where the trench lines of the adjoining regiments did not unite with precision. At each of these Alexander had to scurry across as fast as he could possibly manage, always bent over double so as not to attract any more fire than usual. At many points the most advanced Federal trenches were no more than 100 yards away, so there was precious little margin for error. He managed each crossing without incident by sprinting as fast as he could, but then about halfway through his rounds, and while stopped for a short drink from his canteen, Alexander realized that his pay envelope was missing from his pocket. Disgusted and weary, he slumped down in the trench. He almost felt like crying. Alexander knew, of course, where he had dropped it—at one of the three uncovered intervals.

The thought of going back through the trenches again to look for his pay was beyond consideration—that would double a journey that had already proved fatiguing beyond measure. The stifling heat below ground had already sapped most of his energy, and he feared illness if he dallied in the trenches any longer than necessary. By 11:00 o'clock that morning his head already felt light and his uniform was entirely soaked with sweat.

So Alexander crawled along for a few hundred yards, then turned up a narrow connector trench, and paid a short visit to General Gregg's headquarters, the infantry commander in that sector. He found Gregg in a small hole in the center of his lines, just as hot and worn as the rest of his men. Alexander smiled weakly and saluted.

"I fear I have a small problem, General," he said, rolling sideways into Gregg's tiny hole of a headquarters.

"General Alexander," Gregg replied wearily, "welcome to my humble abode. Can I offer you some fine, red Virginia clay? It's about all we have to eat around here."

Alexander laughed weakly, then dusted himself off. "'Fraid I've picked up plenty of that, General, all on my own."

"Pity," Gregg said with a short chuckle. "It's really all I've got to offer."

Alexander smiled, pulled out his canteen for a quick sip then explained the nature of his dilemma. Fortunately Gregg was able to locate some paper, and with that Alexander quickly jotted a short note authorizing any man who found his pay envelope to deduct twenty dollars as a reward before returning the envelope directly to Gregg's headquarters. That accomplished, he affixed the note to a small stick, and posted it in the trench for all to see.

Alexander wiped the sweat from his face with his handkerchief, took another gulp of water, then checked his watch once more. It was now almost noon, and he still had the better part of a mile of trench line ahead of him. The thought almost made his stomach turn.

He sat for a while, just long enough to catch his breath. Then he shook his head miserably, and started on his way. After all, any undue delay on one end, he realized, would only delay his cool bath at the other.

The sun was almost directly overhead now, and the dry trenches were baking like the lining of a fiery kiln. Not far away the bodies of the Federal dead were beginning to rot in the heat, the stench wafting back into the Confederate trenches, a bleak, ghastly odor.

Porter Alexander continued his scramble south. He was determined to finish it properly, to put each and every gun in its proper position, but also to do so as quickly as was humanly possible. If he closed his eyes for even a second, he could easily conjure the image of a cool, flowing creek, and that thought alone almost magically prodded him forward. It was not generally his desire to urge the enemy forward, to tinker with the odds of death, so to speak, but a few more days like this at Cold Harbor, he thought, and he might soon begin praying for Grant to attack.

He slipped under another blanket, called out to the men underneath, then crawled over another corpse. He gently pushed the man aside then carefully wiped the blood off his hands on the side of the trench.

A shot rang out, and a soldier collapsed nearby with an ugly wound to the head. Several men crawled to where he had fallen.

Alexander closed his eyes for a moment, took another deep breath then crawled off on his way. He had been off to war for three long years now, had seen more misery and death than he could possibly recall, but as he crawled on through the long trench that afternoon, he could not help but wonder just what precisely might be the difference between Cold Harbor and hell.

CHAPTER NINETEEN

JUNE 4TH—MIDDAY

LEE

Lee leaned back against the trunk of a tree, and asked the courier to repeat the message. He was a young lieutenant just in from Wade Hampton's division of cavalry, which was operating along the wings of the army. Robert E. Lee had sent instructions to all of his cavalry divisions urging them to remain vigilant. Grant's army had suffered a terrible defeat, and Lee wanted to know if and when the Federals demonstrated even the slightest inclination toward shifting their position, or perhaps even pulling out.

"Yes, General," the lieutenant replied, going over the message again in his mind before repeating it. "Sir," he began, "I am instructed to inform you that there has been no movement to speak of, either of the Yankee infantry, or their two divisions of cavalry, which remain south of the Chickahominy. Their other division of cavalry, Wilson's, connected with Burnside's right flank a few days ago, and has not budged from that position since. They continue to screen Grant's extreme right flank, and show no sign of imminent movement."

Lee displayed no emotion. "Thank you, Lieutenant," he said. "Tell General Hampton I am very appreciative of his vigilance. You are dismissed." Then he glanced toward Walter Taylor. "All

WINDMILL POINT

the reports are the same. For the time being, at least, Grant appears to be stationary." Lee tapped his foot and thought for a moment or two. "Have there been any reports of the Federal units massing anywhere along the front? Anything at all?"

"No, sir. Not a thing."

"You've checked?" Lee asked.

"Of course, General."

"Good. Of course. And General Alexander is positioning all of Hoke's guns?"

"Yes, sir," Taylor replied with a quick smile. "I delivered that order myself. In fact, I believe General Alexander is out inspecting his front already."

No one appreciated Edward Porter Alexander more than Robert E. Lee. In the early spring Joe Johnston had requested that Alexander be reassigned to his command out west, but Lee would not hear of it. Alexander was one of the few officers whose help and assistance he always leaned upon, quite possibly the finest artillerist in the entire army. So Alexander had stayed on with the Army of Northern Virginia, but Lee had seen to it that his promotion to brigadier general had gone through immediately.

"Yes, that would be like him," Lee said. "He is always prompt and thorough."

"I also explained the situation to General Hoke," Taylor continued, "and he was actually very relieved to hear that General Alexander would be positioning his artillery. The general's reputation precedes him."

"Yes, good," Lee replied. "If Grant decides to attack us here again we must be prepared to make him suffer again. Alexander will see to it."

"Yes, sir."

Lee relaxed for just a moment. He thought of his men, of the food he desperately needed to keep them going, then his mind slowly drifted back again to Grant. He tried to anticipate his adversary's next move. He knew by now that Grant would stay close and fight him—if not again here at Cold Harbor, then certainly somewhere nearby. The only question was where? Lee had been up since early that morning expecting to have a fight on his hands once again, but nothing had stirred beyond a few grey squirrels, and he had wound up sipping his morning coffee in silence.

Pity, he thought. For while his lines were still paper thin in many places, he had secretly hoped that Grant would have come and assaulted them again that morning. Lee felt confident his army could duplicate yesterday's bloody repulse ten times over, and that another shattering defeat might well spell doom for the Army of the Potomac.

But no guns had sounded, and now it was midday and nothing seemed to be happening on the other side of the field. By all reports, the Federals appeared to be as flat as a pancake. Either Grant had been damaged far more severely that Lee had initially presumed, or the Federal commander was contemplating something entirely new. Only time would tell which it might be.

In the meantime, Lee insisted he be kept well informed of every movement by the enemy, no matter how seemingly trivial. He could no longer afford a single error or miscalculation. Both victory and defeat seemed to hang suspended simultaneously in the hot, steamy air above Cold Harbor, the final issue dangling on a razor's edge of possibility. One mistake either way could spell the difference. Surely, with luck, he might destroy the Yankees' willingness to fight if Grant hurled his brigades at his works once again, yet a single misstep could just as easily send his entire army tumbling back to Richmond in one dreadful afternoon. It was a ticklish situation, and victory, he knew, would smile only on the most vigilant.

"Does General Early report any activity on his front?" Lee asked.

WINDMILL POINT

"None at all," Taylor answered. "Not since yesterday, that is, when his command stormed some of the advanced Federal positions. Since then he reports only that the Yanks have advanced in force, and he had to retire against overwhelming odds. The lines are now back to roughly where they were early yesterday morning, and the situation there appears to be at a stalemate."

Lee took a deep breath, thought it over. "Tell him to try and probe the Federal lines again today," he said. "In all the fighting and maneuvering they may have left a gap or weakness somewhere. There may be something we can exploit out there, but we must find it first. We must be very diligent."

"Yes, I understand, General," Taylor replied. "And General Breckinridge has requested permission to move forward and try to force back the most advanced Federal positions along his front. He says in some places they are as close as forty yards, and that the situation is not advantageous."

Lee nodded. "By all means," he said. "Push them back if at all possible. Even there we may well be able to turn a small success into a significant one. If those people over there are as demoralized as the reports we are receiving indicate, well, some of them may not fight at all. We must continue to probe all across the front. If their lines cave somewhere, we must be prepared to move with force rapidly and exploit the situation."

"I will issue the orders, sir," Taylor said. "Oh, and by the way, I thought you would want to know that those vegetables and foodstuffs you requested yesterday are reportedly already being loaded for delivery. A courier came in from President Davis earlier this morning."

Lee sat up straight. "How soon?"

"The first wagons should be arriving by early evening, I'm told. Tomorrow morning at the latest."

Lee displayed emotion for the first time all morning. He could hardly contain himself. "That is excellent," he said.

"Excellent. The men need food, Colonel. With good food we will be able to stave off illness and keep our army healthy. We must make every effort to ensure that the men in the very front lines receive their share of the new rations: good meat and vegetables. *That* is essential. If our army is healthy I believe we will be able to hold off Grant, no matter how often he attacks us."

"You have always held him off, General," Taylor replied. "He has lost the equivalent of two or three full corps to casualties this last month, yet you have never once relinquished the field. You have severely crippled the Federal army, General."

Lee stared at his adjutant for a moment, then frowned just slightly. "The *men* held him off, Colonel," he said. "They have always risen to the occasion."

Taylor beamed at him. "Behind these wonderful entrenchments," he said, "I believe our boys are invincible."

"Yes," Lee agreed. "As our late General Jackson once commented, our men have never been driven from a defensive position. Never. Failed to take one, well, perhaps here and there, but never driven from one. On the defensive they do appear almost invincible. And we must ensure they remain that way," he insisted. "The men have done their best once again here at Cold Harbor, so for now we will simply wait and see what General Grant has up his sleeve, then react accordingly. But we must remain prepared and very wary. I believe the war may be decided within the next few days, Colonel. With God's blessing, and much hard work on our part, it may well be decided in our favor."

CHAPTER TWENTY

JUNE 5TH—MIDDAY

WHITE

Wyman White sat up, set his tools down, and watched as the men filed past. Behind the lines, he had just finished molding the last of his bullets for the day when the bugle sounded and caught his attention. Wyman stood, put his hands on his hips, and watched the short column of troops march off down the road. The bugle had sounded the call to muster-out a number of veteran units whose enlistments were finally up. Few of the men who stood nearby and watched as they filed passed, he knew, did not harbor at least a small sense of envy. Wyman carefully peeled his shirt from the branch where he had laid it to dry after washing, and put what was left of his shoes back on. Then he decided to walk down and see just what all the fuss was about.

After putting his shirt on, he pulled his coat tight around his neck and buttoned it all the way to the top. High above Cold Harbor grey clouds were beginning to pile up in the west once again, dark and dreary in appearance, and the air had taken on a dank and uncomfortable chill. Hot one day, chilly the next. It was nothing if not a prescription for pneumonia, or worse still, the dreaded Chickahominy fever that all the army feared.

Wyman walked down to the open lots behind the division headquarters with Joe Thompson at his side. The fields there had been planted with spring corn, but all of that now was trampled and ruined by the army, with its seemingly endless camps and vast train of wagons. Just ahead the short column had come to a halt, and the boys were now preparing to be mustered out. It was the 3rd Maine, a veteran outfit from his own 1st Brigade. They were all New England boys, and Wyman had come to know quite a few of them over the years. Strangely, he felt both joy and sadness oddly co-mingled: happy to see them off safely, sad that he would not be heading off among them.

Wyman then vividly recalled his last visit home. Having reenlisted, the Sharpshooters had been granted a full thirty-day leave during the early winter of that year, and then that leave had been extended for an additional thirty days so that they could all stay and vote in the state elections. Wyman made the long trip home by rail, with stop-offs in Washington, Baltimore, and New York, before finally arriving at Fitzwilliam Depot one morning in early January. Not a soul knew he was coming, and his father could hardly speak, so overcome by Wyman's arrival had he been. It proved a wonderful time of food, friends, family, and merriment, which he would not soon forget. Many patriotic gatherings and dances were held in their honor. The people of Fitzwilliam had never been more friendly, nor the girls more kindly. The only difficult part had been having to depart.

Despite the gloomy weather that was rolling in, the Maine boys were all smiles, and Wyman could hardly blame them. Just the thought of packing his bags and heading off for New Hampshire again made him suddenly quite homesick. He thought of December snow falling in the mountains near his home, soft, white and wonderfully cold. That thought alone was almost enough to break his heart.

"Say there, Sergeant Wyman," one of the Maine boys called out, "take care of this here war now that you will be missing us, will you? We are all very sorry," he continued, a big grin plastered across his face, "to be leaving all you fine fellas behind."

Wyman smiled, nodded toward the fellow, waved. "Oh, I'm quite sure of that."

"Hey Sarge," another man yelled to Wyman, "be good enough to send us some hardtack and salthorse, now would you. You know we can't survive without those fine delicacies anymore."

Everyone laughed.

Joe Thompson cupped his hands around his mouth. "Listen here, Marvin Wilcox!" he hollered. "Don't you boys go grabbing up all the pretty gals before the rest of us get home."

"Who said that?" Wilcox asked, spinning around to see.

"It was Corporal Joe Thompson of the U.S. Sharpshooters," someone answered.

"Oh, hey Joe," Marvin Wilcox called back. "I will tell you truly, that's exactly what I hope to do—grab up all the pretty girls from here clear up to Maine. That's me alright! I plan on snatching one or two in every state I pass through, from Virginia right on up to Bangor."

"Haaa!" Wyman howled, enjoying himself immensely. "Any nice looking gals who get a good look at you fellas is gonna run the *other* way, for sure! Any of you boys take a close look in a mirror lately?"

The whole Maine regiment broke into a grin. "No," one of them yelled back, "but I can sure see you clear enough, Sarge. So I guess you got a point."

They all laughed even louder.

Wyman chuckled, looked down at the rags his uniform had become, and granted the man the better part of the joke.

The wind came up in a sudden burst, and a light rain began to fall, but it could not dampen the spirits of the Maine boys for even a minute. They were tired and bedraggled specimens to say the least, but this morning their eyes all shined like beacons. It was good to see men happy again. They were going home. The war was over for them.

"Sorry to leave you all alone to fight Bobby Lee without us, Wyman."

"Never mind any of that," Joe Thompson replied. "Just be sure to tell all the folks back at home that we will be along right behind you."

"Not unless you're planning on taking a little French leave, you ain't," Marvin Wilcox added with a wink, hinting that they would all have to desert if they wanted to see home anytime soon.

Joe Thompson slapped the side of his leg. "Oh, yeah, we *will!*" he cried. "We're going to whip old Bobby Lee better without you than if you was with us still."

"Ahhh, listen here, boys!" Wilcox hooted. "Sounds like whisky courage to me!"

A man next to Thompson stepped forward and shouted, "Three cheers for the 3rd Maine! What do you say, let's hear it boys!"

All the boys threw their fists in the air and yelled, "Hurrah! Hurrah! Hurrah!"

Then a brief moment of silence hung between the two groups, those that were leaving, and those who would have to remain behind, until the Maine boys were suddenly seized by what seemed a deep sense of appreciation. The cheer had caught them by surprise. Marvin Wilcox walked straight up to the man who had called for the cheer and shook his hand firmly. Then he whirled around and faced his comrades.

"We can't let these fellows outdo us, lads!" he yelled. "How's about three good cheers for the fellas who are staying on to fight the damned Rebels, hey boys? 'God bless 'em's, what I say!"

No sooner were the words out of his mouth than did the Maine men toss their caps in the air and begin to cheer with all

WINDMILL POINT

their might. It was a wild, raucous whoop. The cheer rolled on for a good minute, men laughing, hooting, and hollering as loud as they could, before the thing naturally trailed off to nothing. They all stood and smiled at one another without saying another word. Both sides were cheered out.

The Maine boys were all mustered out of the service then. It was a simple drill. The drums rolled, their names were called, and they finally stacked their arms. They were going home, and it was a beautiful thing to see. The entire affair was over in just a few minutes, and soon they were all off down the road toward home.

Wyman White stood along the edge of the road and watched them leave, memories of New Hampshire tugging away at him again. Never before had he ever felt so homesick. He watched until the last of the Maine men disappeared into the grey drizzle down the muddy road toward Bethesda Church. As much as he envied their trip home, in many ways it was still a sad sight to witness. There had been over a thousand of those Maine boys back in 1861 when their regiment had first been mustered into the service, and there was no more graphic example of the toll the awful war had taken. Very few had survived. Thin, tired, and worn to the bone from three long years of fighting, there were barely even fifty of them left that morning to start for home. The rest had all found shallow graves, Wyman knew, buried ingloriously somewhere between the Susquehanna and the James.

CHAPTER TWENTY-ONE

JUNE 5TH—LATE AFTERNOON

GRANT

Ulysses filled the glass gingerly to the rim again, slid the cork back into the bottle, and set the glass carefully on the edge of his desk. Then he slumped down on the corner of his cot, some odd, indiscernible intuition holding him back, something he couldn't quite put his finger on stilling his hand. For the better part of a minute he did nothing more than stare at the glass, the golden liquid beckoning—such a lovely opportunity to once again escape Cold Harbor, summoning him from across the smallest divide.

For most of the day he had been gone in one way or another. Early on it had been on the wings of the beautiful, hot alcohol, the whiskey transporting him off to that cloudy delirium that, if not entirely perfect, was at least not Cold Harbor. Rawlins had come to his tent then, finding him around first light, much of the furniture toppled this way and that, maps and notes and papers in the dirt. Rawlins had shooed all the others away, and Grant did not argue. He had never been an angry drunk, and Rawlins had always been a good friend. Sick, was what Rawlins had told them all, just as he had done so many times in the past. The General was sick. It was a term his staff seemed to understand well enough by now, and they all kept their distance after that.

WINDMILL POINT

Rawlins had tossed him onto his cot, and by then Grant had gone obligingly, sleeping it off till well after noon. Now, his head throbbed, his throat was dry, and his whole body ached for another quick taste, just one good taste. One more, Grant was convinced, would surely make it right. Outside, the guns still banged and thumped, the men hunkered low in the trenches, and the bodies still reeked, but for the better part of twelve hours he'd managed to escape all of that.

If he held his hand out straight he could just about touch it, could easily lean forward and wrap his fingers tightly around the cool glass once more. Then he could grab hold and quickly down it all, a few good gulps and the whole thing would be done. That's what he wanted to do. That's what he really wanted to do. But for some reason he didn't.

For a moment Ulysses Grant took his eyes off the glass and let them wander slowly around the interior of the tent. Here were the maps he had accidentally knocked onto the dirt the night before, his broken lantern, an overturned camp chair. Nearby he had flung his coat over the back of his chair, and his eyes slowly gravitated to the gold stars displayed on the shoulders. Those stars. Those awful stars. Did anyone understand just how heavy those stars really were? Could they possibly grasp the weight, the responsibilities, they imposed? He doubted it. Not since George Washington had anyone worn that many stars in the field, and after Ulysses S. Grant had put that coat on for the first time, he soon discovered the terrible burden that came with them. *George Washington... my God*, he thought, *who in the world might ever mistake him for George Washington?*

Congress had voted to restore the old rank of Lieutenant General in late February, and Abraham Lincoln offered him the position in early March. He had accepted, of course, but what he had not known then—what he could not have known at the time—was the almost unbearable weight that came along with the job. It was one thing to simply be called Lieutenant General, quite another to actually walk in Washington's footsteps. One thing to lead an army, another entirely to lead a *cause*. What he had accepted as a difficult task was in fact a monumental one, for Grant soon realized that coming right along with those heavy stars came the inescapable eye of history.

Grant had met with Lincoln in the White House before the public ceremony, and had seen first-hand the awful strain that the war had taken on the President. Withered, stooped, and worn almost beyond description, the President seemed to be carrying alone on his shoulders, not only the hopes of the entire nation, but the faltering aspirations of democracy itself. In a world still rife with czars, kings, and emperors, democratic government was barely ninety years old, and it was no secret that many European governments still eagerly hoped and prayed for its imminent demise.

Grant, of course, had read Lincoln's short, lucid speech delivered at the dedication of the national cemetery at Gettysburg the preceding fall, and without fail Grant returned again and again to the last, startling line: "that government of the people, by the people, for the people, shall not perish from the earth." That, it seemed, had become Lincoln's most profound fear, Grant now realized: that democracy might simply implode and perish as a result of this awful civil war, and that in the end Lincoln's name would become synonymous with nothing more than democratic failure. Now it had become Grant's worst fear, as well.

In just over a month of bloody fighting he had finally come to understand the awful truth. Whether he liked it or not, wanted it or not, agreed with it or not ... his decisions would affect not only his men, the course of the war, and the future of the country, they would also reverberate down through the ages. His judgments—for better or worse—would affect the very breath of freedom for all of history, and that awful burden was

WINDMILL POINT

what made those stars so difficult to wear. Without question, there had been many times over the last thirty days when he had wondered if he was man enough for the task.

Grant looked back at the glass, wanted to take it up in the worst way, to disappear into that incoherent reverie again, but still he held back. Why? He glanced once more at the gold stars, thought of Washington, and wondered... *Did Washington ever stumble so horribly? Did he ever... doubt? Were there times when he wanted to lose himself in the bottom of a bottle? Were there times when, perhaps, he did?*

Grant had studied the great campaigns at West Point, of course, and the truth of it was Washington's army had been routed from the field far more often than it had prevailed. Yet in the end he did prevail, and surely there was a lesson in that. But what? For the entire month of May, Grant had done nothing but try to prevail against the Rebels, and all he had managed to accomplish was to clog all the roads leading north with a sea of caskets, and now to provoke the virtual mutiny of his own army. Grant read the Northern papers religiously. Journalists were calling him many names these days, but "the father of his country" was yet to appear among them.

He reached for the glass, held it tightly in his fist for a few seconds, then put it back down again. It was the recollection of Lincoln, of course—those great, sad, understanding eyes—that would not let him be, would never give him peace. Thoughts of Lincoln almost haunted him at times, had rolled through his drunken thoughts, even the night before. Abraham Lincoln was perhaps the most unaffected human being he had ever met, so straightforward, so genuine. Grant was not naturally a "Lincoln man," although he had read in detail his debates with Douglas, and shared his abhorrence of slavery. Yet it was not until he met the President that he realized just how unique the man really was.

Lincoln seemed to care precious little for all those things that motivated other mortals, but had somehow risen to an entirely different level. He seemed to live only for the country, his every motivation the common good, and as such he had come to personally feel the pain of civil war all that much more. The nation was tearing itself apart, and Lincoln seemed to be slowly dying in the process. Mothers came to his office in tears, and he held their hands. Men wept for their lost sons, and he wept along with them.

That same Abraham Lincoln had asked Ulysses Grant to help bring an end to this national catastrophe, and no matter how many times he had tried to run away and hide in the bottom of a bottle, in the end he could not let Lincoln down. That sad face, those imploring eyes, would not go away, and in the end the simple truth of it was they would not go away because Grant would not let them. He admired Abraham Lincoln too much.

Grant had as much fight and persistence in him as any man, but those qualities would only go so far. Now he had fought and persisted his way into a bloody corner, and his army would not march, and his men would not fight anymore.

He leaned forward, pulled the blue coat from the chair and admired the stars up close. *What would George Washington have done*, he wondered? Grant thought for a moment, closed his eyes, let his mind drift. While it was true Washington had suffered any number of disastrous defeats, it was also true that he had crafted some beautiful campaigns. Trenton, of course, had been Washington's masterpiece, a dramatic strike that was considered a classic of war, still studied in most of the military academies both at home and abroad.

Grant recalled Trenton with clarity. It was December, 1776, and that winter the cause of American independence had sunk to its lowest ebb. Washington's army had shrunk to nothing more than a shadow, and most of those few, remaining

WINDMILL POINT

enlistments were to be up by the end of the month. Men were deserting his Pennsylvania encampment daily, and it seemed that very soon the American effort might wither away entirely. Times were desperate. Washington did not simply have to do something constructive. He had to do something breathtaking, something so dramatic that the whole country would sit up and take heart.

So on a snowy, freezing, Christmas night he took what remained of his beleaguered command—only 2400 men—crossed the ice-choked Delaware River on an improvised fleet of flat-bottomed ore boats, and surprised the Hessian command at Trenton the following morning. He appeared where no one expected him, at an hour when no one was bothering to watch. Weary and hardly expecting the Americans to appear out of such a terrible storm of cold and snow, the stunned Hessians could not have been more surprised had Washington's small band tumbled out of the clouds, and after a brief firefight they surrendered almost to a man.

Within a week Lord Cornwallis personally led a retaliatory mission. Washington had again returned to Trenton, and Cornwallis went out to bag him. Outnumbered and entirely outgunned, defeat loomed once again for Washington's small army as Cornwallis attacked and pressed the Americans up against the banks of the Delaware River. By nightfall it looked as though the revolution was over once again. But desperate men conjure desperate tactics, and no one was better in tight spots than George Washington.

Leaving a small party behind to stoke a long line of abandoned campfires, Washington slipped away under the cover of darkness with the rest of his command. Traveling on back roads unknown to the British, their cannon's wheels muffled with cloth, at dawn they arrived ten miles south of Cornwallis at Princeton. There, Washington immediately surprised, attacked, and routed three regiments of British regulars before marching off to winter quarters in the mountains of central New Jersey.

Those two small victories galvanized the nation, and saved Washington's army. Within weeks, money and equipment arrived from France, and men again began flocking to the cause of independence. In one smashing stroke, George Washington had revived the spirit of a nation. No less a soldier than Frederick the Great, then considered the reigning military genius of the day, had hailed Washington's twin victories as one of the greatest campaigns of all time. It was not only the stuff of myth, it was the stuff of true greatness, and Grant admired it enormously.

Ulysses S. Grant reached out and picked up his coat, rubbed the stars, virtually grieved over whether he even had the right to wear them again. Washington! Only a few years ago Grant had been clerking at a dry goods store owned by his father. Who might dare compare him to George Washington?

Yet Grant knew how to fight, and he knew how to drive himself, and, right or wrong, Lincoln had surely seen something special in him. Now he found himself in a situation almost as dismal as Washington had faced during that dreadful winter of 1776. Yet instead of reaching for a plan that might save the nation, the brutal truth of it was, Grant only seemed capable of reaching for the bottle in order to save himself from his own, pathetic fears.

The thought of his own weakness suddenly infuriated him. A bolt of anger shot through his chest, and he wheeled, reached, and knocked the glass of whiskey off the desk with a swipe of his arm. It flew across the tent, finally clattering to a stop against an overturned chair in the corner. Grant's chest heaved, and his face grew red. *Damn you, Ulysses*, he thought. *God damn you!*

Rollins was suddenly out front in a rush. "General! General!"

WINDMILL POINT

Grant took a deep breath, fought for control. "Yes."

Rollins stuck his head inside the tent flap, stepped in. He surveyed the scene quickly, spotted the upturned glass, the whiskey in the dirt. He looked solemnly at Grant for a few seconds, then nodded. "I will send for coffee," is all he said, then spun on his heels and was gone.

Grant slumped back down on the edge of his cot, struggled to let the anger go. What good would anger do him now? None. He needed action now instead of anger, but he didn't even know where to begin. His army was broken and stuck in their awful holes at Cold Harbor, and he needed a strategy to get them out—a very good strategy. He needed to restore their *spirit*. He could no longer attack, and the longer the army sat in the Chickahominy low country the more his men would fall prey to fever and illness. Grant needed a maneuver every bit as good as George Washington's, perhaps even better, but his head just throbbed, and he was fresh out of ideas.

He picked up his coat again, stared at the stars. *What would Washington have done*, he wondered? Grant closed his eyes, tried to concentrate. *I need to cross the river and hit them at Trenton*, he thought, *on a whole fleet of boats with muffled oars so they won't hear me coming.* Then he tossed his hands futility in the air, and laughed bitterly. For the Delaware River was hundreds of miles away, and the British long gone... still....

There was a sudden commotion outside ... voices ... Rawlins once again at the front of his tent. "General Hancock is here, General," Rollins announced, tossing the tent flap aside. Then he lowered his voice, "and he will not be put off."

Grant stared at Rollins, blinked once. "Very well then," he said. "Show him in."

Rollins tossed back the tent flap again, and Hancock entered. The big man stopped in the entranceway and saluted.

141

Grant returned the salute, grabbed a chair and flipped it upright. "Have a seat, General," he said. "To what do I owe the pleasure?"

Hancock nodded, removed his cap, sat. He looked pale and uncomfortable, and it was obvious to Grant that he was suffering and in pain. "Thank you for seeing me, General Grant," Hancock said stiffly, almost formally. He looked quickly about the tent, noted the disarray.

Grant said nothing... He waited.

Hancock crossed his legs, then cupped his hands together. "General," he said, "it has been almost two days now since our last assault was repulsed, yet there has been no attempt to recover our wounded. We need to do that, sir. There is not much time. The men are dying."

Grant could feel Hancock's eyes probing, questioning, trying to discern his condition. "Yes, of course," he said flatly, giving nothing of himself away.

"Will you write to General Lee?"

"I will," Grant agreed.

"I fear there are very few of our boys still alive," Hancock pointed out. "The stench from the dead is growing worse by the hour. The corpses need to be buried as soon as possible. The situation is ... well, demoralizing. The men ...."

Grant nodded.

Hancock stared at him for a moment then leaned forward. "*Sir*," he said emphatically, "we need to get out of here. The Rebels... they are too well dug in. Their works.... Well, it is impossible...."

Grant smiled thinly. "Thank you, General," he replied. "I very much appreciate your view of things. I will write to General Lee immediately and ask for a suspension of hostilities."

Hancock frowned, had obviously been expecting more than that. "Well, thank you, sir," he said.

WINDMILL POINT

Grant stood, gestured politely, and showed him back outside. "Thank you again for your thoughts, General Hancock," he said finally. "By the way, how is your wound coming along? I've heard that it's giving you some problems."

Hancock scowled miserably. "Not too damned good at all," he replied. "Yes, General, it has become quite painful. The shrapnel keeps slowly working its way to the surface."

"Please take care of yourself, General," Grant said. "I rely on you and your corps a great deal."

Hancock took the reins to his horse from the orderly, saluted, then swung up into the saddle. He glared down at Grant. "We must *move*, General," he repeated forcefully, then turned and rode off.

Grant returned to his tent, slumped down onto a chair; that word still echoing in his ears: move. *Yes, we must move,* he thought, *but where? We have been moving for the better part of a month and now we are stuck as if in the neck of a bottle like a great, fat cork. Do we swing back to the north and give back the ground we have taken after the sacrifice of so many men? Wouldn't that look like a retreat, a failure? The Northern papers are already screaming. Imagine what they will say if I even appear to be in retreat? But if I move south there are two rivers to bridge, and Lee will be waiting to slice us apart as we cross. Yes, I know we must move, General Hancock, but to where am I to move?*

Headquarters mess that evening was very quiet. Grant remained deep in thought, said nothing, noticed no one around him. His mind was working, but nothing seemed to come of it. There was nothing in his mind but a blank, a great mess of confusion. And then...

And then as he sat in his tent at night and thought of Washington again, a plan began to slowly congeal. It was hazy at first, a notion more than a strategy, but then, like the pieces of a complex puzzle, it started to fall into place. The river, the muffled cannon wheels, the strike falling where it would be least expected. *Yes, yes, thank you, George*, he thought. *I can use all of that, all of that and more. It must be bold, it must fool Lee, and it must **work**. God knows, it must **work**.*

That evening Grant returned to his tent, picked up the bottle of whiskey, and put it back in his trunk. No more need for it now. He would save it for a proper celebration. His pulse began to quicken. Grant was feeling better now, the headache entirely gone, his mind beginning to focus clearly again. It was possible. The movement would be vast, dangerous, and complex, but it would still be possible. Yes, it just might work. His foot began to tap, and he slipped deeply into thought again, could see the whole thing coming together like a vast painting in progress.

Finally he stood, walked across the tent, and pulled his coat up from the chair. Grant looked at the stars on the shoulders one last time, nodded to himself, then slowly tried the coat on. Yes, it still seemed a good fit. Then he threw back the flap to his tent and walked out by the fire to where most of his staff was seated. Rollins, Porter, and Comstock were all there. They stopped talking as he approached.

"Colonel...." Grant called to Rollins.

"Yes, General?"

"Please inform General Barnard, our chief engineer, that I would like to see him first thing tomorrow morning."

Rollins put down the cup in his hands, slowly surveyed everyone else seated around the fire, then looked back up at Grant. "General Barnard," he repeated, obviously surprised. "First thing."

"Yes."

"I will see to it, then," Rollins replied.

Everyone was looking at Grant then, wondering....

WINDMILL POINT

"Get a good night's sleep, gentlemen," Grant told them all. "We have a great deal of work ahead of us. And please have an orderly round up some more coffee for me."

Then he walked slowly back to his tent, arms folded behind his back, lost in thought. Ulysses Grant had made up his mind. Yes, there were still many details to work out, and much of it was still hazy, but he had made up his mind. It was a beautiful feeling, and his heart felt free and unrestrained for the first time in many days. He felt alive again. Outside the tent he stopped and glanced up into the tumbling clouds overhead.

"I have your coffee, General," an orderly called to him.

Grant stopped, smiled. "Yes, good. Put the pot inside on my desk, if you would be so kind. I'll need it all tonight."

"Very good, sir," the orderly replied. Then he dropped the tray off in the tent and slipped away into the darkness.

Grant took a deep breath of cool night air. There would be much work, exhaustive planning, but he had never been afraid of work. Once he set his mind to a task he could be like a bulldog, and for this he would need all of the concentration his heart and soul could bring to the task. So be it. He was not going to let anyone down. Not his family, not the country, and not Mr. Lincoln. No, not even himself.

He set his jaw firmly, glanced up into the night sky again, and for a brief moment Ulysses Grant felt a deep, profound sense of connection. Grant smiled up into the dark, swirling clouds. He closed his eyes. *Wait and see, General Washington,* he thought. *I think you will like what I have in store. I owe much of it to you, of course, but wait and see just the same. I promise, on the grave of every soul who has ever perished for the sake of liberty... I will not let you down.*

CHAPTER TWENTY-TWO

JUNE 6ᵀᴴ—MORNING

GRANT

Grant dropped the tent flap shut, pointed to a chair and waited for the engineer to be seated. John Barnard was the chief engineer for the Army of the Potomac, and if there was one branch that had served almost flawlessly throughout the entire war, it had been the engineers. Ulysses S. Grant had the utmost confidence in both Barnard and his men.

"I want to thank you for responding so quickly," Grant said. "Your promptness is greatly appreciated."

Barnard smiled. "As always, General, it is my pleasure."

Grant took a seat. "It goes without saying," he continued, "that what I am about to tell you can go no further than you and I, and those few people who absolutely must know. And they must be sworn to secrecy. We must play this very tight to the vest, General. *Very.*"

Barnard cocked his head just slightly, then leaned forward. "Of course."

Grant shook his head, folded his hands together tightly in his lap. "All right, then. I intend to move this army across both the Chickahominy and the James, and then move upon Petersburg. To say the least, this will require a considerable effort on the part of your engineers. Questions, General?"

WINDMILL POINT

Barnard crossed his legs, thought for a second or two. "May I ask when, sir?"

"As soon as possible," Grant replied. "I would hope within the next week."

"And where do you intend to make these crossings?"

"I will be sending out members of my staff to determine the best locations. We will probably cross the Chickahominy at two points, most likely Jones Bridge and Long Bridge. As far as the James is concerned, I want to cross somewhere below City Point so that we can remain out of sight of the enemy, but not so far east that it will delay our march on Petersburg. Are you at all familiar with the James in that area?"

Barnard nodded his head positively. "Yes, somewhat. I can tell you it is wide there, General. Very wide and quite deep. Probably a good seventy or eighty feet in depth, I would guess. And I would hazard, General, that any bridge crossing the James in that area would have to be almost a half-mile in length." Barnard whistled at the thought, rolled his eyes. "A *good* half-mile."

Grant took a long drag on his cigar, considered what his engineer had to say, then let the smoke slip slowly through his lips. "Can you bridge that distance?"

Barnard nodded. "I have many, many pontoons, General, and the best men in the whole world working for me, if I might say so myself. But let's be honest about it, General. This will be no small task. A floating bridge a half a mile long? To my knowledge no army in the history of the world has built such a bridge, except perhaps Xerxes, if I recall my history lessons properly, and he had a considerable period of time to accomplish the task. I trust we will probably have very little time to accomplish ours?"

"Very little."

Barnard nodded, clapped his hands together once, then broke into a grin. "Well, General this is what engineering is all about. Now, by God, *this* is a challenge! But, yes, yes, we will build your bridge. What an honor! My God, sir, we will make *history*," the engineer continued excitedly, rubbing his hands together. "Just let me know as soon as possible the site you choose. As you requested earlier, I have already gathered most of the equipment we will need. But General..."

"Go on."

"The river is quite navigable there," Barnard went on, turning the whole thing over in his mind. "The Rebels... well, it's my understanding that they still have some gunboats up around Richmond. We could lay a very long bridge and the Rebels could just steam downriver and blow the thing up while a corps of our boys is marching across. Or they could simply ram the damn thing. I mean..."

Grant fretted for a moment, took a long tug on his cigar, then rubbed his chin thoughtfully. "Okay, I'll have the navy there in force," Grant replied. "We'll have the river plugged tight from both ends. That way nothing will get close. Besides, it's my aim to make this crossing without the Rebels knowing anything of it until we're all safely across the river and on our way to Petersburg."

"And the roads, General? Have you picked the route?"

"No, not yet. I'm sure the roads will need work on them too, but hopefully not too much. We will need to cut some routes from here across the low country to the Chickahominy. You can probably get going on that right away."

"Yes, right," Barnard replied. "I'll get the pioneers working on that immediately."

"The bridges across the Chickahominy should be easy enough. The James, of course, will be a different story."

Barnard blinked, looked away, then returned his gaze to Grant. "We will build it, General. Rest assured, the engineers will be ready. For anything you need."

WINDMILL POINT

Grant blew out another long puff of smoke, shook his head. "I will also be sending orders to General Meade to have a separate set of works constructed well behind our current lines, just in case Lee should try something."

"That should pose no problem, General."

Grant thumped the table, liking what he had heard. "Good!"

Ulysses Grant had awoken that morning with a renewed sense of mission, and a soaring intensity thumping in his chest. For the first time in days he felt entirely focused. It seemed the pieces of his plan were almost tumbling together of their own accord. Just that morning, for instance, word had come in that a Federal command under General David Hunter had defeated a small Confederate army of about 5,000 men in the Shenandoah Valley at Piedmont near Staunton. That small bit of information had supplied a crucial piece to his puzzle.

Lee's army was supplied directly from Richmond, and Richmond was in turn supplied by two railroad lines. One of those entered the city from the south via Petersburg, while the other entered from the north through Lynchburg in the Shenandoah Valley. Grant's aim now was to shift his army secretly across the James, join with Butler's army, and fall upon Petersburg, while sending a second contingent to join Hunter in the valley and have that combined force take Lynchburg. If successful, both of Richmond's supply lines would be permanently cut.

Then, as Richmond starved, Lee would have only four choices. He could flee, surrender, dig in and await siege, or come out from behind his works and fight the Federal army on open ground. Grant had little doubt that Lee—with the Confederate government screaming in his ear—would of necessity pick the last alternative, and Grant was confident that, without their trenches and works to protect them, he would destroy the Rebel army once and for all. No more asking his men to charge head first into firing squads. In one sweeping movement, he would simultaneously restore his army's spirit and force the Confederacy into an end game that they could never hope to win.

It was the best plan he had ever conceived. Oddly enough, it was the best plan because in very many ways it was the worst plan. The move south would require him to secretly remove his army from its current position, where the confronting lines were in some places no more than forty yards apart, almost an impossibility to accomplish without alerting the Rebels in some way. He would then have to march his entire command over two rivers on poor roads, while Lee had the shorter route to any one of the objectives. Grant's march to Butler would consist of better than fifty miles, Lee's less than half of that. All the advantages of terrain and distance fell to Lee.

So the movement toward Petersburg would be fraught with danger at every turn, Grant knew, but that was precisely why he reasoned Lee would never expect him to make it. Lee was, without question, one of the world's most preeminent soldiers, so he would be expecting Grant to make the next logical play, not the most logistically taxing and hazardous of all. In all likelihood that meant Lee would be anticipating a quick dash across the Chickahominy, and then another sledgehammer attempt at a turning movement up the Long Bridge Road toward Richmond. That would be in keeping with what had been Grant's strategy for almost the entire month of May. But just as George Washington had foreseen so many years before, the best place to strike was often not the easiest or most obvious, but rather the least obvious and most difficult.

The great fear incumbent in any disengagement such as Grant now planned was that Lee would somehow get wind of it and strike while his army was strung out on country roads or, worse yet, divided by one or more rivers. If the Rebels moved rapidly, Lee might devour Grant's entire army in detail, destroying one unit at a time, before pinning the last,

WINDMILL POINT

beleaguered remnants of the Army of the Potomac against the banks of the James. In short, such a movement might ultimately result in, not just a defeat, but annihilation.

That is why Grant planned on constructing an extensive interior line of fortifications to fall back upon in the event of a Rebel advance; but beyond even that, he had a much better card up his sleeve. Since the very beginning of the war the Confederate cavalry had supplied Lee with sterling reconnaissance and timely information. Indeed, on more than one occasion J.E.B Stuart had taken his horsemen on rides around McClellan's entire army. But under Phil Sheridan the Federal cavalry had finally come of age. Recent victories at Yellow Tavern and Haw's Shop had proved, if not the superiority of the Yank cavalry, at least their parity, and now Grant intended to employ that new advantage to good use.

During his campaign against Vicksburg in 1863 Ulysses Grant had learned the advantages of utilizing his horsemen on strategic raids to confuse and distract his opponent. He had ordered Colonel Ben Grierson to lead his cavalry divisions inland, far behind Vicksburg. That raid had caused near bedlam in the Confederate high command, and while Grierson was off on his dash, Grant had taken the opportunity to slip his army across the Mississippi River virtually unnoticed. That cavalry ploy had worked to perfection, and he planned on doing the same thing now to cover his movement south from Cold Harbor.

Sheridan's cavalry was divided into three divisions consisting of almost 14,000 riders. Lee's contingent of horsemen was considerably depleted after years of war, and many of their mounts were broken down from lack of adequate feed. The number of horsemen Lee had available, Grant knew, in all likelihood numbered somewhere around 8,000. So he could send off two full divisions of his own—almost 10,000 sabers—and still hold back a full division to screen his army's movements.

Lee, on the other hand, would have to react. Whether fooled or not fooled by Grant's gambit, the Confederate commander would be obliged to send off the majority of his horse to counter Sheridan. He would have to defend Lynchburg, his lifeline to the Shenandoah, or risk the permanent disruption of his supply line. No army can survive for long without adequate food and supplies no matter how skilled its commander, and after three long and difficult years at war, no one understood that better than Robert E. Lee. So Grant had every confidence that Lee would respond. With Lee's horsemen off on the chase, Grant's ability to hide his movements and intentions would increase considerably, and the potential for a debacle would be greatly reduced.

Grant's plan out in the Shenandoah was a simple one. Sheridan was to rendezvous with Hunter's army somewhere near Charlottesville. The goal of the raid would be to destroy the train depots at Charlottesville, Lynchburg and Gordonsville, before returning along the line of the Virginia Central and ripping up every mile of track all the way back to the Army of the Potomac. If somewhere along the way Sheridan should meet and defeat a significant contingent of Confederate cavalry, well, that would just be icing on the cake. The main goal was to draw off Lee's eyes and ears. Without that, Grant's gamble might well prove fatal.

Unfortunately, the military brass in Washington also had its own ideas as to what Grant's next move should be. General Halleck had wired him repeatedly, anxious that the Army of the Potomac slip back north and attempt an investment of Richmond from that quarter. But it was apparent that Halleck's concerns were more for the safety of the Federal capital city than the swift execution of the war. Any movement north would require a shift of Grant's supply line from a water route down

WINDMILL POINT

the Chesapeake Bay—which could be easily defended by the navy—to an overland route, which would require a significant portion of his army to guard. That strategy would also isolate Butler's army, appear to all the world like a retreat, and as a consequence bolster the resolve of the Southern people. So Grant decided not to argue with Halleck. Better to simply ignore him.

Late that morning he had a long consultation with Andrew Humphreys, his chief of staff, in order to begin sorting out the logistics of the operation. Humphreys listened intently to every small detail of Grant's plan, his chin perched immobile on his folded hands, until Grant had finally concluded. Then he simply smiled and said "It is brilliant, General. Absolutely brilliant. I have only one, very small suggestion."

Grant, always anxious for good advice, leaned forward curiously. "Yes, yes... what?"

"Well," Humphreys continued, "it's been my experience that men tend to see what they expect to see, General. And when they see what they expect, they react in familiar ways."

"Yes, of course. Please, go on."

"For the past month we have made a series of short, tight maneuvers against Lee's army, each designed to always turn his right flank and place ourselves on the short line to Richmond."

Grant blew a puff of smoke, tapped the ash away on the leg of his chair. "True."

Humphreys smiled, edged closer. "You just told me yourself that you doubted Lee would ever expect you to conduct such a far-flung and dangerous operation as the one you have now conceived."

"Oh, absolutely," Grant replied. "It violates many of the basic principles of war. But that's exactly what makes it so attractive."

"Yes, I agree entirely," Humphreys replied. "But, you see, Lee will be expecting you to perform the same sort of maneuver as you have routinely demonstrated all along—another short, quick attempt to turn his right flank."

Grant took a long drag on his cigar, thought it over, then exhaled quickly. "Yes, I see what you're saying. And I agree with you. In fact, I've thought so myself. Lee will expect us to cross the Chickahominy and advance toward Richmond, probably up the Long Bridge Road. Or somewhere thereabouts."

Humphreys' eyes sparkled. "Exactly!"

Grant shrugged, still lost. "I'm not sure I'm following you, General."

"You told me that after Smith's corps departs by water, you intend to have Warren's corps swing behind us, cross the Chickahominy, and take up a blocking position south of the river. The rest of the army will then pull out and depart for the James behind Warren. Warren will serve as the rearguard."

"Yes, that's the plan."

"But suppose," Humphreys continued excitedly, "that instead of simply taking up a blocking position, we have Warren *advance* just slightly up the Long Bridge Road toward Richmond. Not an attack, mind you, just an *advance*. Say, until he strikes their pickets."

"Grant's eyes narrowed. "Advance?"

Humphreys ran his hand back through his hair, crossed his legs. "Yes," he said. "If that's what Lee expects to see, then why not show it to him? The best way to keep the Rebels put may be to make Lee think we are doing exactly what he expects us to do. If we advance he won't view Warren as a rearguard at all, but the advanced elements of our entire army coming *toward* him. Instead of coming out of his trenches and looking to see where we've gone, he will begin the construction of a whole new defensive position to stop us. And while his men are hurriedly digging a whole new labyrinth of rat holes, we will be slipping away."

WINDMILL POINT

Grant rubbed his chin, put his cigar down, then took it up again. He took a puff, blew it out. "Advance?"

"Yes, sir. Advance."

Grant smiled. "It's so simple, yet it's absolutely perfect. Perfect! I tell you, Andrew, I would never have thought of that myself. It's perfect. You're right. Lee will think we're coming right down his throat again."

Humphreys broke into a grin. "It will work. I'm sure of it."

Grant shook his head, chewed on the end of his cigar. "You bet it will," he agreed. Then he leaned forward. "Listen, General," he said, "*that* is just the sort of help I need."

"My pleasure, sir."

"No," Grant went on hurriedly, "I mean moving this army out of here. Now, quickly. We need to get the men away from all... *this*."

Humphreys grimaced. "I understand."

Grant shuffled his feet. "I'm not sure you do. This is all my... well, let's just say there will be a great deal of work to be done if we're going to get out of this intact. I think the men need rest, you see Andrew, some time to recuperate. This army needs to recover."

Humphreys nodded, seemed to understand. "I have already issued a series of directives, General," he said, "that I hope will address the most serious problems."

Grant looked up at him. "What?"

"I've ordered up food by the crate, fresh vegetables to be carefully cooked and distributed to all the front lines. I've sent off details for good, clean water. I've ordered a fresh shipment of beef brought in, and given strict orders to have all the camps tightly cleaned up and properly policed. New uniforms and shoes are being distributed. That should help. It's at least a beginning."

Grant was thrilled. "Yes. Yes, that's a great help."

"I have also issued orders to have small reconnaissance parties sent out on both flanks to see what the Rebels are up to. I thought that you would want to keep tabs."

"Yes, of course," Grant agreed.

"Anything else, General?"

"No, not right now. But please, stay close."

Humphreys smiled. "I intend to, sir."

Once Humphreys was up and off to his business, Grant went to the front of his tent and took a long look outside. The sun was breaking through the clouds, and the air hung hot, steamy, and still. It would be another scorcher of a day. The stench of rotting flesh was heavy in the air. He pitied the men in the front lines. Grant lowered his head. The truth of it was, it was an appalling scene, and it was a scene he intended to leave behind as soon as possible. Now, at least, he had a plan.

Grant tossed one cigar aside, then reached into his coat pocket for another. He lit it carefully until the tip end glowed red, then took a strong, deep drag. Yes, it was starting to come together. He had gotten them all into this jam, he thought, and now it would be his job to get them out. Well, so be it. His intention was to move the army south, force Robert E. Lee out into the open, and restore his men's morale in a single stroke. But it would have to be done quickly, and it would have to be done right. Failure here or near Cold Harbor could easily result in the destruction of his army, and victory for the South. And that could not happen.

CHAPTER TWENTY-THREE

JUNE 6TH—FORENOON

WHITE

Wyman held the gun's scope steady on the target, then gently squeezed the trigger.... Blamm!

The gun kicked, and without even bothering to check the results, White rolled on his side, jumped to his feet, and made a mad dash for a stand of trees just to his left. He dove headfirst into a maze of bushes and briars then crawled along on his belly, lugging the big gun by his side for thirty yards. Wyman wiped the dirt from his face and carefully rubbed the blood from his fingers. Then he yanked the gun around, slid the barrel through a sticker bush, and took a long look through the scope. He smiled.

White had been dueling with a battery of Confederate artillery for over an hour, their five guns to his one, and so far he had been winning. He'd found a small knoll behind the main infantry line, and while working there along the crest business had been good. Wyman had taken down three Confederate gunners so far, harassed the others half to death, and could tell they were starting to become more than merely irritated. After each of his shots they would toss a solid charge or two his way, but they were always shooting at where he had been, not where he had just scampered to, and they rarely came close.

Hunting him down with those smooth-bored cannons was, of course, like trying to shoot a gnat with a shotgun from a hundred yards off. As long as he was careful and kept his head low, the advantages were all his. Wyman would shoot again and they would duck away, then wheel the guns about and fire. Then it would be his turn to duck, and the little dance would kick off once more, back and forth, on and on. But now things seemed to be getting serious.

Wyman could see through his scope that they had had just about enough of him. All five guns were being rolled into position and aimed at his previous location, and while that was a fair 50 yards away from his current spot, he thought it best not to take any chances. So Wyman found a depression on the opposite side of the small rise where he burrowed low into the dirt. He counted to ten, then stuck a finger in each ear just as the distant guns began to buck and roar.

The ground trembled and the air fairly screamed and hissed with metal, great funnels of dirt tossing into the air and landing in the bushes nearby. For almost twenty minutes they blasted away like that, hurling the better part of thirty shots virtually dead on where he had previously been hidden, but not one came near him now. Wyman just kept his head down and used the extra time to reload. From time to time he looked up simply to catch the lay of the land in order to pick out the next sequence of positions he intended to use. Then, when the cannonading finally ceased, he lay low for a few minutes just to decoy them before sliding away to a new spot by a tree.

When enough time had elapsed so that they might feel comfortable again, he carefully slid the muzzle of the monstrous gun through a few low hanging branches, centered the sight, and drew a bead. He took a deep breath, checked the breeze, let the air slip slowly between his teeth, then squeezed the trigger. Blamm! The gun bucked, and nearly a mile away a Rebel officer toppled backward into the dirt. All the others began to scream and yell. He couldn't hear them, but he sure could see them, and they clearly weren't happy.

But there was no time to waste. Wyman yanked the gun back, and dashed off for his next chosen spot. There he hunkered low and loaded the huge gun again. Once loaded, he whirled about rapidly, shoved the gun up through some fallen logs, and picked another target. Again the gun exploded, and far off a Reb gunner grabbed his arm and went down on both knees.

"Gotcha, Johnny," Wyman whispered to himself.

Then he was off again in a rush, tumbling down a short ridge, and making for the next preselected position. Wyman rested a moment and tried to catch his breath, waiting for the guns to start firing. Surprised when the battery did not retaliate, he pushed his gun through some weeds, and took a quick look through the scope. He watched for a few seconds then grinned. They were limbering up, pulling the guns out of the small meadow across the way, and heading off for some other position. They'd had enough of him. One sharpshooter against a whole Rebel battery, and the plain truth of it was, in the end it had been no contest. He had whipped them straight-up.

The regiment had been roused from bed early that morning, told to eat quickly and pack. After a modest breakfast of hardtack and foul water, the Sharpshooters were marched the entire length of the Union line. Out past the extreme right flank, they went into position along a branch called Matadequin Creek. Here the ground was low, flat, and marshy. The soil was far too wet to dig entrenchments, so while the infantry prepared the position by felling trees and tossing mud up against the logs for protection, Wyman was ordered to harass the Rebels across the way. It was thought the Confederates might be preparing to use the swamps to launch a flank attack on the Federal right, so everyone was warned to remain alert.

What remained of the 2nd U.S. Sharpshooters had been broken up and parceled out all along the front. Some were out on picket duty, while others like Wyman had been placed in strategic areas and given full license to annoy the enemy as much as possible. That's when he'd found his spot behind the lines on the knoll and immediately went to work. They were all busy pecking away at the Rebels around noon, when suddenly the blood-curdling yelp of the Rebel yell rose in the woods off to the west. Wyman watched as the Union infantrymen below leaped for their rifles. Suddenly what seemed like 5,000 men came screaming and crashing through the woods, not in organized ranks at all, but running and leaping in clusters of five or six, all of them howling like demons from hell. The Rebels were headed straight for the new flank position, and many of the pickets out on the skirmish line were taken by complete surprise and gobbled up in the initial surge. The Confederates had apparently heard them moving in earlier that morning, and were coming on hard now to discover in what strength the Federals were deployed. It didn't take long for them to find out.

As the Confederates closed to within a hundred yards they were greeted with a sheet of flame and an explosion of shot from the Yankee line that immediately staggered their advance. Hats flew, flags fell, and Confederates toppled everywhere. Wyman got a few good shots in himself, although he could not reload and fire the big gun nearly as quickly as he would have liked. Down along the Federal line the boys were yelling and hollering, shaking their fists, daring the Rebels to come on again. After the disastrous charge they had all witnessed and endured just days before, the Union troops were anxious to give the Confederates a taste of their own medicine.

The Rebels fared no better than had the Yanks in assaulting a strong position at Cold Harbor, and now their dead littered that thin space between the lines, too. Complicating their attack had been the marshy ground itself, which inhibited movement and coordination between units, and consequently greatly favored the Federal defenders. As far as Wyman was concerned, it was a rare pleasure to see the grey ranks plowed down under the same conditions that the Union boys had suffered just days before, and he did not pity them in the least. The Rebels were repulsed easily, and they quickly appeared to lose any appetite for storming works across open ground. Once beaten back that morning, they did not test the position again.

In the early afternoon Wyman was called to a meeting with Captain Guest at the regimental headquarters. Guest was from a company of Michigan infantry, and was in temporary command of the regiment. Wyman did not care for Guest, for he seemed a very foolish man who generally derived whatever small amount of courage he ever displayed from the bottom of a bottle of whiskey. At night he would often leap up in front of the men whenever shots began to be traded between the lines. Drunk and ridiculous, he would holler, "Flam! Flam! Flam!" at the top of his lungs while swinging his sword overhead and spinning about. It was always a witless exhibition, and while many of the boys took bets on how long Guest would remain standing before being struck down by a Confederate ball, Wyman had always refrained. In the manner of most drunks, he'd noticed, Guest survived easily against odds aligned formidably against him, good fortune seeming to bend over backwards on his behalf for some reason. Such was the strange good fortune of the inebriated.

"We are ordered to send out a squad to reconnoiter the ground to our far right, well beyond the lines," Guest explained, somber and sober once more in the bright light of day. "I've picked a squad of Sharpshooters, and I want you to lead it, Sergeant."

"Yes, sir," Wyman replied. "Just what are we to do?"

Guest pointed due north. "Go as far out to the right as you can safely go and observe the strength and positions of the Rebels in that area."

Wyman followed his motion then looked back. "When are we to leave, Captain?"

"Immediately."

So they started out just after 2 o'clock, passing through the picket line on a heading due north. The afternoon sky was clear, the sun high and hot, but soon they were off into the muffled stillness of the trees, where the air was wonderfully cool and the heat seemed far behind. The squad moved about a mile through heavy timberland and saw nothing whatsoever of the enemy.

They slipped through the timber silent as deer, three men moving while the other three covered from behind. Occasionally, Wyman would send a man up a decent-sized tree for a look far out to the right and rear of the army, but they reported nothing more than long miles of rolling woods, and Wyman guessed that the Rebels had not maneuvered behind them. Everyone was just beginning to relax when Joe Thompson grabbed him by the arm and pointed.

"Look there, Sarge," Joe said. "Riders!"

"Cover!" Wyman called, and the men scattered quickly behind trees and rocks.

It was a small squadron of Rebel cavalry, maybe twenty men in all. They were about 700 yards off across a wide clearing, but closing at the trot.

Wyman rubbed his chin, tried to think quickly. "Alright," he said, "let's give 'em two shots each in rapid form. That should give 'em something to think about."

Everyone took good aim, and waited for Wyman to fire. When he felt he had a good line, he pulled the trigger, and almost instantaneously the other five rifles discharged. Then all six of them tore open the breech of their target rifles, reloaded, and fired again. Small puffs of smoke swirled in the air.

WINDMILL POINT

The Rebel cavalry pulled to an abrupt stop, horses rearing, two riders toppling into the dirt. They jerked their carbines about, and fired a hasty round in response, but they hardly knew where the sharpshooters were hiding and their shots did no damage. Then they quickly turned and rode off.

Joe Thompson stood up and came out from behind the tree where he'd taken cover. "What you think, Wyman?" he asked, watching the Confederate riders disappear into the green thickness of the trees.

Wyman shouldered his rifle. "We caught them by surprise," he answered. "Pretty obvious. At least this time."

"What do you mean, *this* time?" Joe wanted to know.

"Well, I imagine they're out here doing the same thing we are, Joe," Wyman replied. "So my guess is they'll be back to see just what we're about. And next time they'll come with help. Won't be just a few riders, Joe. We'll have our hands full."

Thompson rubbed his chin. "Whatcha think we aught to do?" he asked nervously.

"I don't like it so far out here all alone," Wyman answered, glancing back toward the way they had come. "Too far out. No help out here."

"Yeah, I hear ya." Thompson agreed.

Wyman put his hands on his hips and took a look back over his shoulder again. "Well," he said, "we haven't seen much of anything out this way at all. I'm satisfied we've done our job. A few Reb cavalry don't amount to a hill of beans. Think we should head back while we can."

Thompson nodded vigorously. "No argument here," he said. "Let's get on the go."

They started on the trek back, sweeping just slightly west to see if they could spot any additional Confederate positions or patrols. Most of the territory they crossed was heavily wooded, with small breaks here and there where the woods had been harvested, or burnt out by fires. Every once in awhile they stumbled upon a small farm cut out of the timber, and there were also quite a few tumbling creeks and a few natural meadows filled with sweet-smelling wildflowers.

The sight of the flowers was disarming, their aroma almost intoxicating. While everyone in the squad seemed nervous, for Wyman, the fresh air and woodlands were a pleasant change from the heat, stench, and narrow trenches along the main line. In many ways, the afternoon's march felt like nothing more than a hike through the New Hampshire woods, and he was instantly reminded of home. For a few lovely seconds, the war seemed a million miles distant.

As they crossed a hilltop over an open strip of ground Wyman called the party to a sudden halt. From the summit of the hill he could see for the better part of two miles, and far off to the west he could clearly make out a line of cavalry pickets in advance of the main Rebel line. He glanced north again, but saw nothing, and it was clear to him then that the Rebels had not strayed far from their initial position between the rivers.

Wyman gestured toward Joe. "Look there," he said. "That's everything we got to know. Rebels are off to the west and that's all. None of 'em up north or behind us from what I can see."

Thompson smiled. "Captain Guest will be happy to hear *that*," he said.

Wyman frowned, then spit into the dirt. "Captain Guest don't know Monday from Friday," he replied. "But someone up the chain will be happy to hear it, I hope."

"Let's get going," Thompson suggested, glancing about anxiously.

Wyman chuckled. "You still worried about them Reb riders, are you, Joe?"

Thompson shrugged. "Yeah, why not?" he answered. "You said yourself they'd be back with some help. I don't believe I'd necessarily care to see that, Sarge."

WINDMILL POINT

Wyman smiled. "Yeah, well, you're probably right," he agreed. "Let's pull the boys up tight and..."

Just then a fusillade of bullets exploded from the tree line along the western edge of the clearing. All six sharpshooters dove to the ground, then crawled like mad for cover. As bullets whacked and pinged against the jagged rocks nearby, they began to return fire, but the Confederates were well concealed along the edge of the timber, and could not be easily discerned.

"Can't spot a one of them!" Joe Thompson cried out. "I'm just shooting at sound. You see 'em, Sarge? You see 'em?"

"I don't see a thing!" Wyman called back. "But keep it up just the same! Least it'll make them keep their heads down."

Wyman loaded, fired once at a white puff of smoke, then sat up on his knees and motioned for the men to file off behind him, one at a time. He remained behind, firing as rapidly as he could manage, trying to cover their withdrawal. Once they were all off and well on their way, Wyman stood, fired one last time, then took off running behind them. They all stayed low, using what little cover the ground provided, firing back over their shoulders as they ran. The Rebels had other ideas, of course, and continued a sporadic fire, but their shots were fired in haste, and fell harmlessly in the rocks nearby.

The sharpshooters crossed what little remained of the open clearing rapidly, and everyone kept their head during the passage except Tom Gorman, who had from time to time been a problem in the past. Gorman, Wyman believed, possessed precious little sense or self-control, and he had suddenly become quite agitated as a result of all the excitement. Tom started darting about, and falling out of his place in line. Twice Wyman had to go back and yank him around again, and Wyman was quickly losing his temper. The thought of losing a man or being shot himself because of Gorman's foolish antics infuriated him. He grabbed Tom by the shirt and tried to shake some sense into him.

"You act like a fool, Tom!" Wyman shouted, as bullets hummed passed their ears or ricocheted in the rocks at their feet.

Tom's eyes bulged. "I know!" he answered finally. "But I fear we will be killed before we get back to our men!"

"We will if we all act like *you*!" Wyman blurted. Then he took Gorman by the buttons on his shirt and tossed him back into his proper place in line one last time. "Now stay put, Tom!" Wyman yelled. "I'm done fooling with you! If the Rebels don't get you, maybe I will."

Wyman pointed toward the trees ahead. "Let's move!" he shouted.

They all crouched low, ran furiously, and managed to cross over the last forty yards of clearing in just a few seconds. Finally the squad gained the cover of the trees, breathless and gasping for air, but safe at last. Wyman loaded his rifle, and told Joe Thompson to take the lead while he remained behind to see if the Rebels dared follow. He waited for what he thought was an appropriate amount of time, but the Confederates never showed themselves. The Federal picket line was only a few hundred yards from that point, and perhaps they'd thought better of tangling with a good portion of the Federal army.

Just a few minutes later Wyman ducked back into the woods and headed for the safety of the main line. He passed through the pickets a few minutes after that and found the rest of his squad waiting patiently under a tree nearby. Wyman stopped, looked them all over, and felt a great sense of relief.

"Well now," he said, stepping toward Tom Gorman, "I guess you survived after all, aye, Tom?"

Gorman broke into a happy grin. "Yes, Sergeant."

Wyman put his hands on his hips. "I want you to remember this, Private," he said. "If you listen to orders and do as you're told, you just may survive this war."

"I will try, Sarge."

WINDMILL POINT

Wyman relaxed. "I do not care to yell at you, Tom," he said. "It is not a pleasure for me. I hope you understand that."

"I do," Tom replied.

Wyman smiled at him, felt unusually relieved. He sensed a few drops of sweat on his forehead and quickly wiped them away. He realized then just how hot and tired he really was. The small mission that afternoon had been his very first command, so to speak, and he had not only accomplished his assigned task, but had brought them all back safely, as well. For a few very lonely hours he had carried their lives in his hands, and that responsibility had weighed heavily on him.

The troops back in the trenches often disparaged their officer's tasks, but Wyman understood now that those same boys all spoke without the benefit of any meaningful experience. To know that your men's well-being depends upon your own good judgment is a difficult hardship to endure. How Birney, Hancock, or even General Grant handled such responsibility day in and day out was beyond his comprehension, but he certainly had a greater respect for them now.

The Sharpshooters stood up and began the short trip back to the main line. Wyman nodded as each man passed by him, then he turned to head back himself. As he neared the main line, Wyman spotted the officer in charge of that section and saluted. The lieutenant looked his way, then snapped a sharp salute in return.

Wyman stopped dead in his tracks, held his salute, and sensed an unusual look in the officer's eyes. Wyman White had experienced a wide range of emotions since arriving at Cold Harbor, from terror to despondency, but the clear sense of understanding in the lieutenant's eyes was something entirely new. The look was one of respect, and, for the first time in many months, Wyman felt proud of himself. It was a feeling that he thoroughly relished.

"Good show, Sergeant," the lieutenant said.

Wyman nodded as he walked passed. "Thank you, sir," he replied. Then he started back through the woods toward his regiment, feeling as good as he had felt in a long, long time.

CHAPTER TWENTY-FOUR

JUNE 6TH—AFTERNOON

LEE

Lee took the message from Taylor, unfolded the note, and read it over carefully. It was another message from Grant, seemingly one more attempt at avoiding the inevitable. The first one had arrived late the day before, a request to gather the wounded between the lines, but without the requisite appeal for a suspension of hostilities which, according to the general rules of war, was always a tacit acknowledgment of defeat. Grant was playing games, trying to float the pretense that he had not been whipped, but Lee was not buying. He read again…

>Cold Harbor, Va, June 6, 1864
>General R.E. Lee,
>Commanding Army of N. Va.
>
>Your communication of yesterday's date is received. I will send immediately, as you propose, to collect the dead and wounded between the lines of the two armies, and will also instruct that you be allowed to do the same. I propose that the time for doing this be between the hours of 12 M. and 3 P.M. to-day. I will direct all parties going out to bear a white flag, and not to attempt to go beyond where we

have dead or wounded, and not beyond or on ground occupied by your troops.

> U.S. Grant,
> Lieut.-General.

Taylor folded his hands neatly in his lap, smiled. "May I inquire, General, if our esteemed adversary has changed the wording of his inquiry this time around?"

Lee looked up, handed the message over to his aide. "Read for yourself," he replied. "I believe you will see that General Grant has changed the wording of his message, but not its covert intent. He still seeks to avoid requesting a suspension of hostilities in the hopes, I suppose, that he can use our acceptance of his terms as proof positive for his government that he has fought us to a draw—or perhaps even *defeated* us."

Taylor read the message thoroughly, then nodded. "Does he take us for fools, General?"

Lee considered the question carefully. "No, I don't think so, Colonel," he answered. "I suggest to you that our General Grant is simply a battler, you know: the very combative type. He will fight us over roads, woods, rivers and now even words, if that's what it takes. He will fight over anything and everything. There is no issue he will not contest. In that sense Grant's correspondence is not an insult, Colonel. It's simply a challenge, an invitation to wrangle now over *terms*. But I'm afraid this is a battle he cannot win. For he has been defeated, and now we hold all the cards."

"What will you do, General?" Taylor asked.

Lee shrugged. "Reply," he answered.

"Shall I take a message, sir?"

"Yes, please do, Colonel," Lee said, as Taylor took up a piece of paper. "Tell General Grant that I cannot agree to the burial of the dead or the removal of the wounded in accordance with the

WINDMILL POINT

terms he's proposed, but that when either party should care to do so, that appeal should be accompanied by a request for a suspension of hostilities, and a flag of truce." Lee stared at Taylor for a moment. "He knows all of this, of course, but I will repeat it politely just the same."

Taylor looked up. "What if General Grant sends out parties in accordance with his earlier correspondence, sir? His men will be carrying white flags. They might be fired upon. That would be very unfortunate. How should we handle that?"

Lee frowned. "Yes, you're right, Colonel," he said. "Well, tell him that any parties he might send out will simply be turned back. We must make sure that our men understand that, Colonel. We must *never* fire upon men carrying flags of truce, but they must also not be allowed to wander wherever they please without a proper agreement in place."

Taylor smiled. "Very good, sir. I'll have it properly written for your signature."

Lee nodded. "Please do."

Robert E. Lee took a sip of water, leaned back, and relaxed. He watched as the miles of wagons rolled by on the road below, all up from Richmond, chock full of fresh supplies. Down along the road, much of it was being divided, each division of the army getting their proper share. It did his heart good to see his men finally being taken care of. The finest plans in the world would not move a starving army.

Lee thought again of Grant's note. It was nice to see the Federal commander struggling so, he thought, desperately trying to wrench a victory from the ashes of an obvious defeat, hoping somehow that a war of words might now provide the victory the real war had denied him. Grant's message provided Lee with a very clear indication of just how desperate his adversary was feeling. And desperate men do desperate things, and often in their haste to make things happen mistakes are made. So Lee realized, now more than ever, that he would have to remain vigilant. He must be prepared to take immediate advantage of any opportunities that presented themselves. The war seemed to be moving toward a climax, here, of all places, in this God forsaken no man's land named Cold Harbor. He must be ready for anything.

Around him now swirled a sea of officers and men, their spirits rising, his army's confidence seemingly never more firm. They had stopped Grant and his massive army for over a month. Lee's men were almost jubilant. They all talked now as though they could stop Grant forever.

Yet Lee still had his own problems to deal with. He had just received word of General Hunter's victory in the Shenandoah Valley, and that was a matter of some concern. He could not allow the Federals to roam uncontested throughout the valley for long without severe repercussions.

That morning, as well, he had given orders for Jubal Early to try and turn Grant's right flank, far up north in the swamp, but nothing had come of it. The Yanks had apparently been well posted, and while the reports he'd received all glowed with the usual superlatives, Lee could read well enough between the lines to know that Early had been repulsed—perhaps severely.

No matter; it had been a minor gambit anyway. The real test would come with Grant's next move, and there was no telling from the tone of his recent message just what that might entail. If pressed hard enough by the authorities in Washington, Grant might even stumble headfirst into another all-out assault right here at Cold Harbor. Lee relished the thought. Fresh food had arrived by the wagonload, and his army was growing stronger by the hour. His men had now had an additional two days to strengthen their works, and plenty of ammunition had been brought up and stowed away in the trenches. Robert E. Lee was confident that any subsequent attack on his position would be repulsed in a far bloodier spectacle than even the last. If Grant

WINDMILL POINT

were fool enough to attempt that, the road to Southern independence might well be established by week's end.

"I have it for you, General," Taylor said, handing him the written response.

Lee looked it over carefully then signed the bottom. "Yes, that's fine," he said, handing it back. "And Colonel..."

"Sir?"

"Let's ask General Early to try the Federal's right flank again tomorrow."

Taylor folded his arms across his chest, frowned. "Sir," he said, "I'm not sure we were quite as successful today as..."

Lee held up his hand. "I understand all of that," he replied. "It doesn't matter. Whatever pressure we can keep on General Grant at this juncture, I think will inure entirely to our benefit. Our means are obviously limited in that regard. It pains me to admit that, but I know it's true. So if Early can get on his flank, well, that would be good, but if he is just able to annoy Grant, in the end it may be just as productive."

"To keep him on edge, do you mean, sir?"

"Yes, that's it, Colonel," Lee answered. "You see, I believe General Grant has very few options at this time, and those that he has are not so terribly good."

"May I ask, General, what you expect him to do?"

Lee stretched his legs out, considered the question. "Well, sir, his easiest movement—and therefore his quickest and safest—is simply to move south across the Chickahominy and attempt to turn our right flank again. He has been hammering away at us all spring in just that manner, and I honestly expect him to try it again."

"You mean, cross over the river then move on Richmond from there?"

"Yes, that's it," Lee said.

"But General," Taylor continued, thinking it over, "we have ample works still in place all throughout that area from two years ago when McClellan moved up the peninsula. They are very *strong* works! If we could reoccupy those positions, a fight there would be even better for us than another fight here at Cold Harbor. And our position here is virtually impregnable."

Lee smiled briefly. "Yes, I believe you are correct."

Taylor studied him, broke into a sudden grin. "Yes, I believe I'm starting to understand now, General. So we are going to harry General Grant as much as we possibly can and hope we can influence him a bit into making just that decision. The more uncomfortable we can make it for him, the quicker he might move his army across the river."

Lee smiled.

"And if he makes the move across the Chickahominy," Taylor went on, thinking it through as he spoke, "then you will have him right where you want him. Any assault made by them along that line will no doubt turn into a disaster, another Yankee defeat even worse than Cold Harbor. Could the Federal army survive such a thing?"

Lee rolled his shoulders. "It would be nice to think not, Colonel, but I do not consider Grant to be a fool by any means."

"But he came at us *here*, sir...."

"Yes, well, you are correct on that," Lee admitted.

"And if he moves south, he will surely hit us again. What other option would he have?"

"Very few," Lee agreed. "That's true. But we must not become overconfident, Colonel. That alone could spell our ruin. Even if he does not attack at once, there might be an opportunity for us to pitch into his rearguard as he is crossing the Chickahominy and damage his army severely. That's why I want to keep up the pressure. Under duress Grant may act in haste, and if we are lucky we might force him into a mistake."

Taylor stood. "I will deliver the order to General Early myself, sir."

WINDMILL POINT

"Very good," Lee replied. "And in the meantime we must keep a keen watch on the fords along the Chickahominy. Has there been any enemy activity reported along the river?"

"None that I know of, General. But I will inquire again."

Lee nodded. "Yes, fine. And double the pickets along the river, Colonel. Nothing must escape our attention right now. The fate of our nation may ride on our efforts over these next few days."

"How so, General?"

Lee nodded, sighed. "I believe Grant may be under a great deal of pressure right now, Colonel. Things have not gone well as of late for him, and I'm sure the future appears equally as bleak from his perspective. Yet the war is costing the Federal government a fortune each day to prosecute, so Grant will be feeling a great sense of urgency to act. The more pressure we can apply to the situation, the sooner he may act, and the greater the chances that anything he does will be hasty and possibly ill conceived."

Taylor's eyebrow arched noticeably. "You mean... a blunder?"

"Exactly," Lee affirmed. "A blunder."

CHAPTER TWENTY-FIVE

JUNE 6TH—LATE AFTERNOON

GRANT

U. S. Grant had selected both members of his staff with great care—Porter and Comstock. They were to handle the most critical aspect of the entire campaign. If their mission proved successful, then the great movement would at least have a chance. If they bungled it, then all could be lost. For the first time in years, Ulysses Grant felt an almost overwhelming need to impress upon his subordinates the importance of the task they were about to undertake. He stared at them intently. *This could not be botched.*

Porter shifted uneasily on his chair, apparently sensing Grant's anxiety. Seated next to him, Comstock sat utterly motionless... waiting.

Grant tossed his hands in the air then pointed at them forcefully, one after the other. "I want both of you to undertake a very important mission," he said, "prior to moving this army from its current position here at Cold Harbor."

Comstock's eyes grew wide. Porter blinked, coughed nervously.

"Let me explain," Grant continued, staring a hole through them both. "I have made up my mind to send Smith's entire corps to Cole's Landing on the Chickahominy by means of a forced march. There they will take boats and be transferred to

WINDMILL POINT

Butler at the Bermuda Hundred. These troops will depart without their wagons and artillery. Those will all accompany the Army of the Potomac."

"Accompany the army, sir?" Comstock repeated, grasping for Grant's intent, trying to understand where he was headed.

"Yes, that's right," Grant replied. "For the time being the army will be held in readiness to pull out on short notice, then by rapid marches cross the Chickahominy, reach the James, and prepare to cross that river, as well."

Both subordinates leaned forward, seemed to grasp at once the scope of the movement he was contemplating. They were becoming excited.

Grant tapped the arm of the chair apprehensively. "I want both of you to go to Bermuda Hundred and explain the movement to General Butler—all the details. He must be prepared to render his position secure against any attack Lee might launch while the Army of the Potomac is in transit. That will be the most critical time, as far as he is concerned, so he must be prepared. Butler's compliance will be critical to the success of the campaign."

"All the details, sir?" Porter inquired.

"Yes," Grant affirmed. "General Butler must understand everything. Special orders are now being drafted for you to deliver. They will include all the points he must take care of on his end. In particular, I want him to load a few transports with heavy rock and have it dumped in the James River above City Point so that the Rebels can no longer navigate the river downstream. But there is much more than that, and all of it must be accomplished without fail. All of it."

"When do you want us to depart, General?" Comstock asked.

"Wait," Grant went on hurriedly, "there's more. After you meet with Butler you will then ride east and select the best point along the James River for the army to cross over. To do this you must take into consideration as short a line of march as will be practicable for the army, yet it must be a point on the river far enough downstream to allow for a sufficient distance between it and the present position of Lee's army, to prevent the chance of our being attacked or spotted while making the crossing." Grant took a long puff on his cigar, blew it out. "As I recall, you both have previous experience along the James, do you not?"

"Yes, we do, General," Comstock replied at once. "We were both on General McClellan's staff in '62 when the army moved south from Richmond, and we helped comb the river in search of a feasible location to harbor the army that year. We rode every inch of the James from Chaffin's Bluff east to Harrison's Landing."

"Excellent," Grant said, tossing one cigar aside and quickly pulling out another. "I thought so. That knowledge should serve you well this time around. That is one of the reasons I selected you both." He put the cigar between his lips, pulled out a match and lit it carefully. Then he thought for a moment before continuing. "You should, of course, also be guided by considerations of the width of the river at the point you choose, and the character of the country by which it will have to be approached. Naturally, you will have to consider the network of roads that the army might utilize serving the point on the river you choose. And so on, and so on…. There will be many factors to weigh."

"When would you have us depart, General?" Porter asked.

"The orders for General Butler should be fully completed later tonight. Get a good night's sleep and leave first thing tomorrow. I have already had arrangements made for you to ride to White House Landing and from there depart by transport for the Bermuda Hundred."

Comstock stood, saluted. "Thank you, sir."

WINDMILL POINT

Grant returned the salute and let out another small puff of smoke. For a moment he simply watched it twirl away and disappear toward the top of the tent. Then he returned to the topic at hand. "I cannot impress upon you gentlemen enough the importance of this effort. Leave no rock unturned in search of the proper location. Then return here as quickly as you possibly can. The longer the army sits around in these squalid trenches the worse the situation will get. I want to get out of here as soon as is possible. Do either of you have any questions?"

"No, General," Comstock said. Then the aide glanced sideways at Porter.

"I have no questions either, sir," Porter added. "Thank you for this opportunity, General. We will not let you down."

Grant forced himself to smile. "I know."

He wished them well, then watched as they exited the tent. They were the two best men he had for the task, and he could only trust that they understood the gravity of the job they had undertaken. Then he picked up the message that had just come in from Lee in response to his second request for a truce, opened it with a jerk, and began to read:

> I regret that I did not make myself understood in my communication...

Grant frowned, read no more, simply folded the note back into the envelope, and tossed it back on top of his desk. Well, so much for cleverness. He should have known better, he thought. He'd never really been a clever man. Not, at least, in terms of what made him tick. He was more a banger, a slugger, the straightforward type for whom cleverness never seemed entirely natural, or for that matter, used with anything even approaching deftness. Like the most common of shysters, his attempts at cleverness generally came off as more disingenuous than cagey, the hollow ring of pretension clanging loud and clear for all to hear. He should never have tried it with Lee, and, predictably, it had all come to naught.

So there seemed little more to do now than address the situation straightaway. He picked up the note from Lee, unfolded it, and read it slowly through from start to finish. Then he read it again, tossed it back onto his desk, and picked up his pen. He wrote:

> COLD HARBOR, Va, *June* 6, 1864
> General R. E. Lee,
> Commanding Army N. Va.
>
> The knowledge that wounded men are now suffering from want of attention between the two armies, compels me to ask a suspension of hostilities for sufficient time to collect them in, say two hours. Permit me to say that the hours you may fix upon for this will be agreeable to me, and the same privilege will be extended to such parties as you may wish to send out on the same duty without further application.
>
> U.S. Grant,
> Lieut.-General.

He read it through twice, was about to sign and slide it into an envelope for delivery, when an orderly appeared at the front of his tent. The orderly stuck his head inside the flap.

"As you requested, General Sheridan is here to see you, sir."

Grant looked up, folded the note to Lee, and put it aside. "Yes, show him in."

Sheridan, a short, bandy-legged Irishman from New York, had been a member of the West Point class of 1853, and had made his mark as a commander of infantry under Grant in the Western Theater. Tough and aggressive, Grant thought him just the man to come east and whip the Potomac Army's cavalry into shape. The President had been more amused than impressed by Sheridan's diminutive stature, calling him "a brown, chunky little chap, with a long body, short legs, and not enough neck to hang him, and such long arms that if his ankles itch he can scratch them without stooping over." Yet, since coming east early that spring, Sheridan had acquitted himself well indeed, scoring impressive cavalry triumphs at Yellow Tavern—where his Confederate counterpart, J.E.B. Stuart, had been mortally wounded—and more recently at both Haw's Shop and Cold Harbor. Known to lead from out in front, Sheridan was just the sort of dynamic leader that Grant favored.

Grant returned Sheridan's salute, then pointed to the chair just recently vacated by Porter. "Have a seat, General," he said. "We have some things to discuss."

"I've already read the orders Meade sent over," Sheridan replied. "Looks like a little action is in the offing."

Grant nodded slowly. "Yes, I'm afraid so, and more than a little."

Sheridan smiled. "Well I'm all for that, General. I'm all ears."

Grant got straight to the point. "My intention is to move the army out of here soon, and in so doing draw Lee out into the open where we might have a fair shot at him."

Sheridan nodded vigorously. "The infantry boys, well, they're getting tired of charging earthworks, I hear," he said. "Can't say as I blame them."

Grant sipped his coffee, put the tin cup back down. "Nor I," he agreed. "Now, as your orders stipulate, what I want you to do is to take two of your three divisions of cavalry and raid far inland, clear up into the Shenandoah Valley."

"Yes, I see that." Sheridan answered. Then his eyebrow arched noticeably. "That's quite a ways off, sir. It's a hell of a jaunt."

"Indeed, that's the point," Grant agreed. "Look, Richmond is supplied from the north via the Shenandoah, and from the south through Petersburg. I'm going to move upon Petersburg, and I want you to join with Hunter in the valley and shut down the railroad leading into Richmond from the other end. I want you to move on Gordonsvile, Charlottesville, and Lynchburg. Tear up the track. Once that's done, I want you to rejoin the army by coming back down the lines of the Virginia Central, tearing up every track and tie along the way." Grant pointed at a map hung near his desk. "Take a look."

Sheridan stood, studied the map for a moment or two. "It's a long ride, General," he pointed out. "We'll have to move slowly or else we'll break down our mounts before we even get into action."

"That's fine. Whatever it takes."

Sheridan cocked his head. "The thing is, General," he continued, pointing toward the map, "the whole movement you want me to make will be through Rebel territory. If I move slowly, surely the Rebels will spot us; their scouts and riders are everywhere. Then they'll give chase. My guess is Hampton will be after us with almost everything he has."

Grant smiled. "That's exactly what I want them to do," he said. "Look, I can't afford to have Lee's cavalry snooping all around Cold Harbor while the Army of the Potomac is up and on the move. If they break through our perimeter and find out what we're about, Lee will go over to the offensive at the first opportunity. Then I may have real problems on my hands, especially if he catches us in the midst of crossing these two rivers. So part of your mission—and an important part!—will be to draw off the better part of his cavalry. His cavalry is his eyes, and if they're gone, he won't be able to see what I'm up to. And

WINDMILL POINT

that's just the way I want it." Grant stared at Sheridan for a moment. "Hampton." he said. "He's new to his command. What do you make of him?"

Sheridan thought for a moment, folded his arms across his chest. "Well, my sense of him is that he's a good soldier. Not flashy like Stuart was, but a good soldier."

"Well, I can live without the flash myself," Grant said.

Sheridan laughed. "We'll be moving out at first light, General."

"Yes, fine," Grant said. "Your men have not been heavily involved for a number of days. They should be ready and rested, their horses well fed by now."

"We are, General," Sheridan answered excitedly. "We're ready, all right."

"Good," Grant responded. "I want you to leave one division behind—Wilson's would be my choice—so he can screen the Army of the Potomac as it moves. Have you plotted a tentative course?"

Sheridan nodded affirmatively. "I have," he replied. Sheridan stepped to the map, pointed. "I've already given orders to consolidate at New Castle Ferry on the Pamunkey River this evening. I'm bringing one pontoon bridge, and the engineers are to employ that tonight. We'll cross at first light, and make for the north bank of the North Anna River. The river will cover our flank as we move west."

Grant studied the map. "Yes, good."

"Anyway," Sheridan went on, "it's a good sixty miles or so upriver to this ford." He pointed emphatically. "Carpenter's Ford. That's where we'll cross back over the river, then head almost due south and strike the line of the Virginia Central Railroad. If everything goes right, we should strike the tracks right about here."

Grant crowded the map, squinted. "Is that Gordonsville?"

183

"No," Sheridan replied. "Gordonsville is a few miles further west. This stop on the line is called Trevilian Station. It's out in the middle of nowhere. We'll start there and start ripping up track all the way into Gordonsville."

Grant folded his hands behind his back. "Yes, fine. That should do."

Sheridan smiled, stood back and saluted crisply. "Thank you, General," he said. "I will issue the final orders to my boys at once."

Grant reached out, took Sheridan's hand, gave it a firm shake. "You have never let me down, Phil," he said. "Needless to say, this *has* to work."

Sheridan nodded forcefully. "It will work!" he said. They shook hands one more time. Then Sheridan turned and marched out of the tent.

Grant sat down again, tapped his desk impatiently. Soon the whole thing would be in motion, he thought, his grand design no longer just a jumble of disconnected thoughts strung loosely together, but a real thing of flesh and blood and action. In less than a day he had translated ideas into motion, potential into reality, and now in his mind the campaign was taking on the firm feeling of certainty. In the morning Sheridan would be heading off for the Shenandoah Valley with over 9,000 men, Porter and Comstock off by water for the Bermuda Hundred. He smiled, tapped the desk again, then suddenly felt the envelope intended for Lee under his fingers again.

He picked it up, signed the letter, and called for a staff member to have it delivered through the lines. Then he thought of Lee—probably sitting in his headquarters tent off to the west, perhaps no more than a few miles away. Grant wondered what his adversary might be thinking. Yes, he would admit privately now that Lee had had the best of it so far, but if all went as planned, soon Grant would turn the tables on him once and for all. Lee would not see it coming. If all went well, the Army of

WINDMILL POINT

the Potomac would be across the James and well on its way toward Petersburg before Lee would be able to grasp what had happened, and by then it would be too late.

But Lee was very good; there was no question of that. There had been a time when Ulysses Grant considered the officers in the Army of the Potomac to be just a bit overwhelmed by his adversary's reputation, but no more. Grant had been taught a rough lesson all spring, and it had been a hard one to digest. But he was not about to back away. Now he had cast the dice again, and within a few days the issue would be decided, for better or for worse. So be it. He would either fail and be chewed apart in the process, or force Lee out of his entrenchments and end the war soon on open ground. He had put the whole thing into irrevocable motion now, and in a few days they would all have the answer.

CHAPTER TWENTY-SIX

JUNE 6TH—EVENING

CUSTER

George Custer sat not far from a gentle bend on the Pamunkey River as the last few slivers of scarlet faded and then disappeared from the western horizon. He flicked several annoying mosquitoes away from his face, set his chair firmly in place, and then leaned back comfortably. Custer put his boots up on a small crate, pulled the lantern close, and dipped the tip of his pen into the ink. George Armstrong Custer thought for a moment, then began a short note to his new bride:

> Again I am called on to bid you adieu for a short period. Tomorrow morning two divisions, 1 and 2, of this Corps set out on another raid. We may be gone two or three weeks. I will write the first opportunity. Keep up a stout heart, and remember the successful issue of the past. God and success have hitherto attended us. May we not hope for a continuance of His blessing?

He read it twice, signed it affectionately, then set the letter aside for a moment to allow the ink to thoroughly dry. He glanced up, and for as far as his eye could take in, the red flicker of campfires dotted the hills and fields around him. Custer smiled. The cavalry was once again on the move, and the mere thought of action made his blood dance.

They had ridden north from the Chickahominy River that afternoon, on back roads all the way to New Castle Ferry, where they'd gone into bivouac on the banks of the Pamunkey. Two thirds of the cavalry corps was now assembled nearby, and it was a sight to see. They'd been told to draw 100 rounds of ammunition and three days' rations, but no one knew what for. Ever since Grant had come east, secrecy had been the word, and not even the division commanders had an idea as to where they were headed. But they were obviously headed somewhere. Camped along the banks of the river were almost 10,000 riders, their mounts, well over a hundred wagons, ambulances, and an entire brigade of horse artillery: some twenty cannon and three hundred artillerymen. Their final destination was a mystery, and if Grant had his way, not one of them would know where they were going until they got there.

Custer picked up the note, tested the ink, then folded it carefully away into an envelope. He'd send it back with a courier to be posted, and could only imagine when he might see his wife, Libbie, again. He had met her while on leave in Monroe, Michigan, after the first battle of Bull Run, and had fallen instantly in love. Elizabeth Clift Bacon was the prettiest girl in town and the daughter of a prominent judge. George Armstrong Custer, on the other hand, was no more than the son of a blacksmith, but his humble beginnings hadn't stopped him from pursuing her. By grace and pluck and persistence he had wormed his way into her affections, and they had finally been married in the early spring of 1864. By then Custer was known far and wide as far more than the son of a blacksmith. He had already become a legend.

George A. Custer had been born in the small Ohio settlement of New Rumley in December of 1839. Smart and energetic, footloose and lighthearted, he'd gained entrance to

West Point in 1857 when the father of the girl he had been wooing was so desperate to see him gone that he pressed the necessary congressman for a favor. Thrilled by the appointment, Custer was off quickly for the military academy in New York, soon to find out, however, that he and military discipline did not exactly get along.

For four years George Custer barely skimmed by in his class work, while racking up an unprecedented volume of demerits. He was in trouble for almost everything, from his foolish notions of fun, to his inability to stomach authority. In1861 he finally managed to graduate, dead last in his class academically, first in total demerits. Only five days after graduation he was arrested and charged with neglect of duty for allowing two incoming cadets to fight. A court martial found him guilty, and under normal circumstances he might even have spent a few days in the stockade, but with the Federal Army desperate for trained officers, he received only a reprimand and was quietly shipped off for service. But from small acorns do mighty oaks grow, and thus began one of the most remarkable careers in American military history.

Tall, athletic, and possessed of extraordinary energy, Custer quickly displayed a natural instinct for war, and a fearlessness that knew no bounds. Early in the conflict he had been attached to the staff of the legendary Phil Kearny, from whom he learned the necessity of rigid discipline. Later he served on the staff of General Winfield Hancock, and, later still, on George McClellan's. Always daring and aggressive, Custer's rise through the ranks had been nothing short of astonishing, and in 1863 he took the extraordinary leap from captain to brigadier general at the tender age of only twenty-three.

Just like that, he was in command of a full brigade of Michigan cavalry, and it didn't take Custer long to show everyone just what he was about. He had received his promotion to general just prior to the Gettysburg campaign the previous summer, and he had wasted no time displaying his uncommon aggressiveness. On June 30th his brigade tangled with J.E.B. Stuart's column en route to Gettysburg—over 5600 men—in the streets of Hanover, Pennsylvania, and two days later at Hunterstown he personally led no more than fifty men in a full-fledged assault on Wade Hampton's entire cavalry division. That daredevil assault was blasted to pieces by the waiting Rebels, and Custer's horse was shot right out from under him as he charged. He escaped almost certain death when, at the last moment, a trooper noticed Custer on the ground and helped pull him to safety. Together they made a wild dash for the rear, somehow avoiding the avalanche of small-arms fire aimed in their direction. That harrowing experience might have tempered many a soldier's taste for combat, but not George Custer's. Indeed, it seemed only to increase it.

The following afternoon he deployed his entire brigade below a long ridge a few miles east of Gettysburg, and then—when he spotted nothing more than a glint of metal in the trees above—led it pell-mell into the teeth of Stuart's whole corps. His charge initiated a furious cavalry engagement that rocked back and forth across wood lots and farm fields for hours. When it was finally over Stuart—bloodied and beaten by Federal cavalry for the first time in the war—withdrew from the field. Ever since then stories of Custer's dash, mettle and, yes, extraordinary good luck, had been swirling throughout the Army of the Potomac.

The "boy General", they called him affectionately now, and that suited George Custer just fine. Much like Kearny and Stuart, this boy general had a taste for glory and a pure and simple love of action. Outfitted in a tailored uniform with gold piping, a red kerchief tied rakishly around his neck, and long blond curls flapping behind in the wind, Custer was an unforgettable sight on any battlefield, and that's just the way he wanted it.

Custer glanced up, caught a whiff of dinner cooking in the pot. "What's that?" he asked

"Chicken cookin'," Eliza answered. A runaway slave, Eliza Brown worked as his cook in camp. Funny and irreverent, she followed Custer's wagon in an old, improvised carriage, and was loved by Libbie and all of his men. "The Queen of Sheba" they called her as she bounced along behind his train of wagons, and his headquarters could not run without her. Custer's camp was always well supplied and comfortable, Eliza preparing special meals for his staff, while the young boy, Johnny Cisco, washed his uniforms, gathered firewood, and performed odd jobs. To Custer they were just family. That's just the way he treated them, and they loved him for it.

"Hope you got plenty cooking there, Eliza," Custer joked, "this may be our last real meal for awhile, you know."

"Don't you worry about your stomach, Gen'l George," she answered.

"Just asking," Custer said, grinning back at her.

"You know we got plenty of food," she replied with a wink. "Liza keep you fat so you can shoot the Rebels." She smiled across the campfire. "You know where we's off to, Gen'l?"

"Wish I did," Custer admitted. He shrugged. "Shoot, only three days' rations. Maybe it won't be so far this time."

"Or maybe they don't want us carrying so much to slow us down."

Custer nodded. "Could be. Who's to say? Could be headed anywhere, I guess." He smiled, leaned back in his chair. "I reckon we'll find out soon enough."

"Maybe we's headed straight on into Richmond. You suppose? Catch old Jeff Davis sitting right at his big desk. You could arrest him, Gen'l George, and send him up to Mister Lincoln as a fat ol' prize. I'd like that!"

WINDMILL POINT

"Haa!" Custer laughed. "That'd be fun, alright, now wouldn't it? But I don't guess so, Eliza. Probably headed west to hit the railroad is my guess. Or maybe curl back around and sneak up on Bobby Lee from behind. Grant's got some kind of a plan in the works, but he won't tip his hand. Not till he's ready."

"Well, whichever," she continued, tasting a spoonful of chicken stew, "you'll be well fed and plump as a rooster when you get there. I promised Miss Libbie I'd keep you fat as could be."

Custer chuckled, rubbed his stomach. "Yeah, well, that could take some doing."

After a fine dinner of chicken stew, ham, and potatoes he slipped away from the campfire and checked on his pickets. Everything was quiet, the evening air still, stars blinking in the heavens as clear as he'd ever seen them. He took a deep breath, felt wonderful. The thought of a clash with the Rebels was almost intoxicating. He could hardly wait for dawn. It promised to be a hot one come morning, and heat was never fun for a long column of riders, dust and cotton dry mouths the usual order of the day. But none of that bothered Custer. Come morning he'd take his brigade across the Pamunkey River at first light, and, just like that, they'd be on their way to another scrap with the enemy. It didn't matter in the least to him just where they were bound, only that there would be Rebels and riding and action. The truth of it was, George Custer had come to love war as much as he loved his new bride, and if he were to fight a battle each and every day for the rest of his life, that would be just fine with him. For George, nothing was more exciting than the prospect of battle. As a young boy he had read countless books on the romance of war, and he'd always imagined soldiering to be one of life's highest callings. Some men, he understood, considered war to be the scourge of the earth, but for George Custer war had become nothing less than an infinite pleasure.

He curled up by the fire early that night, determined to get some rest before they all moved out in the morning, and in just minutes Custer was sound asleep. He slept deeply, dreamt of long lines of cavalry horses thundering across green, open hills, of carbine fire crackling in the air, of the earth shaking and rocking from the steady boom of artillery, of men screaming, shooting... falling. He slept well. They were, after all, pleasant dreams.

CHAPTER TWENTY-SEVEN

JUNE 7TH—MORNING

LEE

Robert E. Lee whisked the last piece of beefsteak from his plate, chewed it slowly, then washed it down with a few gulps of hot coffee. Everything tasted wonderful. Someone in Fitz Lee's command had stumbled upon and plundered a few Yankee supply wagons, so for the time being they even had a small amount of sugar for their coffee along with an assortment of preserves for their morning bread. Lee was beginning to feel stronger now, good food, rest, and, yes, victory working their magic on both his body and mind. Another night had passed with no serious fighting, and each hour of inaction only served to rest and strengthen his army that much more. Truth be known, Lee drew as much strength from his men as they drew from him, and as his army slowly healed, his health gradually returned.

Taylor had just handed him the latest message from Grant, and he'd taken the time to read it thoroughly. His adversary had finally decided to accept defeat and call for a suspension of hostilities after all. That accomplished, Lee saw no reason to prolong the debate. He would allow a cease-fire for two hours between 6 and 8 o'clock that evening. That would provide plenty of time to alert his own commands, and allow for the message to return to Grant so that he, too, could make the necessary arrangements. Lee had won the battle on the field, and now he had prevailed in the war of words. It was surely a minor victory, but a victory nevertheless, and against someone as obstinate and combative as Grant, every triumph, no matter how small, was to be prized. Yes, the future was looking bright.

Lee put his reply to Grant in an envelope, then handed it over to Taylor. "Please see that this is delivered to General Grant as soon as possible," he instructed.

"Yes, of course, sir."

Lee took a deep breath, felt the strength of a good breakfast begin to boil up in his body. "Have there been reports yet from our pickets down along the Chickahominy?"

"Nothing, sir."

Lee turned, stared at Taylor. "No activity at all? You're sure?"

"No activity at all, General. I personally checked earlier this morning. The pickets report nothing and I doubled them last evening, just as you asked."

Lee thought for a moment, folded his arms across his chest. "Well," he said, "that's interesting. I would have thought that Grant would have been up and on the move again by now. That *has* been his history—I will give him that, Colonel. He generally does not spend much time crying over spilt milk, so to speak."

Taylor smiled. "And General Grant has spilled a whole lot of milk over the last four or five weeks, sir."

Lee relaxed, tried to think of every angle. "Is it possible we've underestimated the damage we've inflicted on those people here at Cold Harbor?"

"It's hard to say, sir. But surely they remain inactive at this point."

Lee shook his head, thought better of it. "Unless the Federal war machine is broken down entirely—which I seriously doubt—something will be happening somewhere soon. Grant cannot afford to simply sit and while away his time as if on holiday.

WINDMILL POINT

The conditions for his troops are deplorable, the water here is very poor. No, he will be up and moving soon." He stared at Taylor again. "We must not become complacent, Colonel."

"Sir," Taylor answered, "we have pickets, cavalry, and scouts out everywhere. If he moves, we will detect it."

"Yes, good," Lee replied. Then he glanced up into the low-hanging clouds outside his tent, saw the first streaks of blue and shafts of sunlight beginning to slice through. "The sky is clearing," he said. "It appears today will be another hot one, another dreadful day for the Federal soldiers out in their trenches." He shook his head slowly. "Good. Even the weather appears to be conspiring against General Grant. The hotter it remains, the sooner he will have to move his army or lose it to sickness and ill health. It appears even God is with us today."

"Yes, sir."

Lee shifted uneasily, was beginning to feel anxious despite all the good news. Aggressive by nature, waiting had never been one of his strong suits. "But God will not spot the Federal army moving for us," he said sternly. "*That* is something we will have to do for ourselves, Colonel. And quickly."

"If they move, we will see them, sir."

Lee nodded emphatically. "We *must*."

CHAPTER TWENTY-EIGHT

JUNE 7TH—FORENOON

CUSTER

Custer slipped away from the main column and rode to the crest of a small knoll overlooking the line of march. There he reined his horse to a stop and yanked his canteen around. His mouth was dry as newspaper, so he tilted his head back and took several long gulps of sweet, cool water. With his thirst now at least moderately quenched, Custer wiped his mouth with the back of his shirtsleeve, plugged his canteen, and watched the men as they passed slowly below.

They had been on the march since 5 o'clock that morning, almost ten thousand sabers along with all their wagons and baggage. It was an impressive sight. At first light the bugles had sounded "Boots and Saddles," and once the men were all mounted and assembled, the column had quickly crossed the pontoon bridge over the Pamunkey River and struck a northern course across the Virginia countryside. Rumors buzzed throughout the long column, many of the men convinced they were bound for Washington or even Maryland to aid in the defense of that region. They all hoped to leave Virginia behind.

Custer watched as the column slipped by. They moved at the walk only, fearful of breaking down their horses in the heat, and many of the men had already dismounted and were making the march on foot in order to spare their mounts. The rules were

WINDMILL POINT

simple, if somewhat brutal: any horse that broke down was to be shot immediately and left behind. Sheridan had no intention of allowing the Rebels to nurse Federal horses back to health, and then face them again on some future field of battle. Once a horse had been shot, the trooper would simply toss all of his gear into the closest wagon, and continue the march on foot. Fearful of just such an outcome, most of the cavalrymen had become far more mindful of their horse's good health than they were of their own. Riding much of the way to Maryland, after all, was one thing; walking all the way quite another.

Some eight miles in length, from Custer's vantage point the immense column appeared more like an enormous cloud on the move than an accumulation of horses, troops, and wagons. A long funnel of dust filled the sky for as far as the eye could see and tumbled south behind them now, like smoke trailing a giant locomotive. It made for a long and miserable trip, dust and horsehair filling every nook and crevice—pockets, to underwear, to mess kit—but that was life in the cavalry.

Gregg's division had taken the lead, Custer's brigade starting close to the rear that morning, and thus for them the volume of dust had been considerably magnified. Like swimming in a sea of sand, for many of the boys the trip was near suffocating, dust and dirt clouding their vision and covering their faces, uniforms, and gear. They lived only for the slightest breeze that occasionally swept down across the hills and for a brief and blissful moment or two blew the cloud aside. Add to that a temperature that seemed to be climbing toward ninety by noon, and it was no small wonder the men were already worn and miserable.

Custer turned toward the south and spotted two riders approaching. Their uniforms were so covered with brown dust they could easily have been mistaken for Rebels. It was Major James Kidd, commander of the 6th Michigan Cavalry, along with one of his scouts. Kidd, only twenty-four years of age and one hell of a fighter, was one of Custer's favorites. They reined to a stop just below him and saluted.

Custer returned the salute, smiled briefly. "To what do I owe the pleasure, gentlemen?"

Kidd removed his cap, slapping away at the dust on his pants and shirt for a moment or two, sending small spouts spiraling into the air around him. Then he replaced his cap, wiped his face once with his sleeve, and looked up at Custer. "Well, General," he said, "Walker here reports that he ran up against some Confederate outriders or scouts back a ways. Oh, you remember Corporal Walker, don't you General? He's my best scout."

Custer studied the scout, recognizing him as a very reliable man. "Sure do," he answered. "Now, tell me, what's up?"

"Okay, tell him," Kidd said.

"Well, sir," Walker started, "we was working out off the main column, maybe eight hundred yards or so—me, Worthan, and Miles, that is—when I looked up and saw five, maybe six riders out a quarter mile or thereabouts. They was Rebs alright. Shot at us, they did. Right off, too! But they was too far off to hit anything, and we chased 'em away easy enough. They're scared of our Spencers, you know. We can out-shoot 'em every time, General, and they know it. Anyway, they moved back out of our range, and I didn't consider it wise to push out too far after 'em. This is enemy territory, after all, and who's to say what's over the next hill."

"That's right," Custer told him, listening calmly. "So... go on."

"Yes. Well, sir, we chased 'em off a good bit, but they's been tailing us ever since. I reckon that's what they's been told to do, 'cause every time we push out a bit and try to get close to them, they just back off again. And so on."

Major Kidd nodded vigorously, wiping the sweat from his forehead with a dirty handkerchief. Then he yanked the top off

WINDMILL POINT

his canteen, and took a long, almost furious drink. That accomplished, he capped the canteen, and wiped his lips clean. "Yeah, but that's not all," he added. "Tell him the other...."

Walker cocked his hat up a notch, stared at Kidd's canteen and licked his lips hopefully. "You mind if...?"

Custer chuckled. "Go ahead."

The scout pulled his canteen around and had a long drink for himself. Kidd and Custer waited patiently. Finally satisfied, Walker tucked the canteen away and got back to business. "What the major means," he said, "is that the Rebs have been popping at the rear of our column for most of the morning. Running in and taking some shots, then fading back."

Custer nodded. "Anyone hit?"

Walker shook his head. "Not yet, as I have it. They're more a nuisance than anything, but I thought you would want to know."

Kidd shook his head vigorously. "They're onto us, General. That much is clear. Wherever we're headed, we're not going to surprise anyone once we get there, it looks like to me."

Custer frowned. "Column eight miles long moving at the walk through Rebel territory.... Well, I didn't expect we'd fool them for too long. How could we?"

"Just the same, General," Kidd went on, "they're watching us every step of the way. It's right clear to me that that's not good news."

"No," Custer admitted. "No, it's not." He turned back toward the scout. "Good work, Walker. I'll send word of your report up the line. I'm sure General Sheridan will be more than a little interested. I'll be sure to mention your name."

"Yes, sir. Thank you, sir," Walker replied.

"In the meantime," Custer continued, "keep a good eye out for any more activity. Scouts are one thing. I expected scouts. But if you see anything more than that, any indications of a force moving this way, check it out closely, and send back immediate word."

Kidd looked at him intently. "You mean Confederate cavalry?"

"Yes, of course."

"What, may I ask, do you expect, General?" Kidd asked.

"I expect a whole bunch of Rebel cavalry to be on our trail, and pretty soon, too," Custer answered.

"Yeah, that's just what I was thinking," Kidd replied. "They can't hardly let a force this size go wandering around the countryside unopposed, now can they? I imagine they'll have Hampton after us real soon."

Custer smiled. "I hope so," he said. "We whipped him at Haw's Shop, and we'll whip him again if he comes calling."

"You got any idea yet where we're headed, General?" Kidd asked hopefully.

"None."

Kidd glanced up at the sun. "We been moving due north all morning," he said. "A lot of the boys, well, they seem to think we're bound for Maryland. Maryland would be nice, I think."

"I doubt that's where we're headed, Major, but I can't say for sure," Custer answered.

Kidd smiled, shook his head. "I sure wouldn't mind Maryland," he said. "Nice break from this red Virginia dirt, as I see it. Gals there were sure friendly, as I recall," he added with a wink. "Plenty of pretty ladies, good food, and splendid, rich fields upon which to graze our horses. Couldn't ask for much more than that."

Custer smiled back at him. "Don't get your hopes up, Major," he said. "I don't guess General Grant just all of the sudden decided to send ten thousand riders off on vacation, now do you?"

"Well, the boys..."

WINDMILL POINT

Custer laughed. "The boys," he repeated. "Yeah, the boys are always dreaming. But the fight's right here in Virginia, and I'm guessing we're bound for that fight somewhere hereabouts."

Kidd frowned, slapped at his dust-caked trousers again. "Well, I kind of had my heart set on bathing in the Potomac, General. You know, washing out this grubby uniform, and dabbing on some of that fine perfume I bought back outside of Fredericksburg last month. I'm guessing you're right, of course, but I'm hoping you're wrong, just the same."

"I understand," Custer told him. "And if I hear anything for sure, I'll let you know first thing. But in the meantime, if I was you I'd keep your pistol handy and that perfume packed away."

Kidd grinned. "You know me, General!" he replied. "I've never objected to a good brawl. Wouldn't mind one right now at all!"

"I know," Custer answered. "So go ahead and re-post your scouts. And if, by God, we cross over the Potomac River into Maryland, I promise I'll give you time enough to get that bath of yours, and dab on all the perfume you can manage."

Kidd rolled his shoulders. "I'm guessing that's not going to be much of a promise to make good on, General," he said with a wink. "But I'll sure hold you to it just the same."

"Yeah, you do that," Custer told him.

Custer watched as the two rode off, then turned and headed back down the short knoll, bound for the head of his own brigade. The head of the main column had already passed through Aylett's Crossroads, and was now bound for Sharon Church, on a course that would have them close to the Mattapony River by sundown. All around, the choking dust swirled above the horses in brown, suffocating clouds. He glanced up into the sky. The sun was arching higher, the temperature rising, and the enemy inching closer by the minute. Custer smiled thinly, snapped the reins, and hurried along.

CHAPTER TWENTY-NINE

JUNE 7TH—EARLY AFTERNOON

ALEXANDER

Porter Alexander rode up with his staff to the banks of a small creek that ran along the rear of the Confederate works, and there began scanning the open fields for General Gregg's headquarters again. The sun was high, the air thick, the day already hot. Alexander had been far too busy that morning to make his usual inspection of the trenches, but as he rode behind the lines with his staff, he had the sudden urge to see if, by some stroke of good fortune, his pay envelope had been returned. Rather than wander back through the long trenches, stumbling over hundreds and hundreds of men on the errand, he decided instead on a strategy of direct approach.

Gregg's headquarters trench was easy enough to identify. There was a small persimmon tree on one side that provided a modicum of shade during the middle portion of the day. Amid the muddy, stark landscape of Cold Harbor, that small tree stood out like a sore thumb, and was easily recognizable from hundreds of yards away. The distance from the creek up to Gregg's headquarters was about 500 yards, but the ground sloped back from a small hill crest toward the creek, thus at least a good portion of the approach could be made while completely out of sight of the Federal sharpshooters.

WINDMILL POINT

Even in the area where Alexander and his staff had stopped to reconnoiter there was still some small danger that spent rounds fired by the Yanks from above would slowly curve back to earth and strike the ground well behind the lines. But, despite the unprecedented volume of sharpshooting being engaged in by both sides, the danger of being struck by a spent ball was minimal, and Alexander did not overly concern himself with that. The real danger in the approach would be the last 50 yards or so as he made his way up the incline to the point where his head, shoulders, and then finally his full torso would slowly become entirely visible to the Federal marksmen. In order to negotiate that last 50 yards he would have to first crouch low, and then proceed in a sort of duck walk for perhaps twenty or thirty yards.

But even that would not suffice for the remaining few yards, where he would finally come into full view of the enemy. To traverse that last distance unmolested would require getting down on his hands and knees, or possibly even crawling on his stomach like a snake. Neither of those approaches was an exercise that particularly appealed to him, but Alexander certainly wanted his full month's pay back and those strategies —though obviously somewhat compromising for an officer of his distinction—were nevertheless superior to taking a ball in the forehead.

Each member of his staff begged to be allowed to make the trip in his place, but Alexander considered them all far too young and insufficiently experienced in the dangers of the battlefield to appreciate the necessary caution that such a venture would require. The possibility that one of them might be struck down while on an errand on his behalf, yet unmindful of the dangers involved, was not a thought he cared to entertain. And besides, it was his pay envelope, after all.

"No," Alexander said, waving them all back toward the trees behind the creek. "You hold the horses and stay down here well out of sight." He pointed toward the far bank of the stream. "Back behind some of those trees would be my idea of things," he went on. "That way you'll be far less likely to be struck by a spent round."

"We're not concerned with any of that, General," one of his aides objected.

Alexander chuckled. "Yes, well, I'm afraid that's just the point, Lieutenant," he replied. "I am, you see. In fact, I am cognizant—I should say *fearful*—of a great many dangers that you are not even aware of. I have served in this war since First Manassas, and I've seen far too many good men die for lack of proper attention. Besides, gentlemen, it's my pay that's missing."

So he handed over the reins of his horse and started carefully up the low incline toward the trenches, mindful every step of the way that the Federal works must always remain entirely out of his view. The logic was obvious. If he could see them, then they could see him, and once they had spotted him he would be in every Yankee sharpshooter's sights in a matter of seconds only.

As he closed to within 100 yards of the persimmon tree he began to crouch, and when Alexander got to within 50 he kneeled down for a short rest before the final push. At that point he knew he would either have to crawl forward slowly, or make a wild dash for Gregg's headquarters as fast as his legs could carry him. Uninspired by the prospect of crawling through the muck like a reptile, and realizing that the Yankees would not spot him entirely until the very last few yards—and also that they would then have considerable difficulty striking a fast-moving target—he passed on the crawl, and opted instead for the sprint.

Alexander took a deep breath, grabbed hold of his sword, and leaped to his feet. Then he ran straight for the persimmon tree as fast as he had ever run in his life. When he got to the edge of the trench he simply dove forward headfirst, as if taking a plunge off a rock into the soothing waters of the Chesapeake Bay. Instead of a wonderful splash into cool bay water, however, Alexander landed with a loud thud in the dirt. Then he looked up with a smile, happy as could be that he had no noticeable holes in his body. Unfortunately, General Gregg and his staff were nowhere to be found. His smile disappeared.

Alexander had landed directly between two dead Texans, each with a fresh bullet hole through the forehead. A third Texan, an older fellow with full whiskers, a toothy grin, and a jovial air, sat comfortably on the other side of the trench. He beamed brightly at Alexander.

"By gosh!" the old fellow said, "you has to be mighty careful how you shows a head around here, or they'll get you certain!" He nodded toward the dead soldiers. "Thar's two they got already this morning!"

"Yes," Alexander replied, "I see. But where's General Gregg's headquarters? It was right here just the other day."

"Oh," the man replied, still jolly as could be, "he moved last night down thar somewhar, nigh that little branch." The Texan nodded positively. "You go thar and hunt. You'll find him."

"Yes, well, thanks," Alexander told him. He glanced quickly at the two dead men in the trench, then looked away. Cold Harbor, he thought, seemed just another synonym for the eternal abyss.

"I reckon I'll just sit and rest a spell, then head back down to the creek," Alexander told the Texan. "I certainly appreciate your help."

"That's fine."

Alexander leaned back against the side of the trench, then took a few deep breaths. His flying advance had all been for naught, and now he would have to duplicate it again on his way back downhill. He was not anxious to test fate quite so liberally, but, under the circumstances, he appeared to have but little choice. He nodded toward the Texan. "Keep your head down," Alexander said, then grabbed hold of his sword once again. He took two deep breaths and wiggled his legs to get them good and loose. Then in a single burst he leaped over the top of the trench, legs churning beneath him, and in just moments was safe by the creek with his staff once more.

Alexander was able to locate General Gregg's new headquarters easily enough, now well back behind the lines and tucked away in the shade of the trees. And sure enough, the general had his pay envelope in hand, every last cent accounted for; except, of course, for the twenty dollars Alexander had pledged to whoever turned it in. He took it gladly and tucked the envelope away in his hip pocket for better safekeeping this time.

That chore finally accomplished, Porter Alexander rejoined his staff and mounted for the ride back to his bivouac. Here and there the guns still sounded, and occasionally a spent ball would go whirring into the woods over their heads as they made their way south, but no one seemed to take notice. Alexander let the junior officers lead the way, and slipped behind deliberately to ride by himself in the rear.

War, he had learned many years ago, was not a natural time for philosophizing, the ever-demanding business of life and death generally consuming each and every second of a man's time and energy. Food alone was enough to occupy most men's thoughts for weeks on end. Good soldiers, after all, did not generally question orders or challenge the natural order of things. That sort of business was left for others. But there were times that simply imposed themselves on a man's consciousness, events that kicked in the door of daily complacency, so to speak, and demanded answers to questions that were difficult to fathom. For Edward Porter Alexander, this was just such a time.

WINDMILL POINT

To say the least, he was confused. Just what sort of a creature, he wondered, was this thing called man? Human nature was most certainly a profound mystery. Here was a creature willing to live happily in a hole with the dead, to shoot at anything that moved, day after day, month after month, yet at the same time perfectly willing to return a man's lost pay envelope without the slightest hesitation, when pocketing the entire thing could never have been traced or possibly adjudicated. Dreadfully ruthless, yet moral to a fault.

Was there any making sense of it? He didn't know, and for Alexander it was surely the mystery at the heart of all mysteries. *Why do people act the way they do?* In the end he suspected the answer to that question was probably far more complex, convoluted, or even crazier than he might ever imagine, and he realized as well that far more sophisticated minds than his own had pondered the same dilemma without satisfying results. But there still were times when he wished he had the answer, and this was most certainly one of those times.

His staff rode on in silence. Alexander trailed slowly behind, lost in thought, the sound of the guns momentarily forgotten.

CHAPTER THIRTY

JUNE 7TH—LATE AFTERNOON

GRANT

Ulysses heard the commotion outside his tent and cocked an ear to listen. George Meade had been wandering around between the headquarters tents for some time now, swatting his boots with a riding crop while pacing back and forth anxiously. He was making everyone nervous. Meade appeared to be in utter disarray, his Army of the Potomac seemingly beaten and uncooperative, and he had no idea where to turn. Confusion and demoralization appeared to have beset much of the officer corps, and Grant knew that none of these problems augured well. And Meade's angry response wasn't helping.

"Wilson!" he heard Meade shout.

"Good afternoon, General," came the reply, and the voice was one Grant recognized at once. It was Jim Wilson, the cavalry commander whom he had selected to remain behind and screen the army as it moved. For Grant, it was always a pleasure to see Wilson. Grant listened closely.

"Tell me, Wilson," Meade went on, "just when is Grant going to move on Richmond?"

There was a long, awkward silence. Finally Wilson replied sheepishly, "Whenever the generals and troops in this theater all work to that end."

WINDMILL POINT

Wilson's response generated another long, pregnant pause. Then Wilson, obviously somewhat flustered, said, "Excuse me, General."

Grant grimaced, then rubbed his face with both hands. The morale of the army and his officer corps was in tatters, and all the planning in the world would not change a bit of it. He had to get them all up and moving, away from the graveyard Cold Harbor had become. Judging by the reaction of Meade and many others, the sooner they were all in motion the better. But it would be days, at least, before Comstock and Porter returned, and he could only pray that the situation would not deteriorate even further before they did.

Suddenly Rollins pulled aside the flap to Grant's tent and looked in. "General Wilson to see you, sir," he said.

Grant nodded.

Wilson entered, saluted stiffly.

Grant returned the salute, pointed to a chair. "Good to see you, General."

"Good to be here, sir," Wilson replied.

Grant smiled weakly. "So tell me, when is Grant going to move on Richmond?"

Wilson turned slightly red. "What was I to say, sir?" he asked. "I mean ... may I ask ... just what in the world is going on around here?"

Jim Wilson had served on Grant's staff at Vicksburg and Chattanooga, and before that had served with McClellan in 1862. Grant considered Wilson—who was a young, headstrong West Pointer—to be tough, smart, and aggressive. He trusted him completely.

"You've seen it for yourself, haven't you?" Grant asked. "Surely you've noticed the condition of this army."

"I have," Wilson acknowledged. "I'm shocked."

"So," Grant asked, "tell me, Wilson. You've known these men and officers for years now, right? What do you make of all this?"

Wilson grimaced, reached up and grabbed his nose. "Maybe it's the stench around here, General," he said. "I've never...."

Grant frowned. "I've been trying to take care of that," he replied, "but Lee has been very difficult. We've finally been able to work out an agreement for a truce, however, and the medical teams and burial crews will finally be headed out later this evening."

Wilson shook his head. "Well, sir, if my nose is any judge at all, then it's not a moment too soon."

Grant nodded in agreement. "So, go on... tell me what you think."

"Well, on the face of it, General, it does seem somewhat desperate around here."

Grant stared at him closely. "Desperate?" he repeated finally. "I'll say it's desperate." He tossed his hands in the air. "Wilson, what is wrong with this army?"

The cavalry officer rolled his eyes. "General," he answered, "there is a good deal the matter, so much so that it would hardly do to go into detail."

"That tells me nothing," Grant objected.

Wilson shrugged. "Well, I may not be able to easily detail all the individual problems, General, but I *can* offer a good remedy for what ails this army."

"A solution, aye?" Grant said. "Go on, I'm all ears."

Wilson grinned at him. "Take Parker," he said, referring to Colonel Ely Parker, the full-blooded Native American on Grant's staff, who was the reigning chief of the tribes known as Six Nations, "and give him a scalping knife and a tomahawk. Send him out to bring in the scalps of a few of your major generals."

WINDMILL POINT

Grant laughed out loud. "Some *solution*," he cried. "Can you at least tell me which *ones* he should go after?"

Wilson frowned, then shook his head. "That doesn't matter so much," he said. "Just tell him to attack the first ones he comes to and not quit till he's attacked at least a half dozen. After that you will have a better army."

Grant chuckled, blew a puff of smoke across the tent. "By better do you mean, ready to fight?" he asked.

"Well, maybe not ready to fight," Wilson admitted. "But better nevertheless, I should think. A sort of addition by subtraction."

Grant snorted. "Well, with all due respect to Colonel Parker," he said, "a few more days of this and I just might start scalping a few of them myself."

Wilson grinned from ear to ear. "Now *that's* just the sort of medicine we need around here!" he proclaimed. "I will tell you, we have corps commanders, General, who are so lazy they will not even ride their own lines, but will not hesitate for a moment to order their men to attack the enemy, no matter their strength or position. You know who they are!"

Grant shrugged. "Yes, I'm afraid I do," he agreed. "But there's no time for changes right now. We're going to be moving soon."

Wilson's head snapped up. "Moving?"

"That's right," Grant answered.

"May I ask where?"

"South," Grant told him. "I'm going to take this army across the Chickahominy, then the James, and move on Petersburg. If all goes as planned, I will pry Lee out from behind his entrenchments and force him into a straight-up fight on open ground, probably somewhere south of Richmond."

Wilson's eyes grew wide. "The James, General!" he exclaimed. "Well ... it's just that the James River is very wide up this way."

"General Barnard assures me it can be bridged," Grant replied. "We've already discussed it in some detail."

"But where?"

"Porter and Comstock are off now locating a suitable point. I suspect it will be somewhere around Fort Powhatan."

"When?" Wilson asked eagerly.

"Very soon. A few days at the latest. We can't afford to sit around here and rot anymore than we already have. This morning I gave orders for Warren's entire corps to quietly disengage, pull out from the lines, and begin moving toward the Chickahominy. That corps will serve as the rearguard for the movement. That's where you come in."

"Of course, sir," Wilson said. "So Warren is already on the move...?"

"Yes."

"Do you have orders for me?"

"General Meade will have them for you," Grant replied. "Your division will first have to storm the Chickahominy fording points, secure the river, and then screen the army as it moves off toward the James. Needless to say, we *can't* let Lee's cavalry get through your screen and determine what we are up to. If Lee finds out... well, things could get very rough."

"I understand," Wilson said. "My boys are ready, General."

"Good. I'll be counting on you. Of course," Grant went on, "you know Sheridan is off with two full divisions bound for the Shenandoah."

"I knew they were off, General, but I didn't know their destination."

"Well," Grant said, "my plan is to cut Richmond's supply lines from both ends, and to force Lee to move once that happens. But I'm also counting on Lee having to respond to Sheridan's departure with cavalry of his own. If we can draw off most of their cavalry, it should make your job here that much easier."

WINDMILL POINT

"Yes, that should work, General," Wilson agreed.

Grant nodded. "So keep an eye out for Rebel cavalry on the move. I want to know if they take the bait."

Wilson smiled. "You bet."

They talked for a while longer, Grant filling Wilson in on the scope, strategy, and anticipated timetable of the new campaign. When they finally parted company, Grant felt both energized and relieved, the young officer's sense of strength and enthusiasm rubbing off on him. It was, after all, the Wilsons, Hancocks, Comstocks, and Gibbonses who would ultimately lead the Army of the Potomac to victory if there ever was to be one. Grant could do little more than set a sensible course; the rest would have to be carried out by others. The finest plans in the world were meaningless without the men capable of turning them into reality.

His meeting with Jim Wilson satisfactorily accomplished, Ulysses Grant tossed an old cigar aside and quickly took up another, a brief respite before getting back to the unending detail of such a far-flung movement of men, equipment, and supplies. He penned an order to General Abercrombie, in command at White House Landing, the army's supply depot on the Pamunkey River, instructing him to pull up all the iron from the York River Railroad and put it on barges, ready to be shipped off to City Point on the James when needed. Then he leaned back, took a few long puffs, and opened the latest dispatch from General Henry Halleck in Washington. He and Halleck had never gotten along, and their mutual animus went back to Grant's first days in the war out west. So he had saved the message until most of the hard work had been completed, so it would not dull his most recent surge of enthusiasm. But Halleck could not be put off forever. He unfolded the dispatch and read:

> I inclose a list of troops forwarded from this department to the Army of the Potomac since the campaign opened—48,265 men. I shall send you a few regiments more, when all resources will be exhausted till another draft is made.

Grant winced, read the note slowly one more time, then tossed it aside on his desk. It was, of course, a not too subtle rebuke from Halleck for the loss of so many men. He was making it clear to Grant that Washington had already sent him virtually every available unit— veterans and new enlistments— and that Grant's spring campaign had gobbled them up at a rate faster than they could possibly be replaced. There were no more replacements left to send, and, for obvious political reasons, the administration could not even consider another draft until after the fall elections. The Army of the Potomac's severe losses that spring continued to be a political hot potato, so, for the time being, Grant would have to make do with the troops that he had.

Well, alright then, he thought. Grant had made up his mind, crafted a new campaign, and as of that morning the army was already in motion. So now he had little choice. He would fight it out for as long as he could with the troops at hand, be it two hundred or two hundred thousand. Warren's entire corps was moving south toward the Chickahominy, and Sheridan's columns had crossed the Pamunkey and departed for the Shenandoah earlier that day. Grant's facial features hardened into place. Halleck or no Halleck, losses or no losses, there would be no turning back.

WINDMILL POINT

General Robert E Lee

General Grant

General George Custer

General Wade Hampton

WINDMILL POINT

Wyman White

Brigadier General Edward P Alexander

Federal Army crossing the James River

WINDMILL POINT

Federal Artillery Emplacements

CHAPTER THIRTY-ONE

JUNE 7TH—EVENING

WHITE

Wyman checked to make sure his rifle's chamber was empty, then set the Sharps up against the side of the trench. He flexed his fingers anxiously and leaned back firmly against the dirt. A cease-fire was to go into effect any minute now, and for the time being most everyone was just... waiting. In the trench many of the men were complaining bitterly of Grant's behavior —that perhaps thousands of good men had been left to die in the sun for days simply to maintain the ridiculous pretense that the Army of the Potomac had not suffered a terrible defeat: a fact so obvious that anyone with eyes could see it for themselves. Many of the boys were loud and resentful, and Wyman White understood.

To ask men to die as heroes was one thing; to leave them abandoned, to roast away in pain after they'd given their all, another entirely. It seemed to most of the men a profound moral failure on the part of their commander, and a breach of a solemn bond. Thousands had been condemned to suffer and die so that Grant might try and polish his image in Washington. Were they nothing more than a herd of sheep or beef cattle, their lives to be used at his whim? While some of the troops argued that the delay was due to Lee's foot-dragging, in the end

WINDMILL POINT

few placed the blame on anyone other than the Commanding General himself—Ulysses S. Grant.

Wyman had drawn normal picket duty that afternoon, so he had traded in the big sharpshooting gun for his usual target rifle and headed out with the rest of the regiment into the trenches. But things along the lines had settled down a great deal that afternoon, and there hadn't been much in the way of action. Heat and flies were the main aggravation, keeping his head down his principle concern. The hours had passed slowly.

Then at 6 o'clock the white flags were posted, and—with both sides having been informed well in advance—the guns immediately fell completely silent. It seemed a strange and eerie peace at first, unnatural after so many weeks of steady, thunderous warfare, and for a moment or two Wyman felt virtually disoriented, so radical was the change. He hadn't realized just how accustomed to the sound of guns he'd become, how fighting seemed to have seeped right through his skin like a poison, to contaminate his entire frame of mind. But he recognized it now.

Then he noticed many of the men beginning to stand and clamber up over the sides of the trenches, walking out into that terrible wasteland between the opposing lines. So he slowly inched his head up above ground level too, and when he saw the Rebels out of their trenches and walking freely, he climbed out and joined them all. The sun was still well above the horizon, the air thick and hot.

Wyman walked out amongst the dead, curious at first, but his curiosity quickly turned to disgust. Now for the first time the true magnitude of the slaughter became appallingly clear to him. Here were bodies—if they could even be called that anymore—blackened and bloated beyond all recognition, literally stacked upon one another. He looked up toward the north, and then turned and faced south. Between the trenches the landscape was the same in both directions for as far as the eye could see—appalling. The scene was grotesque, the odor rancid beyond description. The bodies were so torn and decomposed that no father, brother or friend could hope to recognize them now, and the scene evoked in Wyman a sense of horror far more than pity. He had come out to see if he could help, or at least to pay homage to his fallen comrades. Now he just wanted to get away.

He stumbled down a short knoll and joined a small group of sharpshooters in one of the few areas where the bodies were less thickly strewn. Nearby several Rebels had wandered close, mostly in search of trade. Joe Thompson stood nearby and, as the Rebs approached, he pulled a toothpick from his lips, and cocked his head. "Where you boys from?" Joe asked.

"We're with the 19th Mississippi, Harris's Brigade," one answered, seeming friendly enough. "I'm from Yazoo City myself." The Reb smiled, nodded toward Joe Thompson. "Don't suppose any of you Yanks would be willing to trade up some of that good coffee you-un's carry, now would uzz?" he asked, trying his best to sound pleasant.

Joe Thompson nodded slowly, stepped toward the Rebel who'd asked. "Could be, Johnny," he replied, putting the toothpick back between his lips. "Just what you got in mind?"

The Reb smiled broadly. "Well I got me some fine tobacco, and I sure got some decent whiskey, if that's what you would be hankerin' on."

"What sort of whiskey, Johnny?"

The Rebel fished through his sack and pulled out a pint-sized bottle. "This here's fresh as day-old berries, and hot as lightning," he said, handing the bottle over.

Thompson pulled the cork from the top and took a whiff. "Oh Lord," he said, plugging the cork back quickly. "I could piss better whiskey than that, Johnny," he said. "You boys make that yourselves now, did you?"

The Rebel laughed appreciatively. "That's right, Yank. Ain't real smooth, but it's got one hell of a kick. Steadies the aim a good bit, if I do say so myself."

"You know, we got the real stuff over here, Reb," Thompson told him. "Fresh out of the sutler's wagon, too. A few of them just come up from well behind the lines yesterday. Good New York rye whiskey's what's we got."

The Rebel rubbed his chin, rolled his eyes lovingly. "I could sure use a taste of that real New York whiskey," he said. "How 'bout tobacco? You like a good smoke or chew in exchange of a bottle, Yank?"

"Maybe. Let me see what you got." Thompson answered.

The Rebel obligingly went back into his sack and pulled out a wrapper full of tobacco. Then he handed it over. Joe Thompson carefully un-wrapped the bundle and took a good whiff. Then he whiffed again.

"My-oh-my," Thompson crooned. "Now that's *good* tobacco alright, Johnny." Then he thought for a moment. "Tell you what," he said finally, "I'll trade you straight up, two wrappers of that good tobacco for a full bottle of New York rye whiskey. That's a *full* bottle, Johnny. Not some little cut-off bottle like you got there."

"Done!" the Reb exclaimed merrily. "And how 'bout some meat, Yank? We could all sure use a good taste of beef or pork over this way. Whadzz ya say?"

Thompson grinned. "Possibly."

Wyman smiled, but hung back from most of the chatter. He rarely took part in the trade that went on between the pickets, thought it strange that men who only minutes before had been struggling desperately to kill one another could suddenly be swapping food and jokes like old friends. The whole business seemed unnatural to him.

Two of the Mississippi boys were standing just a few feet off from where Wyman stood. One, a skinny, scruffy-looking private by all appearances, eyed Wyman for a moment, then began to grin. He elbowed the other Johnny at his side.

"Guess we done shot you-uns up real good," the scruffy Rebel said to Wyman, sort of cackling all the while. "I reckon you-uns won't be fixin' to come up against us any time soon. Try us, Billy, and this here's what will happen to ya'll." The other Rebel stared at Wyman for a second or two then laughed out loud.

Wyman White felt anger rise up in his chest like a red-hot poker. Making light of the dead before they'd even been buried and then taunting him about it was as low as he could imagine, and he wasn't going to let it go unchallenged. His face turned red. Cease-fire or none, he was just about to go after both of them when another Confederate—a burly looking sergeant—strode across a small open area of grass right up into Wyman's face and promptly held up both hands.

"Set tight now, Yank," the Reb sergeant said. "Ah'l tek ka-hya this he-ah business."

Then the sergeant turned and walked over to the two mouthy Rebels, and placed his hands sternly on his hips. "I done heard your fat mouth, Winston Broone," he said with disgust to the scruffy Reb. "I reckon I should just let that big Yank whoomp the bejesus out of youse both, but we got us a cease far he-ah now, and I gots my orders. You hain't got the sense of a jackass, Winston, belittlin' the dead in front of their own. I'fer twas the other way round, I'da sure put a bullet in youse and think noten' on er. Nahh git!"

The two nervy Rebels appeared suddenly crestfallen. Then they turned away and started to walk off slowly.

"I sayed *git*!" the sergeant yelled again, and the other two took off at a quicker pace.

Then the burly sergeant whirled about and marched right up to Wyman again. "'Pologize, Yank," he said. He was not quite as big as Wyman, but thick and strong as an ox, with

WINDMILL POINT

bright red hair and piercing blue eyes. "Don't need no 'splaining what we's got a few fools of our own, now does it?" he went on. "But they ain't but a few. Mostly we's respectful."

"I understand," Wyman answered, his anger slipping away.

"Only a fool says such a thing as that. I could see you was mad, but no madder than I was myself, truth be told. War's bad enough without that kinda talk."

Wyman nodded. "I reckon that's right," he said.

The sergeant stared at Wyman for a moment, then looked away. "It ain't what like ahh got's a warm place in my heart for your kind, Yank. Understand? Cause I don't. But I *am* respectful, and I don't take kindly to those who ain't."

"I understand," Wyman replied. "No hard feelings."

The Confederate sergeant smiled sheepishly, seemed suddenly unsure of himself now that the immediate problem had been resolved. A few awkward seconds passed. It was obvious he didn't care to stand and talk to one of the enemy, but at the same time he didn't want to appear impolite. The Reb had been caught in unfamiliar circumstances. "See you're a sergeant too," he said finally, almost struggling for words. "How long, Yank? How long you worn them stripes?"

Wyman glanced quickly at the chevrons on his arm then smiled back. "Few months."

"Hard job, ain't it?" the Rebel said.

"It is."

The Rebel rubbed his hand down along the side of his trousers then held it up to Wyman. "Reckon ahh nevah met me no Yank up close," he said, somewhat apologetically. "Almost forgot my manners. My name's Jacob McCabe, Yank. Sergeant Jacob McCabe."

Wyman took the man's hand, shook it firmly. "Wyman White."

"Where you from, Wyman? Can I ask you that? Would that be okay?"

"Sure," Wyman said. "New Hampshire."

The Rebel's eyes flew open wide. Then he pushed the cap back on his head, and threw his arms up in the air as if lightning had just struck him directly in the forehead. "New *Hampshaa!*" he cried. "Well now, don't *that* beat all! Reckon ahh neva thought ahh'd be talking to no Yank from New *Hampshaa!* Pennsylvania, yeah, or maybe New York or Ohio, but neva New *Hampshaa*. Ahh think of New Hampshaa, Wyman, and I think of green mountains, and cold winters, and beautiful, blue lakes. Ain't that 'bout right, Wyman? You tell me now."

Wyman chuckled, stuck his hands in his pockets. "That's about it," he said. "Cool, dark woods where you can go and hunt for hours."

Jacob McCabe winked. "An' I know you's a good shot, Wyman. You's one of them U.S. Sharpshooters, ain't you? I can tell by that green uniform. Or least what's left of it."

"That's right, Jacob," Wyman said, taking a sudden, natural, liking to the man. "And how 'bout you? Where you from?"

Jacob McCabe smiled warmly. "Mississippi's my home, Wyman. Carter City on the Yazoo River. Ever been there?"

"Not hardly," Wyman said. "Before the war I never traveled out of New Hampshire all that much, Jacob."

Jacob frowned. "Me too. Ain't never been up to the North. You a regular, Wyman? A professional soldier?"

"Me? No. Before the war, well, I just worked in the sawmill. Cut lumber. Kinda miss it now."

Jacob smiled sadly. "I know just what you mean, Wyman." Then he pointed. "Best we step aside. Burial crews coming along now. Gonna be some ugly business round hea'."

Across the field of battle burial crews were frantically digging shallow trenches and burying in long rows those corpses they could manage to move. Most were unmovable, however, decomposition having already taken its gruesome toll.

WINDMILL POINT

Most corpses simply fell apart. For those, nothing could be done except to toss a few quick shovelfuls of dirt over the remains and then move on to another. Many of the workers were overcome by the task, and themselves collapsed. Those men had to be placed on stretchers and taken to the rear, casualties now themselves.

"Over there...." Jacob said, nodding toward a small incline a few yards off. "They's a spot where we can sit. I seen it before. No bodies there, Wyman. You Yanks must have marched around that little hill, see?"

"Sure," Wyman agreed. "Why not?"

Jacob led the way, and they quickly located the small knoll and sat on the opposite slope, facing east toward the Federal lines. Here the grass was still green and long, unmarred by most of the fighting. There weren't so many bodies around the small incline, either, so the view wasn't as bleak and disturbing.

"I don't want to talk on the war, Wyman," Jacob said right off, pulling his knees up under his chin. "You gots your reasons for fighting, and I gots mine. Ain't likely we'll solve that problem any time soon, as I see it. So why don't you just tell me a little about New Hampshaa, and I'll tell you about my home in Mississippi. That way maybe we can pass this little cease far cordial-like, and learn a little something we didn't know before. I always like to do that—learn something, I mean. That sound okay to you, Wyman? Hell, I'd love to hea' a whole bunch mo' about New Hampshaa."

Wyman smiled. "Sure."

Jacob slapped his leg. "You know," he said, "when ahh thinks of home ahh think of beautiful gals all gussied up for a dance, or my mama's cooking, or maybe even fish jumping in the river at dusk. What ahh'm saying is that I tend to think of something *special*. Understand what ahh'm saying? *Special*. So tell me then, Wyman," he said, carefully picking a blade of grass and positioning it between his teeth, "what special do you think about when you thinks of home?"

Wyman screwed up his face and thought hard for a second or two. Then he had it. "Snow mostly, I'd have to say, Jacob."

"*Snow!*" Jacob cried merrily. "Hell, Wyman, I ain't *neva* hardly seen *snow*, as best I recall!" Jacob McCabe stretched out on his side and smiled. "Now that I'm entirely comfortable, please do tell me about New Hampshaa snow, Wyman. I'm all ears."

Wyman closed his eyes, could see it then in his mind's eye, as clear as if he were standing at Fitzwilliam Depot in late December: white and dazzling, swirling all around him, pooling, piling... beautiful.

"Oh Jacob," he said, "think of an afternoon gone all cold and grey, and as silent as you could possibly ever imagine. Then think of the whole sky filled with small, white flakes—like a sky full of cotton, I guess—and all of it tumbling around you, soft and, you know, soundless as a ladies petticoat passing in the grass. And as it falls it piles, six, twelve inches deep, or maybe even higher...."

Jacob appeared transfixed, eyes aglow, utterly lost in the vision.

Then suddenly a faint tune rose up to them from behind the Federal lines, and both men turned to listen. It was slow and indescribably mournful, a sorrowful tribute to the dead offered by one of the regimental bands, and the notes seemed to hang over that repugnant field like the breath of death itself. Wyman stopped speaking, just listened. Jacob sat up, cocked his head. Beautiful, yet heartbreakingly melancholy, the music seemed to sink into their souls like the soft drops of a requiem rain, dragging them low, reminding them both of the awful business they were really about. Wyman lowered his head.

Jacob reached out and touched Wyman on the elbow. "No," he whispered. "Tell me about the snow, Wyman. Finish it. Please...."

Wyman looked Jacob in the eye, tried to gather his thoughts. "Okay," he said finally. "You're right, Jacob. Let's try and forget all of that. Well, okay.... In the late afternoon sometimes the snow stops, see, and the sky goes over from a kind of depthless grey to a striking, clear blue. In fact, this often happens, Jacob. Then the sun comes out almost like magic, and paints the white snow with a deep, golden glow. And the whole world is suddenly golden and quiet and as still as you could ever imagine. It's, well ... beautiful, I guess."

Jacob was propped up on one arm, eyes closed, listening intently. "Yes, I can almost see it now, Wyman, please do go on...."

"Then you can go out deep into the woods," Wyman continued, recalling it all now with loving clarity, "and stand deep in the snow, by yourself in this vast sort of cathedral of dazzling whiteness, and watch as the sun sets, at first all gold, turning then to deep amber, then finally violet. And nothing moves then, Jacob, and the mountains just seem to rise up and touch the heavens. If a branch snaps a mile away you can hear it clear as a bell, Jake, and, I swear, if you stand long enough under the snowy canopy of the trees far out in the woods, it's like God reaches down and touches you directly, and your soul stretches out for miles and miles. There ain't nothing in the whole wide world more peaceful than that... than snow in the woods. Wyman nodded slowly then looked down at the ground. "And that's what I recall of snow in New Hampshire. ... And, you know what, Jacob?"

"What?"

"I miss it."

"Well..." was all Jacob could think to say, still momentarily lost in his own vision of crystal whiteness. Then he sat up quickly. "Ahh don't know if I can come even *close* to that, Wyman," he said, "but I think I understand. You see often I go down to the river—the Yazoo River, Wyman, just a stone's throw from my front door—and go fishing. I go by myself most of the time, and in the springtime, I will tell you, the wild flowers are out so thick in the meadows near the river that my heart almost starts to sort of sing, and...."

So as the burial crews dragged the corrupted, unknown remains of thousands of shattered lives toward their final resting places, or covered them with a few hastily tossed shovelfuls of dirt, or ignored them entirely due to the exigencies of time, Wyman and Jacob enthralled one another time and again with recollections of home. As the band continued its sad funeral dirge, Jacob spoke of wide fields of cotton shimmering in the moonlight, and as the decaying corpses were laid out side-by-side in long trenches, Wyman recalled bucket upon bucket of maple sap hauled gleefully home from the depths of the forest.

Between the lines at Cold Harbor, life and death continued their sacred, eternal dance. Who could say why, or even if there was any meaning to it all. As men with shovels collapsed from the stench and strain of their grisly task, Jake remembered with vivid clarity pretty girls at a dance he'd attended three Mays prior, and Wyman fondly recalled nothing more than chopping wood in the back yard with his father. They laughed and slapped each other's arms as bodies were dumped and covered by the thousands.

The sunlight slipped away slowly, the music finally faded, and suddenly 8 o'clock loomed on the horizon. For a delicious two hours there had been no shots, no death, no war at all, and for Jacob and Wyman the time had passed almost like a pleasant dream. Now the dream was over.

The white flags were coming down, and all the troops were being recalled. The time they'd spent together had gone by so quickly and enjoyably that both men were shocked by the sudden knowledge of its passing. Neither knew what to say. They had met almost as brothers might meet, as attuned to one another's stories and memories as old friends, and the ease of their mutual camaraderie now left them both at a loss for words.

Wyman stood, and put out his hand. He felt very awkward. "Jacob," was all he could think to say.

Jacob McCabe took the hand offered to him and shook it firmly. "Wyman," he replied. "Well... it has been a pleasure."

"Likewise," Wyman agreed.

"I reckon if ahh ever gets on up to New Hampshaa I will have to look you up," Jacob offered, knowing all the while it would never happen.

"Yes, please do that, Jake," Wyman replied in kind. "I would really like that."

They shook hands one last time, then parted company. Neither man looked back.

The trenches filled rapidly again, and the last of the burial crews scurried off the field. A lone cannon fired on the Confederate side, announcing the end of the cease-fire. Wyman White slipped into his trench, and took up the Sharps again. The last of the white flags finally came down, and darkness descended upon the field.

In a different world, Wyman thought, he and Jacob McCabe might well have become good friends. Yet it seemed that that was an odd thing to think of the enemy, and it made him feel uncomfortable. He wasn't sure why. He leaned back against the side of the trench, and at that moment knew without question that the short time he'd spent with Jacob would stand out forever in his mind as one of his most vivid memories of the entire war. And that was a troubling realization.

But there was little time left for reflection. Soon the ground began to shake, and the heavy rumble of artillery rose again over Cold Harbor. Wyman loaded the Sharps and stretched his legs out across the bottom of the trench. And under his breath he prayed silently but fervently that the day and hour would never arrive when he would have to kill Jacob McCabe.

CHAPTER THIRTY-TWO

JUNE 7TH—LATE EVENING

LEE

Lee walked back slowly toward his tent through the flickering light, the dim dance of lamps and smoky campfires the only illumination along the way. The aromas of wood smoke, magnolia, and kerosene had pooled above the headquarters' tents like a fragrant cloud, and it served for Lee now as a distinct reminder of the very taste and feel of an army at war. He stopped in the darkness for just a moment to drink it in, and the murky scene stamped upon his memory an image that he sensed he would never forget. Men stepped aside, removed their caps, or nodded respectfully as he approached, and Lee took the time to quietly acknowledge each and every one of them. He was pleased. It seemed his army's strength and morale was beginning again to peak. Yes, if there was such a thing as good times to be had amongst the horrors of war, then this was surely one of them.

Yet, above all else, Robert E. Lee was a realist. He had never allowed his fondest hopes to interfere with his best judgments. Seeing the war clearly—for better or worse—had always been at the heart of his success; a thorough analysis of the cold facts always far more preferable to fond or even vain assurances. Yet now he could not help but think that Grant's army was in trouble, while his own was growing in both strength and confidence. All the signs were there. Surely, it had been a difficult six weeks, and they had lost many good men and officers. But, in the end, his Army of Northern Virginia had never been bested even once on the field, and now, as a consequence, it appeared that the enemy's will was beginning to wane.

Lee stopped short, watched through the smoky darkness as Taylor dismounted and handed the reins of his horse to an orderly nearby. Lee had finally conceded a two-hour cease-fire to Grant, and Taylor had ridden forward to see to its implementation. More than that, however, Lee knew that Taylor would attempt to get a sense of the enemy's morale, and whether it was true that their fighting spirit had been damaged. That might well be the most important fact of all. By the spring of 1864 it had become painfully apparent that the war would be won by far more than numbers alone, and thus every last effort had to be made to discern, if possible, the enemy's willingness to fight.

Taylor spotted Lee standing alone in the darkness, and smiled broadly. "Good evening, sir," he said.

Lee returned his aide's salute. "I trust the cease-fire went off as expected, Colonel?"

"It did, General," Taylor replied. "Precisely as expected. I am pleased to report that there were no problems or foul-ups at all."

"Fine. Yes, I'm glad to hear that."

"We were able to go out and retrieve a number of our boys, General," Taylor continued. "I'm happy to report that at least a few of them were still alive."

Lee listened patiently, then crossed his hands behind his back. "I trust they have been removed to the hospitals?"

"Yes, sir."

"And the Federals?"

"Well, sir," Taylor answered, folding his arms across his chest. "I must say, I don't recall having seen quite so ghastly a

WINDMILL POINT

field anywhere before. The Yankees lost thousands upon thousands of men, General. It was a terrible sight. Remarkably, they did discover a few still alive, even after all these days under the sun, but the vast majority were long gone, and most of the bodies were very corrupted. The stench was literally sickening. I personally observed quite a few of the men working in their burial details collapse from the effort."

"Yet some few were still alive, even after all they'd been through, you say?" Lee asked.

"Yes, sir," Taylor answered. "A few only. Most remarkable, really."

"To say the least," Lee agreed. "They must have endured a terrible ordeal. I would not wish that upon anyone."

Taylor nodded vigorously. "As I have it, sir, one of the wounded Yanks recovered was said to have survived on nothing more than sucking the dew in the morning and eating grass after sundown. An incredible story."

"Really?" Lee said, shaking his head. "Amazing. I do hope he survives and that they quickly ship him home to his family. He surely deserves it."

"Yes, sir."

"And how would you categorize the morale of those people over there?" Lee asked, nodding east toward the Federal lines.

Taylor frowned. "I really can't say, General," he replied. "I did not speak to any of the Federal troops or officers directly, and most of what I saw was simply their burial crews hard at work. None of our officers spoke with the Yanks, but I'm sure many of the rank and file did."

"I see," Lee said. "But you say they have clearly suffered a horrendous defeat?"

"A staggering loss, sir," Taylor confirmed. "Truthfully, General, seeing their dead laid out row upon row as they were, well, it is hard to imagine just what sort of generalship went into it."

"Yes, I agree, it is hard to say," Lee said. "General Grant does seem to favor the frontal assault, no matter what the situation."

"Yes. Well, I can tell you, he paid dearly for it this time."

"Very good," Lee said, thinking it over. "Tell me, Colonel, was there any word or indication at all of a Federal move or redeployment? Anything at all?"

"None, General," Taylor replied. "None at all. From what I heard, the Yanks are just as tired, bored and sick of these trenches here around Cold Harbor as our men are."

"I see. Very well then," Lee replied. "And the pickets down along the Chickahominy?"

"Nothing new as of this afternoon, sir," Taylor told him. "But I will check all the reports once more this evening."

"Very good," Lee replied. "Please let me know if there is word of any movement at all. Anything, Colonel. I fear things are becoming far too quiet around here. It is not at all like General Grant to sit and fiddle. I fear he will try and get the jump on us, and we cannot allow that to happen."

"I understand, General."

Lee slipped back to his tent then, vowing to get the last of his paperwork done, and finally write a letter home to his wife if time permitted. He worked steadily until just after midnight, when his mind finally began to blur and he was forced to give up for the night. He ordered all of his staff off to bed then, and stepped outside into the black night one last time. He took a deep breath of the cool night air, and listened contentedly as his army slept. It was a good feeling. *Sleep well*, he thought. *Soon there will be work enough for all of us, and for that we must be fit and rested.*

Then Lee slid back into his tent, removed his coat, and prepared for bed. He sat on the edge of his cot, said a short prayer, then blew out the lantern's flame. He lay down and closed his eyes, felt the weariness cascade up his legs in small

WINDMILL POINT

waves and knew that he was getting too old for the travails of the campaign. But there was no one else to take his place, to carry the load, he thought. No one else.

Suddenly there was the muffled sound of footsteps near the front of his tent, light and soft, just as a scout moves through the darkness. He opened his eyes.

"General?"

It was Taylor.

Lee sat up.

"General?"

"Yes, Colonel. I am awake."

The flap parted, and his adjutant came in and knelt on the ground directly in front of the cot. "So sorry, General, but I knew you would want to know."

Lee's heart began to beat quicker. "Know what?"

"Reports, sir, from the pickets down on the Chickahominy."

"Yes, yes. What?" Lee demanded.

"We have a report from the 35th North Carolina, sir. They report that Yankee infantry occupied the opposite bank of the river late this afternoon."

Lee took a deep breath, listened quietly. "Have those Yankee troops been identified?"

"Yes, sir. They report two divisions of Warren's Corps—the Federal 5th Corps—now on the river. Those troops directly across the river from our North Carolina regiment are the 118th Pennsylvania."

Lee closed his eyes, could begin to see it all taking shape. "Very good, Colonel. Yes, very good. Be sure to tell the pickets to keep a close watch. I believe Grant has begun to move. He is up to something, and I'm sure there will be more changes in the Federal dispositions very soon. Do keep me informed. We cannot afford to miss a thing."

"Yes, sir. I will."

Lee laid back down then and closed his eyes, but sleep would not come. *Two divisions*, he kept thinking, over and over again. *That is too many troops for a simple redeployment, and both Federal divisions were pulled from their far right. Warren's corps.... Why? If Grant was simply extending his lines, there would be far simpler ways of doing it. No, Grant is moving, and it looks as if he is preparing to move south in order to cross the river. That is fine*, Lee thought. *Move south, General Grant. If you cross the river and come toward Richmond, once you get there you will find us waiting for you again, behind stout earthworks, just as we have always been waiting for you. And you will have little choice, of course, but to attack, and when you do we will make Cold Harbor look pleasant in comparison. We will crush you again, and then, on that very day, you will be beaten for the last and final time, and we will end this war for good.*

CHAPTER THIRTY-THREE

JUNE 8TH—EARLY MORNING

HAMPTON

Wade Hampton was out watching the first glimmers of sun creep through a low, tumbling bank of mist, the enormous red orb ascending slowly through flimsy sweeps of fog as the eastern sky gradually resolved from slate grey into a dazzling rose. Soon, he knew, the mist would burn off entirely and the day would clear. Then the temperature would spike, and the awful heat would be upon them again. But all of that would come later. For the time being the day was mild and pleasant, and Hampton took a deep breath and enjoyed the coolness of the dawn.

The sunrise was a beautiful, almost breathtaking sight, and for a moment Hampton felt virtually transported in time, whisked away somehow to his native South Carolina, the lovely, forested Piedmont near Columbia, and the carefree days of his youth. He thought of the Deep South in June, of carriages clopping lazily down Charleston's narrow alleyways, and of catfish pulled from a nearby pond, fat as a man's thigh. He was instantly reminded of his home, Millwood, of his loving wife and family, and the smell of honeysuckle hanging so dense outside the open window on June nights that often he'd sworn he could actually taste it on his tongue. He closed his eyes and for one sweet moment Wade Hampton was home again, the feel and smell of Millwood so clear and distinct in his mind that he could almost sense his wife's presence hovering in the mist nearby.

For Wade Hampton—born to some of the most affluent circumstances that the antebellum South could possibly provide—the Civil War had come as a nightmare. His grandfather had been a hero in the Revolutionary War, his father an astute and aggressive businessman, and by the time all the hot talk of secession had finally come to rock South Carolina, his family was known as perhaps the wealthiest in all the South. Wade had been raised on a lavish plantation outside of Columbia, had graduated from South Carolina College, and had later entered politics and won a seat in the state senate.

Yet Wade Hampton was anything but the typical planter aristocrat. Many of his views differed markedly from the majority of the Carolina elite. Hampton, for instance, openly criticized the institution of slavery on the senate floor, and later argued strenuously against secession and war—ventures he considered both ill thought-out and hopeless. But when war finally arrived, Wade Hampton swallowed his differences, and at the age of forty-three offered his services to the state of South Carolina. He could not, after all, fight against his home, friends, and family. His offer was quickly accepted, and he immediately raised and outfitted his own Hampton Legion.

While Wade Hampton had been well educated and schooled in the social graces, he had also been an avid hunter and outdoorsman, and he was both a physical and athletic giant when compared to most of his contemporaries. A bear of a man with great combative instincts, soldiering came naturally to Wade, and his rise through the ranks of the Army of Northern Virginia from colonel to major general mirrored his competency far more than his social background. Wounded at Bull Run, Seven Pines, and then again at Gettysburg, Hampton had returned to the cavalry corps the preceding fall after a period of convalescence, to resume command of one of Stuart's three horse divisions.

Since J.E.B. Stuart's death in May, Hampton had served as de facto head of the entire cavalry corps, but with no commensurate promotion from Lee, or even acknowledgment of his service. Over this Hampton had become bitter. It was almost, Wade thought, as if General Lee were biding time in an attempt to steer the command of the cavalry corps toward his nephew, Fitz Lee. The junior Lee was a man Hampton considered little more than an arrogant incompetent, and all this was taking place despite the fact that Hampton clearly outranked the junior Lee, and was eminently more qualified.

Wade Hampton had been privately stung by this, of course, and saw in it the Commanding General's consistent Virginia bias, a prejudice that had always favored the Virginia officers and units over those from the deeper South, no matter how well the latter performed. From promotions, to duties, to supplies, the Virginia regiments always fared far better than those from Georgia or the Carolinas, and on more than one occasion Wade Hampton had gone straight to the top and complained bitterly to Lee about it. Those outbursts had probably not sat well with the Commanding General, but Wade Hampton was not one to set either principle or fact aside to further his own advancement, so complain he had.

But now the army was fighting for its life around Cold Harbor, so for the time being all of that unpleasantness had to be set aside. Hampton had received orders to screen the army's flanks, and for the past few days he'd posted his division on the north side of the Chickahominy River, with Fitz Lee on the south, to accomplish that task. For the cavalry, the fighting had been light in comparison to the infantry, the climate far less intense, but all of that, he knew, might soon change.

There was a sudden clatter of hooves down along the road. Wade Hampton tensed and opened his eyes, and all thoughts of

Millwood suddenly evaporated like mist before the sun's warming rays. In an instant he was back in Virginia again. How sad. He took a deep breath, sighed once, then peered out toward the west as four riders came bounding through the slippery mist and up the road toward him.

One of the men he recognized at once as Thomas Conrad, Chaplin of the 3rd Virginia Cavalry, and one of the finest scouts in his division. The others he was unfamiliar with, but he could feel the sense of tension and urgency in all their movements. Hampton realized this was no casual visit. Wade instantly forgot about the dazzling sunrise, and started down the embankment toward them.

The four riders reined to a stop on the road: Conrad, two other cavalrymen, and a black soldier wearing a Yankee coat. Conrad saluted.

"Good morning, General," Conrad said, puffing hard as he struggled with his horse, forcing it to settle. "Sorry to disturb you at such an early hour."

"No bother, Captain," Hampton replied. "I was up and about anyway." He noticed the sweat soaking through the scout's shirt. "I see you've been riding hard," Hampton said. "What, may I ask, brings ya'll out this way at the crack of dawn?"

Conrad nodded solemnly toward the black man wearing the Yankee blue. "This here fella just slipped away from a large column of Yankee cavalry headed west, General. Coley Miller's his name."

While the fighting along the flanks had been less spirited than in the trenches at Cold Harbor, there had still been ample fighting. But recently those encounters had dropped off considerably, and for the past two days Hampton had worried that the Yankee horsemen might have somehow given him the slip. His eyes narrowed on the black soldier. "Go on, Captain," he said.

WINDMILL POINT

"Well, sir," Conrad continued, "I ran into him real early this morning on the other side of the Pamunkey while I was out scouting. At first I thought I was going to have a little fight on my hands alright, but then he just waved and approached me and asked if I was a Confederate officer. I said I was, of course, and he asked if I knew the whereabouts of General Rosser."

"Rosser!" Hampton repeated, referring to one of his own brigade commanders.

"Yes, General," Conrad continued. "Seems that early in the war Coley Miller here worked for General Rosser, and he told me that he had a good bit of information that he wanted to pass on. Said he'd just snuck away from the Yankees that night, after traveling with them a good distance."

"That so?" Hampton said, his curiosity piqued.

"So I up and took Coley here directly over to General Rosser's headquarters, and the general came out of his bed straightaway to talk with us. He recognized Coley at once, and heard him out for a good long while. When they was finally done chatting, the general told me to bring him directly to you and to tell you that he—General Rosser, I mean—would personally vouch for Coley's story. He wanted me to tell you that this man has a great deal of information concerning the Yankees that he thought you would want to hear. Said Coley's a good man and is to be trusted."

Hampton nodded, starting to feel a small pool of excitement knot in the pit of his stomach. He smiled deliberately, then glanced at the black soldier again. "Well, Coley," he said, "slipping away from that Yankee column must have been some dangerous work for you, I guess, now, wasn't it?"

"Yes, sir, General Hampton, sir," Miller replied. "But I waited till they's all sleeping, then I kinda loosened a horse from the line and walked him a good piece before I saddled up. I already seen where the pickets was placed, so I just slipped in between 'em. Wasn't so hard as it sounds."

Hampton nodded, appreciating the man's valor. "Still, it was a brave thing to do, and I commend you for it. Now, what can you tell me about that column, Coley? Do you know how many men the Yankees have mounted?"

"Yes, General," Coley Miller replied. "Last night I was right there at Sheridan's campfire. I was bringing in the kindling, see, and I heard a whole lot."

"Sheridan!" Hampton exclaimed. "You say Sheridan is in command of this column?"

"Yes, General. I seen him myself."

"And how many men has he got?" Hampton asked, suddenly becoming nervous. If Sheridan was in direct command of a large force of cavalry, then it was reasonable to assume the Yanks were up to something big.

"Two full divisions, General," Coley Miller answered. "Torbert's and Gregg's."

"That's a lot of sabers," Hampton replied, turning the whole thing over slowly in his mind. "Do you know what they're up to? Where they might be headed, I mean?"

Coley Miller nodded his head positively. "Sure do, General. Last night the Yanks was talking up a whole storm about where they's headed, General. I heard 'em say they's going up to Gordonsville to tear up the railroad track real good. They packed themselves three days' rations, and they's got beef cattle, plenty of wagons, ambulances, and cannons too. I seen it all myself."

"Artillery, you say?" Hampton asked, stepping forward slightly. He was becoming very excited. "How much artillery, Coley? Did you get a chance to count the guns?"

"I did," Coley answered. "At least twenty, General. Dat's how much I counted. Twenty."

Wade Hampton thought for a moment then kicked at the dirt. "They're headed out to destroy the railroad line in the Shenandoah," he proclaimed, talking to himself as much as the

WINDMILL POINT

others. "Too many men for anything else, I think. The north side supply route into Richmond. That's what they're after. Two full divisions. Well, that's a big raiding party, alright."

"Yes, General," Coley continued. "We done crossed the Pamunkey early yesterday, and camped at Aylett's on the Mattapony River last night. They moving real slow so's not to break down their horses, though, General. I mean real slow."

Wade Hampton turned back to Thomas Conrad. "Get up as many men as you need, Captain, and track that column closely," he ordered. "Find out how many men they have and anything else you can about them. Keep me informed. If you can nab a few stragglers, bring them right to me straightaway so we can question them closely."

"Yes, General," Conrad replied.

"Good work, Coley," Hampton went on. "You stick around and I'll see to it that you're properly rewarded for your effort."

"Thank you, General," Coley said.

Hampton dismissed Conrad, then turned and walked directly to his tent, mind awhirl. This was major news: just the sort of information General Lee would need to hear at once. Grant was surely up to something major. And if Sheridan was at Aylett's last night, then it would appear he was taking a long loop north and west toward Gordonsville, leaving Hampton the shorter and more direct route north. If Hampton moved quickly he might still have enough time to cut the Yankees off before they got to the railroad. But if he was going to stop them, he would have to respond in strength, and he would have to move very quickly. He could feel the sweat on his palms.

Wade Hampton immediately dashed off a note to General Lee, clearly outlining everything he had learned, and promising to follow up with additional information as soon as anything became available. Then he handed the message to a courier with instructions to ride as hard as he could to Lee's headquarters.

Hampton didn't have to wait long for a response. Before noon a dispatch arrived from the Commanding General, ordering him to take his entire division along with one other and follow Sheridan north.

That afternoon Wade Hampton issued all of the necessary orders for his division to prepare to move out. He also sent word to Fitz Lee to be ready to move his division early the next day. They would depart promptly at 2 o'clock the following morning with at least three days' rations cooked and packed away. Then he took a long look at the map.

First Hampton imagined Sheridan's probable route to Gordonsville, then he traced with his index finger the course of the best roads winding north from Cold Harbor. Each time he did this his finger intercepted Sheridan's anticipated line of march at the same location, a small stop along the Virginia Central Railroad just east of Gordonsville.

If all went as he conceived it, Sheridan would be riding the bow or circumference of a flattened circle, while Hampton would have the benefit of traveling along the inner diameter of that same bow. Where those two geometrical representations intersected one another there was bound to be a heated collision. After his third effort rendered the same result, Wade Hampton circled an area on the map with his pen, near where he expected to encounter the Federal cavalry. In the center of that circle was a small station on the Virginia Central he had never seen or heard of before, but for better or worse it was now his cavalry's objective. Then he tossed the pen aside and walked out of the room. The name left beneath the hastily scrawled circle was "Trevilian Station."

CHAPTER THIRTY-FOUR

JUNE 8TH—EARLY EVENING

WHITE

Wyman White finished the letter to his mother and father, read it twice by the flickers of a small candle, then stuffed it into an envelope. He would post it first thing tomorrow, but for now Wyman just slipped it away into his haversack, between the sleeves of his last clean shirt, for safekeeping. That way it would be clean for posting come morning. Then he leaned back against the side of the trench and relaxed. It had been another hot, stifling day at Cold Harbor, and while it had been close to unbearable in the trenches, none of that bothered Wyman anymore.

Around 3 o'clock that afternoon the regiment had been relieved, and for the first time in days allowed to go well behind the entrenchments in order to rest and bathe. About a mile behind the lines two small streams tumbled together, and what with all the rain and thunderstorms that had been roaring out of the west as of late, the water that afternoon had run high and fairly clear—a wonderful break from the usual Chickahominy muck. The boys all piled in, soap in hand for those who had it, but soap or not, the water was nothing short of a much-needed pleasure. Men bathed and washed their hair for the first time in weeks, and the difference in everyone's attitude afterward was nothing short of astonishing. Joe Thompson laughed out loud as he pulled himself out of the water, and Wyman thought Joe's laughter sounded like music, so long had it been since he'd heard it. Most of the boys washed out their clothes and hung them on short branches to dry in the sun. Once they were all dressed and ready for dinner, they felt almost like human beings again. Almost.

Then came the best part. After drying off, the regiment was marched back to a grand meal of beefsteak, fresh oysters, boiled potatoes, onions, and canned corn. Wyman had always been partial to beefsteak and the meal was almost enough to make him cry. Beefsteak with gravy never tasted better. For desert the cooks had prepared fine chocolate cakes, and they all washed the cake down with pots of fresh boiled coffee laced with honey and sugar. It may not have been a home-cooked meal in Fitzwilliam, New Hampshire, but Wyman White was not about to complain.

Joe Thompson made a big show of shucking and eating his oysters, and the boys all enjoyed his good humor. "Now here goes the fine Rebel ship Merrimack down to the bottom of the bay!" Joe cried, pulling an oyster from the half-shell and swallowing it whole.

Wyman laughed to watch him, but then Tommie Gorman got it into his head that he'd shout the same thing, but, typical of Tommie, he confused and twisted and botched the whole sentence. The rest of the meal he'd call out "Let's pray for Miss Merry Mack's fine Rebel bottom!" with every mouth full he consumed, and while a few of the men considered his inadvertent misconstruction reasonably stupid and laughed accordingly, very few fancied it funny in any true sense. After the sixth time Tom yelled it, Wyman became distressed.

"Let's pray for Miss Merry Mack's fine Rebel bottom!"

Finally Wyman felt it necessary to leave his beefsteak in mid-career to go over and tell Tom to be quiet. Not being one to mince his words, Wyman simply said: "Tom, you are nothing

WINDMILL POINT

but a fool," and let it go at that. Tommie did not understand, but at least he finally shut up.

Later they all returned to the trenches, and while the entrenchments were always confined and depressing, after a bath and fine meal they didn't seem quite as harsh as before. Then an even more remarkable thing occurred.

The same regimental band that had performed the sad funeral dirge the night before during the cease fire rumbled out over the ragged ground in their wagons and set up shop not far behind the lines. Chairs were set in the muck, and instruments hauled down from the wagons. The Rebels, grasping the situation immediately, thankfully held their fire. For a while the band practiced and tuned their instruments, then, once everything was in good order, finally began to play. By then the activity along the front had trailed off to almost nothing anyway, and the music washed out far across the field and over the Rebel lines. The music was loud, crisp, and striking. Everyone sat up to listen.

Across the way heads began to pop up over the Confederate works, and soon men were lined-up, sitting along the tops of the entrenchments as if it were nothing more than an evening in the park. No formal agreement was necessary, and no white flags were required to convince everyone to lay down their rifles. It just happened.

The band played every song they knew—*Red White and Blue, The Star Spangled Banner,* and *Yankee Doodle* among many others. For the better part of an hour the tunes filled the air, and men on both sides of the field tapped their feet merrily or sang along if they happened to know the words. Men smiled and laughed. It was a rare delight.

Then once the Union band was entirely played out, lo and behold, a Rebel band set up directly behind their lines and began a long series of their own. Everyone turned around to listen. Now it was time for *Dixie, The Bonnie Blue Flag,* and other Southern favorites, and all the boys from the North sat politely and listened appreciatively. No one cared what side the music was from. The band played on into the night, and while the music filled the air not a shot was fired nor a harsh word spoken. Soldiers from both sides relaxed and enjoyed the lull as if on holiday, and in a sense that's just what it was.

Wyman White was bound and determined to refrain from looking across the way for Jacob McCabe, but from time to time he couldn't help but sneak a peek. It was good that he didn't spot him, though. No use getting fond or attached to one of the enemy, a man you might have to kill someday, especially for a sharpshooter. If the fighting were close Wyman had already decided he would never pull the trigger on Jacob unless, of course, Jake were about to pull the trigger on him. But Wyman generally killed at a distance, sometimes close to a half mile or more, generally shooting at nothing more than movement or the first thing that entered his sight. At that distance he could shoot Jake six times and never know it was him. So the less he saw of Jacob McCabe the better. He did not want to fret over such a thing. He did not want his conscience to be bothered. But then, of course, he was already fretting, and his conscience was already bothered.

CHAPTER THIRTY-FIVE

JUNE 9TH—LATE EVENING

LEE

Lee sensed the winds of change in the air just as one might anticipate the approach of a summer thunderstorm by the first, gentle shift of the breezes high in the tops of the trees. Two nights before, he had gotten word of Federal infantry moving down along the banks of the Chickahominy, and yesterday morning a courier had arrived from Hampton with a report of a large column of Union cavalry on the roads leading north. Lee knew now that the long days of waiting, sharpshooting, and tension were about to end. Grant was on the move. He could feel it. Just exactly what his adversary had up his sleeve was still unclear, but it already appeared fairly obvious that Grant was hoping to force Lee to shift forces to meet additional threats, thus reducing the Confederate strength available in the Richmond Theater. Divide and conquer; it was a military dictum as old as the hills.

Grant had Sheridan, with ten thousand sabers, on the road, and while there was still debate amongst his staff as to their ultimate objective, Lee had little doubt where they were headed. The only strategic target of serious value north of Richmond was the Shenandoah Valley, with its railroad that fed the city. The small Federal army under Hunter had scored a recent victory near Staunton, and Lee assumed that Sheridan was on his way to join forces with Hunter, destroy the railroad, and then return to Grant, perhaps along the south side of the James. That sort of freewheeling destruction could not be allowed.

So Lee reacted immediately. He at once sent instructions to Hampton to take two full divisions of cavalry and go directly after Sheridan. He also dispatched General Breckinridge's Brigade to the valley to oppose Hunter. Both, of course, were undermanned and outgunned, but for the time being it was the best he could do. The Shenandoah was the Confederacy's breadbasket, after all, and he could no more allow a Federal army to go marching through it unopposed than he could allow Union soldiers to rummage about in his wife's pantry in Richmond. The capital city was already dangerously low on supplies; the Army of Northern Virginia had been close to starvation for weeks. A serious disruption in the flow of supplies would have a far more damaging effect than even Grant being reinforced by two full corps of fresh infantry. So something had to be done.

Lee had already informed Jefferson Davis of Sheridan's departure, and that evening he received a letter from the president in return. He thoroughly read the dispatch—a cogent assessment of the tactical situation—then began a reply. As to Sheridan's intentions, Lee wrote:

> I have received no definite information as to his purpose, but conjecture that his object is to cooperate with General Hunter, and endeavor to reach the James, breaking the railroads &c, as he passes, and probably to descend on the south side of that river.
>
> I think it necessary to be on our guard and make every arrangement in our power to thwart his purpose and protect our communications and

WINDMILL POINT

country. I have directed Genls Hampton and Fitz Lee with their divisions to proceed in the direction of Hanover Junction, and thence, if the information they receive justifies it, along the Central Railroad, keeping the enemy on their right, and shape their course according to his. The pause in the operations of Genl Grant induces me to believe that he is awaiting the effect of movements in some other quarter to make us change our position, and renders the suggestion I make with reference to the intention and destination of Genl Sheridan more probable.

Lee read the letter twice then set it aside for a moment so that the ink might dry. Then a sudden, radical notion blossomed in the back of his mind. If Grant was now going to operate far and wide, so to speak, then perhaps he could do the same, and beat the Federal commander at his own game. There seemed to be, after all, a certain basic assumption built into this newest Federal strategy, the notion, for instance, that the Confederacy had now been knocked back on its heals by Grant's hammering blows, and was as a result incapable of mounting anything beyond the most limited offensive operations. Thus Grant's entire strategic initiative may well be predicated upon the unspoken belief that Lee would not come out from behind his works and try anything rash. But false assumptions often engender corrupt calculations, and it may well be that Grant's Achilles' heel lay in his presumption of Confederate impotence. Time would surely tell, but it was certainly something worth keeping in mind.

Lee smiled, liked the plan that had just occurred to him, but knew it was still too soon for anything that drastic. He would have to wait and see, bide his time and determine just exactly what the Federal commander was up to, and then coolly fashion a response. But if Grant fancied the Army of Northern Virginia incapable of going over to the aggressive, then perhaps this was exactly the time to fashion a plan that was the most aggressive of all, something that neither Grant, his generals, or the government in Washington would ever expect. Yes, he liked that idea, but for now he would just keep it tucked away in his pocket.

Lee took up the letter he had written to the President, signed it, then handed it over to Taylor.

"See that this is delivered as soon as possible," he said.

"Of course, General."

Lee leaned back for a moment, watched the candle light flicker gently on the inside of his tent, and carefully considered the situation. Good strategies predicated upon false assumptions, he knew, almost always backfire. Often men see only what they expect to see, thus responding to shadows instead of facts. So if Grant had misjudged him, then he must use that confusion to his benefit and quickly turn the tables on his adversary with a stroke that the Federal commander would never see coming. Then Grant would miss or misinterpret the movement, not because he wouldn't detect it, but because he wouldn't *believe* it. The great blunder Lee had been hoping for all along might soon be right at his fingertips. Not a blunder of movement, tactics, or strategy, as he had been anticipating, but something far more basic, and therefore even more potentially lethal: a blunder of simple judgment.

CHAPTER THIRTY-SIX

JUNE 10TH—EVENING

HAMPTON

Hampton rode up to a large tavern overlooking the railroad tracks and leaped from his horse. He had just arrived at the junction of the Gordonsville and Fredericksburg roads. In two days his division had traversed the sixty-odd miles from Yellow Tavern, driving both horses and men equally hard. The first day they had passed through a driving rain as fierce as anything Wade Hampton had ever seen, but the second was a clear, breezy day that was a wonderful joy in comparison.

They had ridden at a steady pace, Hampton's division leading the way, Fitz Lee's following close on their heels. North of Richmond they had turned onto the Telegraph Road, and ridden that out to Hanover Junction where they had struck the rails of the Virginia Central. At that point they had turned west and traveled roughly parallel to the tracks along the Gordonsville Road, first through Beaver Dam Station, then Frederick Hall, and finally Louisa Court House. Pushing hard, they'd made up two full days on the Yankees, and had now managed to get out slightly ahead of them. Riding at the very front of his long column, Wade Hampton reined to a stop, dismounted, and took a good, long look at Trevilian Station. There was not much to see.

A train station, tavern, dry goods store, and a few scattered houses were about the size of it. But not far away the Fredericksburg Road led directly north, through Clayton's Store to Carpenter's Ford on the North Anna River, a distance of no more than seven miles. His scouts had confirmed late that afternoon that the Yankee column had already forded the river and was now bedded down for the night in the vicinity of Clayton's Store, just a few miles away from the tavern where Hampton now stood. In the morning the Federal divisions would be converging on Trevilian Station—just as he had anticipated days ago—but it was no longer his aim to simply stop them. Now Wade Hampton planned to destroy them.

Just off to the west and running north, was the Blue Ridge, now looming dark and majestic in the fading light of day. The area surrounding the station was rich with ridges, thick woods, tumbling hills, and swift mountain streams. It was beautiful, green, rolling country, but hardly suited to classic cavalry operations. But that didn't matter. The Yanks would be coming down the Fredericksburg Road in the morning, so in that sense they had already picked the field of battle, and there was little he could do to change any of that. His orders from General Lee were to defend the railroad "at all hazards," so Wade Hampton would fight in the treetops if that's what it would take.

While the ground in and about Trevilian Station was hardly ideal for cavalry maneuver, the lay of the land didn't bother Wade Hampton nearly as much as it would have his predecessor, J.E.B. Stuart. Stuart had loved the grand charge and the sight of sabers flashing in the sunlight, the pounding, dirt-tossing spectacle of a thousand horsemen moving together in wondrous concert across an open field toward the enemy. Stuart had been all dash and audacity, a flamboyant cavalier to the very end, and the cavalry raid had become his signature tactic.

WINDMILL POINT

Hampton had learned much from Stuart, of that there was little question. But the Yankee cavalry now came equipped with new Spencer seven-shot repeating carbines, and they had learned to use them to their advantage. No longer did they favor the grand charge, but rather they used their horses only to move swiftly, then deploy like infantry behind rocks and trees, or works of timber and dirt if they had the time to throw them up.

Times had changed. A cavalry charge against a thousand well-armed men with repeating weapons was simply suicidal. Hampton had taken note of that fact, and altered his own tactics accordingly. Now he, too, deployed his horsemen behind trees and rocks, and while they did not have the advantage of repeating carbines, in an equal fight they were still a match for anything that the Yankees could throw at them.

The old, hulking, vacant Netherland Tavern sat behind him at the intersection, and after taking a look around, Hampton decided it was as good a place as any to establish his headquarters. "This will do," he called to his son, Wade IV, nodding toward the dilapidated structure. "It commands the ground and is centrally located."

"It's not exactly Millwood," his son pointed out sarcastically, brushing aside a thick patch of cobwebs as he walked toward the entrance.

Hampton laughed appreciatively. "No, that it's not, Wade," he agreed, feeling a sudden pang of homesickness come upon him. He couldn't help but wonder if his son missed South Carolina as much as he did; if the war and his father's ambitions had drawn him away from something far more dear to him. Suddenly homesickness turned to regret. "But you know we'll see home again soon, Son," he went on. "I promise you that."

His son smiled, looked away. Then he quickly began issuing instructions for the other aides to begin unpacking, and the headquarters started coming together. Hampton watched for a moment, then decided to get busy himself.

Light was fading, the night cooling, and just outside the front door of the tavern he found a reasonably serviceable carpenter's table. So he had a few chairs dragged out from inside, put a lantern on the table, and dashed off a quick message to Fitz Lee, whose command had gone into bivouac on the Gordonsville Road at Louisa Court House, about three miles east of Trevilian. He made sure that Lee was apprised of all the unit positions, and that he understood that Hampton would send fresh orders at first light, once the Yankees' intentions had been clearly discerned.

The rest of his brigades were coming up now—Rosser, Butler, and Wright—banging, clanging, and kicking up dust as they arrived on the road to Gordonsville. As each weary command approached, Hampton stood in the intersection and directed them off to an area of large, open farm fields, just south of the tracks. There they went into bivouac, tired troopers collapsing onto the ground, many asleep before their heads touched their blankets. There would be no cooking fires tonight. It would be too risky with the Yankees so near. By midnight everyone was accounted for, and he was glad to know the men would have at least a few good hours' rest before dawn.

From the few Federal captives that had been brought in by his scouts, Hampton knew that Sheridan was not even remotely aware of the large Confederate presence that had hurried north to Trevilian Station. Good. He would use that ignorance to his advantage. He also knew that Sheridan was moving with almost 10,000 horsemen and a full compliment of artillery, while Hampton had at best 6,000 riders. But the numerical disadvantage didn't bother him. Wade Hampton had conceived a simple plan. Besides, the Confederates had always fought with the odds stacked against them, anyway.

WINDMILL POINT

As the Federal cavalry approached Trevilian Station come morning, Hampton intended to sweep straight up the road and meet them head on. Taking the enemy by surprise, he hoped to drive them back toward the vicinity of Clayton's Store, where another road forked off to Louisa Court House. He would then have Fitz Lee's division come up on that road and strike the disorganized Yankee cavalry directly in the flank, thus turning confusion and disorganization into bedlam.

Then the two Confederate divisions—now unified—would drive the panicked Yankee horsemen up against the banks of the North Anna River, pinning them against the river, and eventually destroying Sheridan's entire column. It was a sound plan, aided principally by the element of surprise, the pattern of the local roads, and the favorable lay of the land.

Throughout the long ride north, Fitz Lee had stopped at each of the train stations that they had passed through, to telegraph his uncle reports on the Confederate column's progress, along with the latest intelligence that they'd managed to gather on Sheridan's movements. While Hampton was pleased that his commander was being kept well informed, the truth of the matter was, it seemed to him but one more flagrant example of the Virginia partisanship he had come so much to distrust.

It was Hampton, after all, who had been directed by General Lee to take two divisions and proceed after Sheridan, not the commanding general's nephew. Yet at each step along the way, Fitz appeared to be acting as though he was either operating under an independent command, or in charge of the entire mission himself. While Wade Hampton realized that this was certainly no time to begin carping again about what he perceived to be flaws in the command structure, it was clear to see that unless the situation were remedied soon, the discipline and effectiveness of the cavalry corps would no doubt be compromised. Fitz Lee, Hampton thought, was simply inveigling for high command, and unless he was promptly put in his place, the situation might well blow up in both their faces.

But, as usual, that would have to wait, and, for the time being at least, Hampton tried to put it out of his mind. The Yankees were in bivouac only a few miles away, their mission now apparent, their morning's objective—Trevilian Station. Come sunrise he would have the fight of his life on his hands.

Wade Hampton walked slowly back up the slope to the tavern, only to find most of his staff already sound asleep. He chuckled to himself, then felt a rush of weariness wash over him, too. They were all exhausted from two hard days in the saddle, so he slipped outside in search of a place to bed down.

He rummaged around for someplace dry, but it seemed that all of those had already been spoken for. So he wandered along the front of the tavern looking for anything remotely comfortable. After a quick appraisal revealed nothing of promise, he finally decided the carpenter's table would do. Hampton quietly removed the lantern, blew out the lamp, and rolled himself up on top. Hard, but at least dry and flat, it felt almost comfortable. Wade Hampton pulled his hat down over his face, and within minutes was sound asleep.

CHAPTER THIRTY-SEVEN

JUNE 10TH—LATE EVENING

CUSTER

George Armstrong Custer laughed out loud as Johnny Cisco danced an abbreviated jig around the campfire, while Eliza banged a small pot with a large spoon to keep time. The fire was warm, there was food aplenty, and Custer was feeling good.

"Whee-ew!" one of his aides yelped, clapping his hands as Johnny circled and kicked.

"There you go now, Johnny!" Eliza yelled.

Custer clapped, tapping his heel in rhythm as Johnny strutted, spun, and then bounced wildly around the flames.

Johnny had just invented what he called the chicken jig, a brand new dance to commemorate the fine hens that were now boiling in Eliza's biggest pot. Brought in by one of the foragers earlier that afternoon and promptly put to use, the sweet scent of a plentiful supper now hung over the camp like a delicious cloud. So enticing had the aroma become that Johnny could no longer contain himself, and had leaped to his feet and begun the odd frolic in what seemed to be a moment of pure inspiration. Like an Apache warrior petitioning the spirits for success, he now expressed all his fondest hopes through a humorous series of kicks, steps, leaps, and jumps as he circled the blazing campfire. Finally complete, he tossed both arms in the air triumphantly and yelled, "For this evening's entertainment of the Michigan cavalry, I give ya'll Johnny Cisco's famous *chicken jig!*"

Everyone stood and clapped, while Custer stomped the ground with both feet. "Bravo! Bravo, Johnny!" Custer yelled.

"Encore, Johnny!" Eliza insisted. "You can't quit now!"

Johnny, huffing and puffing, shook his head to the contrary. "Done *now*, Liza," he said. " 'Fraid I'm whipped."

"Ahh, come on," Johnny," Custer cried, "I'm sure you got one more kick or bounce left in you. A serious chicken jig is bound to have a beneficial effect on our supper, not to mention the morale of the entire brigade. Aye, Eliza?"

"Course it would," Eliza agreed, grinning from ear to ear. "Nothing better than a fine dance to set off a good meal."

Johnny wiped the sweat from his brow with his handkerchief. "Well, this one's gonna have to get by on what's already been done," he replied. He shook his head forcefully. "Can't overdo the chicken jig, you know. Bad luck. Don't want any of *that* around here, now do we?"

Custer laughed, clapped his hands. "Well, I guess if you say so, Johnny. You're right, of course. Sure don't need any bad omens brought down on our heads for overdoing such an esteemed thing as the chicken jig. You did a fine thing here, Johnny," Custer conceded. "I reckon you earned your supper tonight."

Johnny broke into a broad smile. "Thanks, General. I just gave in to the power of the moment, you see."

"I understand."

Johnny returned to his seat by the fire as Eliza began spooning dinner onto the men's plates. It was a cool, clear evening, the west wind having blown away a sizeable rainstorm the day before, and now it seemed unusually crisp for June in Virginia. But the fire was warm, the wagons chock-full of confiscated food, and the Rebels still far away, so none of that seemed to matter.

WINDMILL POINT

They had been on the road for four days now, the whole column crossing the North Anna late that afternoon, then splitting up down the roads that led south toward Trevilian Station. The main body was bivouacked on the Fredericksburg Road, while Custer's brigade had forked off and gone into camp just south of Buck Chiles' farm on the Marquis Road. The station lay just down the pike a few miles, and in the morning Custer anticipated orders sending his brigade forward to begin tearing up the track. They had run into a few stray groups of Confederate scouts and militia along the way, but nothing of substance had so far been spotted. So Custer anticipated that the morning's work would be easy, and then they would move on toward Gordonsville and hit the railroad there.

"Saved the best for you, General," Eliza said, handing him a plate full of chicken, beef, stuffing, hot bread and fresh picked berries.

Custer pushed his hat back on his head and admired the feast. "Life is good," he said, taking a chicken leg in hand and having a quick taste. "Yes... very good."

"Well, thank you, General," Eliza replied with a wink. "As long as the boys keep bringing in the food, I will keep a-cooking."

Custer took another bite, tried the stuffing. "Yeah, well, there's plenty food for the taking," he said, "but then I don't reckon the locals exactly appreciate our presence hereabouts."

Eliza's eyes grew wide. "You can say that again!" she exclaimed. "I seen them boys hung up in the trees back by the river, General." She shivered miserably. "Terrible sight, you ask me. Just terrible!"

Custer frowned. She was referring to several foragers the locals had grabbed, then lynched on the road leading across the North Anna. Left dangling from the branches of a giant oak, they were an ugly warning to any Federal soldier unfortunate enough to get cut off and gobbled up by the citizens or local militia. Sheridan's foragers had been raiding the farms and homesteads for miles around, making off with whatever they could find in the way of food for the army, and leaving many of the locals virtually destitute in their wake. And while the foraging parties were instructed to mind their manners, Custer knew that many of them took considerable advantage of the power they wielded, and that shootings, burnings, and rapes were often sadly attendant on the army's foraging expeditions. Then enraged citizens responded with atrocities of their own, and the ugly mess just escalated.

"Stick to the main column, Liza," Custer said, "and you'll be fine. That goes for everyone. Johnny, you hear me?"

"Yes, sir."

"Good," Custer said. "Tomorrow in all likelihood we'll move on into Trevilian Station, tear up the track, then probably head on up toward Gordonsville the next day. Don't anyone go wandering off so they can snatch you. Stay close and it won't be a problem."

"You know I will," Eliza answered, picking at a chicken bone. "I ain't ending up swinging from no *tree*."

Custer chuckled, took a deep breath of cool night air. Looking south down the road he could see only darkness, while on all the surrounding hills and pastures the campfires of his Michigan brigade blazed and flickered through the black night. "A few angry citizens is one thing," he said, "Rebels, another. But for the time being there's no sign of the Confederates in any strength. So tomorrow should be easy pickings for us."

"Where you reckon the Rebs are, General?" Johnny asked, stuffing his mouth with gobs of beef and berries.

Custer rolled his shoulders. "Don't know," he admitted. "But they'll be along. They can't afford to let us tear up their dear old railroad, and they've got to know we're out this way by now. So they'll be along, Johnny. Then I'll need you to hold my extra horses again, 'cause when they get here we'll have a fight on our hands, for sure." Custer looked up, smiled.

Eliza laughed at him. "You sure likes fighting, General. I will say that about you."

Custer nodded his head. "I guess that's right," he replied. He took a quick sip of coffee, smiled again.

Eliza beamed at him. "Well, it's good we got someone who does, you ask me," she said, "so we can win this here war. Then all of us will finally be free."

Custer nodded, but in truth, for him it had little to do with any of that. He was simply a soldier, and it was a soldier's business to fight. The best of them fought well, and since Custer was without question among the very best, he not only fought well, but was fortunate enough to count himself among that rare, privileged few who thoroughly enjoyed it.

Custer glanced south again, and for a moment almost thought he'd spotted a movement on the hills off in the darkness. He blinked and blinked, staring a hole through the night, but could not be sure. Finally he looked away. Too bad. It would have been nice to know that the Rebels were out there—that come dawn the guns would thunder again. Still, he had an odd feeling....

Eliza laughed, shook her head, then tossed away the last of the bones from her plate into the tall grass nearby. "You something, General George," she said with a snicker. But Custer was staring off intently towards the south yet again, and wasn't listening.

CHAPTER THIRTY-EIGHT

JUNE 11TH—FIRST LIGHT

HAMPTON

Wade heard the footsteps, but faintly, like whispers in a dream, near but undefined. He snorted once, swallowed then licked his lips.

"General? Excuse me,... General?"

Hampton opened one eye, then the other. His back was sore, face cold. He sat up slowly.

"Good morning, General. Sorry to disturb you."

Wade Hampton sat for a moment as mute as a statue, as his mind whirled to catch up with his body. At first he did not even know who he was, much less what he was doing. For a moment or two he just stared off into a dark sea of trees and blinked.

"Yes, General, so sorry to wake you."

Hampton blinked again, looked sideways. There standing next to him were Thomas Rosser and Matt Butler, two of his brigade commanders. Hampton shook his head slowly. "Well," he said finally, "Look here, I guess I'm awake."

The two men laughed. Rosser tapped the carpenter's table Hampton had used for a bed. "Lovely mattress, General," he said in jest. "You must consider making this sort of luxury available to all of your officers."

Hampton smiled. "When you're tired you can sleep on anything, Tom," he said. He stretched slowly, then rubbed his

WINDMILL POINT

back. "Not so bad, really. I've had worse." He rubbed his back again. "A little stiff, but not so bad."

"General," Rosser went on, "my boys have been up and ready since the first shimmers of light in the eastern sky. What, may I inquire, do you intend to do here today?"

Hampton licked his lips, rubbed the sleep from his eyes. Then he looked directly at Rosser. "I propose to fight."

Butler folded his arms across his chest. "General Hampton," he said, "the ground around the station here is wooded, and unsuitable, in my opinion, for cavalry operations."

Hampton found his hat and put it back on his head. "Well, let's ride out and reconnoiter a little," he replied. "Is there any coffee ready yet? I smell something?"

Butler nodded toward a fire nearby. "I believe your son has some cooking now."

"Wonderful," Hampton said. "Let me have a tinful of coffee, then we'll go out and have a look around."

Just then the sound of bugles became clearly audible on the morning breeze. Rosser's head turned toward the distant trees. "The Yankees are blowing reveille, General," he said. The sound grew, and soon filled the northern sky. Rosser frowned. "Sounds like a lot of them getting up this morning. A whole lot."

Hampton shrugged. "'Course," he answered. "Good ten thousand of them, from what I understand. So what?"

"Is there a plan, General?" Butler asked, rubbing his hands together to warm himself.

"They don't know we're here," Hampton said. "So I'm gonna hit them hard as they come down the road. Then Lee's whole division will sweep up the road from Louisa and get on their flank. Once we've got them stunned and confused, we'll run them right back into the river."

Both men nodded. It sounded like a good plan.

Hampton swung around, stood on his feet. He saw his son, the coffee boiling—he smiled. "Got some good Yank coffee here, boys," he said. "Smells awfully good. You gentlemen care to join me?"

Both officers shook their heads no.

"Well, I won't be but a minute. Food I can do without. Coffee, never."

Hampton took the steaming cup and sipped it lovingly, feeling the heat instantly boil through his limbs like a fresh bolt of energy. His mind started to clear.

He looked north, seeing the sky beginning to brighten, the first faint trace of the oval sun dancing on the eastern horizon. The day was very cool, the ground covered with a thick, slippery dew. Odd for June, he thought. More like October.

"What do the scouts say?" Hampton asked.

Rosser pointed up the Fredericksburg Road. "The Yanks are camped up that way a couple miles," he said. "Then there's another road over yonder," he continued, pointing slightly east, "and they're up that one too. They're headed for the station here alright."

Hampton nodded, sniffed the air; he could smell the Yankee's breakfast fires on the light morning breeze. It seemed a pleasant aroma.

Rosser turned suddenly, smelling it, too. "Bacon?" he said. "I believe those damned Yankees are cooking bacon. Can you smell it, General? Oh, my! Smells delicious. I'll bet its damn *good* bacon too."

Hampton sniffed again, could smell it clearly now, even from miles away. "Oh, my yes," he said, his stomach suddenly grumbling jealously. "Well," he went on, "they'll be finished with their breakfast soon enough. Then they'll be coming down our way."

Hampton finished his coffee, set the cup down on the carpenter's table. "Let's go see what the ground looks like a mile or so out, before the Yanks get done eating." He turned, looked at them both. "Matt, you come with me. Tom, why don't you go

WINDMILL POINT

back and bring up your brigade. Let's get ready to give General Sheridan a surprise he won't forget."

Butler and Hampton found their horses and started out on the road toward Clayton's Store. But they didn't ride a half-mile before they struck trouble.

A small squadron of their skirmishers came tumbling down the road toward them at an urgent clip, horses lathered, men breathing heavily. The two generals stopped in the center of the road as the squadron approached on the fly. Hampton recognized Abner Mulligan, a captain in the 4th South Carolina Cavalry. Hampton smiled, tried to project a sense of calm. "Well now, Captain Mulligan," he said, "I'm guessing this is a fine morning for a horse race."

Mulligan smiled briefly, saluted. "Yes, if you care to race the Yankees clear back to Trevilian Station that is, General."

The squadron had been posted on a vedette line—small groups of forward sentinels—and had apparently encountered trouble.

General Butler spun around in the saddle. "What's the problem, Captain?"

"Well, sir," Mulligan went on, still puffing hard, "the Yankees are coming up right behind us. "They're in considerable force, General. We hardly had time to grab our guns, jump on our horses, and get out of there."

"Could you identify any of them?" Hampton asked.

"No, sir," Mulligan replied. "No time for that. Had to get."

Butler stared at the captain. "Were they deploying for battle?"

"No sir," Mulligan answered. "Not a lick. They were riding slow in four long columns. Plenty of 'em too. But I don't think they know we're here, or they wouldn't be riding so casual like."

Hampton clapped his hands together sharply. "Fine, then," he said. Then he whirled toward Butler. Hampton knew that Butler's brigade was armed with long-range British Enfield rifles that made them essentially mounted infantry, and, so armed, would be a match for any Union cavalry. "Matt," he said, "I want you to bring your whole brigade up and go right after whoever is coming this way. Drive straight up the road into their faces. That's what I want. Meanwhile, Rosser will serve as a temporary reserve. Now, listen here, you've got to get going. There's not much time!"

Butler snapped a salute. "Yes, sir!" he cried. Then he gave his horse the spur and went bounding back down the road toward Trevilian, small spouts of dust filling the air behind him.

Hampton's mind began narrowing on the fight that was coming. "Wade!" he called out, looking for his son.

"Sir!"

"Get down the road there," Hampton went on, pointing off to the east, "and tell Fitz Lee I want his whole division to advance up the Marquis Road toward Clayton's Store immediately. He must cover our right flank. Just like we talked about last night. Do you remember?"

"Yes, General."

"Good. Get to it, then."

Then Hampton turned and reached for another aide. "Listen, go back to the station and make sure the wagons are all pulled together. I don't want them in the way of the fighting." Hampton pointed. "There, in that small hollow just behind the tavern. Do you see?"

"Yes, sir."

"Go!"

Hampton turned, trotted slowly back toward the station, taking in the lay of the land as he moved—the hills, woods, and ridges, the open fields of fire, and the best placements for his artillery. As he trotted south, Butler's brigade was already in motion, the South Carolinians hurriedly deploying just north of the railroad tracks.

WINDMILL POINT

The one-legged Butler—a solid shot had blown his foot clean off at Brandy Station—was all business now, shouting commands as the regiments came up and dismounted. The troops began spreading out into the trees on both sides of the road. Another squadron of cavalry was sent directly out, seeking contact with the Yankees, while the wagons began to gather behind the station. Everywhere horses were bucking and braying, men leaping from their mounts, loading, laughing, cursing. Sergeants were shouting orders, artillery limbers bouncing across open fields, dust rising everywhere, spiraling, obscuring the red morning sun. Wade Hampton took it all in—the crazy, chaotic, frenzy of battle—and felt a great calm descend upon him.

Soon a small squadron of Confederate riders came racing back down the Fredericksburg Road, even faster than they had gone up, a few Yanks giving chase behind them, pistols blazing. The Yankees thought they were pursuing no more than a renegade group of militia. Then they rounded a curve at full gallop and came pounding right into the rifle sights of Butler's entire brigade. An explosion of flame and smoke poured from the trees all around the Federal riders, and when the clouds and twirls of smoke finally cleared the Yanks were all down on the road, dead, a few horses still flopping and braying in bloody agony. The battle for Trevilian Station was on.

It did not take long for Sheridan's troopers to figure out that they had tangled with far more than a few stray militia. They promptly began pouring down the road and deploying in the trees, almost within spitting distance of Hampton's men. The rattle of carbine fire grew in intensity, smoke billowing from the woods just as a wildfire leaps and grows in its fury. But Butler already had the edge, his men in position and moving forward before the Yankees had even begun to deploy, and soon the volume of fire along the entire front became deafening.

It was working. Butler was pushing the Yankees back. The Federals had been caught by surprise, and now they were beginning to give ground. Soon they would panic; Hampton was sure of it. Then they would break. Wade Hampton's jaw tightened. He looked at his watch: 5:23 in the morning. Once the Yanks regrouped he would throw in Rosser's entire brigade and stampede them again. He glanced anxiously at his watch once more and wondered *Where is Fitz Lee?*

CHAPTER THIRTY-NINE

JUNE 11TH—DAWN

CUSTER

George Custer stopped dead in his tracks... stiffened. "Quiet!" he yelled. George leaned forward just slightly and cupped a hand around his ear. He heard it clearly then, the unmistakable sound of heavy carbine fire straight down the Marquis Road. The first few splatters quickly grew into a steady rumble, and Custer knew from the volume of gunfire alone that his men camped forward on the road had somehow run into trouble where no trouble was supposed to be. Something had gone wrong. He took a deep breath, felt his heart begin to quicken.

"Lieutenant Shanahan!" Custer yelled.

The lieutenant tossed his coffee into the grass and came running. "Sir!"

"Do we have reports of Rebels in any strength nearby?" he asked, glaring down the road toward the unnerving commotion.

"No, sir. Nothing."

Custer pointed toward the sound of the gunfire. "Then get down there and find out what the *hell* is going on. Fast!" He glanced quickly at his watch: 5:41

"Yes, sir!" the lieutenant replied, but before he had taken three steps a courier on horseback came pounding up the road, jumped a small creek, and splashed to a stop in the dust near

Custer's campfire. It was a young corporal from the 7th Michigan. Everyone ran to him.

Custer grabbed hold of the horse's bridle and yanked the courier close. "What the hell is going on down there?"

The boy swallowed hard, blinked.

"Well, come on!..."

"G-General," the courier sputtered finally, gathering his thoughts, "Colonel Brewer says to tell you that we have been attacked by at least a full brigade of Rebel cavalry, sir. We have formed a line in the woods and are holding, sir. But there are a whole lot of Rebels. Colonel Brewer requests that you send support. Immediately... sir."

Custer's eyes grew wide. "A whole God damned *brigade*?" he yelled incredulously. "Who the hell is it? Does Brewer have any idea who he's fighting?"

"Yes, sir. The 1st and 2nd Virginia Cavalry, General. That's who we have identified. It's Wickham, sir."

"Wickham!" Custer cried. "Wickham's got a goddamned brigade under Fitz Lee, if my memory serves me. He spun on his heals, looked toward his aide. "Shanahan!" he yelled, "Wickham?"

"Yes, General. You're right. He's got a brigade of cavalry under Fitzhugh Lee."

Custer put his hands on his hips, then spit at the fire. "Well, damn it to hell!" he hollered. "If Wickham's here, then Fitz Lee is here, too. Does that make sense? And if Lee is here, then goddamned *Hampton* has got to be here as well." Custer tossed his hands in the air. "They're in front of us, for Christ sake. How the hell did Hampton get in *front* of us?"

"No one was out there last night, General," Shanahan replied emphatically, shaking his head. "We had pickets out."

Custer cooled down, thought for a moment. He spit again, smiled. "No, they were there."

"No, General," Shanahan said, "we—"

WINDMILL POINT

"No, they were *there*. I could almost *feel* 'em, God damn it. Last night. Out there in the darkness. I knew it!" George Custer shook his head. "Well, too late now." He slapped the courier on the leg. "Listen here," Custer said. "You get the hell down the road to where the 1st Michigan is camped. You see where I'm pointing?"

The boy wiped the sweat from his forehead with a handkerchief, then followed Custer's gesture. "Yes, sir."

"Good. You go over there and tell Colonel Stagg to form his regiment and get down the road damn quick in support of the 7th. Tell him what you just told me. Now, get!" Custer slapped the horse, and the boy galloped off. Then Custer kicked at the dirt. "Should've known! Shanahan!"

"Sir?"

"Let's get everyone up and in the saddle. Now! Then you go down the road and see what the *hell* it is we have on our hands here."

"Yes, General!" Shanahan shouted in response. Then the lieutenant turned and cupped his hands around his mouth. "Bugler, blow Boots-n-Saddles!" he bellowed. "Let's go, boys! It's Boots-n-Saddles!"

The bugles began to peal, and men began running, dousing fires, leaping toward the horses, gathering their gear. The enemy was near, and all was sudden motion. Galvanized by necessity, his Michigan brigade was on the move, and Custer could feel the great, throbbing intensity of war rise in his chest. It was a hot, exciting feeling.

By the time the brigade was mounted and ready to move out, Shanahan was back with word that Wickham had broken off the engagement and retired back down the Marquis Road.

"Is Brewer sure of this?" Custer asked. "Wickham's gone?"

"I saw it for myself," the lieutenant replied. "What does it mean, General?"

Custer sat his horse, thought for a moment. "Wickham was probing," he replied in time. "He didn't know about us any more than we knew about him. So he ran headfirst into us then backed off."

"What do we do now?" Shanahan asked nervously.

Custer smiled. "I have orders to take Trevilian Station. And that's just what I'm going to do."

"What about Hampton, General?" Shanahan asked.

Custer shrugged. "We'll find him or he'll find us, that's for damn sure. We're here to destroy his railroad, and he's here to protect it. So I imagine we'll cross one another's paths sooner or later, right?" Custer grinned, turned in the saddle. "Fifth Michigan in advance, followed by the 6th, 7th, and 1st. Those are my orders. Down the road into Trevilian Station. Let's go!"

The brigade moved out in good order, the slap, clank and jangle of sabers, saddles, and rifles a jarring reminder of war in the cool morning air. Dust soon rose over the hindquarters of the horses, dry and blinding as the cavalry moved out. Just over a mile south of Clayton's Store they struck the Nunn's Creek Road and the column turned west on the direct route into the station. Two miles beyond that, the Michigan brigade finally came upon the Gordonsville Road, no more than a mile east of Trevilian.

As the column turned toward the station the sound of heavy gunfire almost directly ahead became clearly audible. Custer quickly halted the brigade, sent out skirmishers, and ordered the construction of a line of works in the woods nearby. He rode along the edge of the woods, and was watching the men work when a courier sent from Captain Hastings of the 5th Michigan galloped up.

"General Custer!" the man called out. "Captain Hastings begs to inform you, sir, that there is a large train of Rebel wagons due east of the station. They appear entirely unguarded."

WINDMILL POINT

Custer's ears perked. "Large? How large?"

"Captain Hastings believes it is Hampton's entire train, sir. And it is almost entirely unguarded."

"Unguarded?"

"Almost entirely, sir."

Custer thought for a moment, then guessed as to what had happened. The Rebels had gone up the other road to take on Sheridan's advance and left their wagons behind unguarded. Coming in on the Nunn's Creek Road as he had, his Michigan cavalry had simply had the good fortune to ride in unnoticed and stumble upon the prize. Custer realized that to bag Wade Hampton's entire train of wagons and supplies would be a huge success, and a significant feather in his cap. He became excited.

"Go back and tell Captain Hastings to charge with his entire regiment, and take that train at once," he ordered. "There can be no delay. I will be up in a minute."

"Yes, sir," the courier replied and then galloped off.

Custer looked at Shanahan. "You see what's happened, don't you?"

The lieutenant rolled his shoulders.

"The Confederates are occupied with Sheridan's cavalry while we have come in directly behind them. Now we will take the train and create havoc for General Hampton. This is a great opportunity, but we must move very quickly if we are going to take advantage of it."

Shanahan grinned. "Yes, General."

"Let's go."

Custer gave his horse the spur, bounded forward with his staff, and, just outside of Trevilian Station came upon the 5th Michigan forming in a wide field for the charge. Over four hundred men, sabers unsheathed and held aloft, suddenly came rumbling across the field, dirt and dust flying behind them. It was an inspiring sight.

Custer stood in his stirrups as the riders raced past. "Go, you Wolverines!" he yelled, waving his hat overhead. "G-o-o-o!"

The 5th went flying passed him like a hurricane, yelling wildly as they closed on the few surprised guards near the Rebel wagons. Shots rang out, and sabers flashed in the first warming rays of the morning sun.

"Go with them, Lieutenant," Custer yelled to Shanahan, "while I send back word for the other regiments to come up!" Custer sat and watched as his Michigan boys swept through the wagons like a bolt of lighting, then began chasing the stunned Rebels across the fields beyond the train. Sabers were flashing in the sun, pistols were popping, and Custer loved every minute of it. Soon Shanahan was back, breathing hard, but grinning ear-to-ear.

"General!" he cried, trying to catch his breath. "We have taken them by complete surprise. I count over fifty wagons, forty ambulances, quite a few caissons, and I would bet at least a thousand horses. It's the jackpot, sir! It must be Hampton's entire train."

"Excellent!" Custer hollered. "Now go to Major Kidd and tell him that I want his regiment to charge in support of the 5th. I want everyone up!" Custer's eyes were bulging. "Everyone up!"

Custer rode forward into the melee around the wagons, pulled his pistol and began firing. Soon Kidd's regiment came up along the Gordonsville Road and swarmed into the fields near the railroad, too. Not far behind were the 1st and 7th Michigan regiments, and it was not long before the blue riders had the wagon train entirely in their control and began consolidating their position.

He had his prize in hand, and Custer was ecstatic. But his was but one brigade, alone behind the enemy's lines, he knew, and now entirely exposed. If he was going to hold onto his spoils he would have to be prepared to fight.

WINDMILL POINT

"I want barricades thrown up!" Custer barked as his horsemen poured down the road and into the open fields around him. "Everyone move! I want barricades everywhere. We've taken these damn Rebel wagons. Now we've got to hold them!"

CHAPTER FORTY

JUNE 11TH—EARLY MORNING

HAMPTON

Hampton was sitting his horse calmly on a knoll just north of the Netherland Tavern, watching Butler's men drive Sheridan's troops backward, when the courier arrived. He was a captain from Rosser's division, a young man with dark curls springing out from under his cap. He came on in a great rush, saddle bouncing, hair flopping, his horse in a lather. The captain's face was drawn and ashen. It was easy to see he was upset.

Hampton sensed bad news. "What?"

The man stood in his stirrups and pointed furiously down toward the station. "A message from General Rosser, sir!"

"Yes. Go on."

"The Yankees have taken our wagons, General, and are swarming out over the railroad tracks. They are *behind* us!"

Wade Hampton felt the air in his chest implode like a balloon deflating. He whirled around. "*Behind* us?!"

"Yes, sir," the courier said. "You can see for yourself, General."

Hampton yanked his horse around, could see the blue troops below him then, scurrying amongst the wagons and over the tracks, piling timbers across the roadway. It had all the markings of a disaster. Attacked now in both front and rear, for

WINDMILL POINT

all Hampton knew he might be surrounded within minutes. "Whose troops are those?" he demanded, yanking out his field glasses for a closer look.

"It's Custer's Brigade, sir."

Hampton's jaw knotted. *"Custer!"* he repeated, virtually spitting the name between his teeth like a rancid grape. It had been Custer's brigade that had inaugurated the cavalry action at Gettysburg, and it was Custer who had reportedly led the charge in which J.E.B Stuart had fallen at Yellow Tavern. Then, again, it had been Custer who had come up and barreled through his troops at Haw's Shop, and Custer's brigade that had just recently stopped the Confederate infantry advance that first day at Cold Harbor. Custer was nothing if not a thorn in the Confederacy's side. Hampton did not care for Custer, and now that same officer—that *boy* general with his oversized hat, ridiculous uniform, and silly red bandanna—had snuck into his rear and taken his wagons. Hampton's face turned red with anger, but anger, he knew, would get him nowhere. He had to act, and he had to move very quickly if he was going to avoid a calamity. The threat had to be contained. And fast!

Hampton glared at the courier. "Return to General Rosser," he insisted, "and tell him...."

The captain shook his head, pointed west along the railroad tracks.

Hampton followed his motion and could see for himself a large group of grey clad cavalry moving with dispatch along the Gordonsville Road toward Trevilian. Tom Rosser, grasping instantly the potential nightmare that Custer's unwelcome presence represented, had his entire brigade up and moving toward the critical spot. Rosser, a fine soldier, required no orders to respond. Thank God for Rosser! Wade Hampton let the air slip from between his teeth. With a full brigade on the way to contest Custer he could breathe at least a little easier.

"Okay, fine," Hampton said. "But Rosser will barely even the odds," he told the courier. "Listen, you ride down to General Butler and tell him I need his Phillips Legion and the 6th South Carolina. Tell him what has happened, and that we must respond immediately or all may be lost. He'll understand. Now go!"

"Yes, sir!"

Hampton rubbed a hand nervously through his beard, looked back toward his son. "Where is Fitz Lee?"

"I don't know."

"You delivered my orders this morning?"

"Of course."

Hampton felt the anger rise in his chest again. Custer, he knew, must have slipped between his own and Lee's divisions, and had Fitz Lee been diligent, it would never have happened. "This should never have occurred! Had Lee followed my orders, it *wouldn't* have!"

"Yes, sir."

"Alright then," Hampton went on, fighting to regain control of his emotions. "Listen, Wade, I want you to go to Colonel Waring and tell him I need the Jeff Davis Legion to change fronts and charge Custer."

"Yes, Father."

"Then get back down to Louisa Court House and find out where Lee is. But watch out, Wade. There are Yankees all over the damn place now."

"I will."

"But, wait!"

"Yes, Father?"

"If you find Lee, tell him to get his division here as fast as possible. Tell him what has happened. And look, if he comes up the Gordonsville Road now, he'll come in *behind* Custer. Do you see it? Rosser in front, Lee from behind. Then we'll have him."

"I understand, Father."

WINDMILL POINT

"Then go fast. And... Wade!" Hampton yelled as the boy turned away.

"Sir?"

"Be careful."

CHAPTER FORTY-ONE

JUNE 11TH—MID MORNING

CUSTER

Custer spotted the storm of dust rushing towards him on the Gordonsville Road west of Trevilian Station, and knew at once that his little escapade had been discovered.

"The fences!" Custer bellowed. "Quickly now!" He waved his arms and pointed. "Pull the damn fence rails down and pile them up! Quick, boys, quick!"

The men were all racing around the wagons, piling up anything they could get their hands on as barricades, heaving artillery limbers over on their sides for protection. Others were rummaging through the wagon train, or herding the Confederate prisoners into the ambulances for safekeeping, unmindful of the storm that was rapidly approaching. The whole scene was one of dust, frenzy, and confusion.

"General!" a sergeant yelled. "What should I do with all these prisoners?"

"Put them in the ambulances for the time being!" Custer yelled back.

"There's hardly any more room in those, sir! Most are already taken up, and those that are left are broken down. If I put the Rebels in at one end, they'll just tumble out the other."

"Then herd them someplace and put them under guard."

WINDMILL POINT

The man stepped forward. "I am the only guard, General," the sergeant whispered. "There ain't no one else."

Custer shrugged, had no idea what to tell the man. "Then do what you can," Custer told him. "But move them now, Sergeant. We're about to have a fight on our hands."

"Yes, General," the sergeant answered. "Alright now, boys. You all heard General Custer address the topic at hand. Now, let's us move it along nice and peaceful like."

Custer turned away, watched as his men frantically threw up hasty barricades between the wagons. They were flimsy and would provide little in the way of real protection, but it was all they had time to do. Behind him on the road his artillery rumbled to a stop and began to unlimber their guns on a small knoll—Pennington's Battery. *Thank God*, Custer thought.

He glanced west, spotted the tops of the Rebel flags as they approached on the road, then their hats, and finally their horse's hooves as they came pounding along through the dirt. He could tell from the flags snapping at the head of the column that it was Tom Rosser's brigade—the Laurels, they were called—and Custer knew them to be some of the finest horse soldiers in the Rebel army. He and Rosser had been good friends at West Point, but Custer doubted that their friendship would earn him any sympathy today. The Laurels would come at him with everything they had.

"Cavalry!" Custer yelled, pointing up the road as some of his men ran for their horses. Others slipped behind the barricades and quickly loaded their carbines. Knives were pulled from belts, swords unsheathed, pistols quickly loaded. It was all happening too fast to control.

A lieutenant ran past him on the fly, saber in hand. "Get ready, boys!"

The Laurels filed from the road across the open field opposite the wagons and quickly deployed in two long lines. There they stopped and pulled their sabers. Suddenly both lines lurched forward as one, the thunder of almost a thousand horses bearing down on the wagons booming in the air: terrible, beautiful, deafening. Dirt was flying, swords glinting in the sun, riders screaming.

For a moment Custer froze, dazzled by the sheer power of the scene, carried away by the almost irresistible force of the spectacle approaching him. Then he pulled out his revolver and aimed. "Come on, you bastards," he said under his breath. Custer sighted down the barrel of his pistol. "Ready!" he screamed.

All along the Michigan line carbines and pistols were raised and steadied, the metallic clack of hundreds of hammers being cocked suddenly audible around the wagons.

The Laurels were hurtling across the clearing now, riding low in the saddle, hats bouncing behind, hair flying, no more than 100 yards distant.

Custer closed one eye, took a calm, steady breath. "Aim!"

Now they were almost on top of the wagons, coats flapping, sweat flying, and he swore they were so close he could almost read the letters on their belt buckles. *Now*, he thought, and he yelled with all his might: "*Fire!*"

A blast ripped across the length of the wagons, hot and focused, smoke lofting back up and over the canvas tops. Custer pulled the trigger again... again... and emptied his revolver into the closing mass of horses and men.

Some of the Laurels flew backwards, falling with dreadful thumps in the dirt. Others toppled sideways, grabbing their heads or chests, blood spraying in the air. Horses reared, screaming in agony, or pitched headfirst into the dirt, sending their riders sailing forward face-first like a child's doll, limbs smashed and broken by the fall. Horses kicked and writhed on the bloody ground. Many of the men who had been unhorsed were simply trampled in the violent storm of hooves that followed.

WINDMILL POINT

But the volley had not even dented the Laurel's momentum, and the Rebel cavalry churned over the last few yards and struck Custer's Michigan brigade from end to end like a furious, grey tidal wave. They smashed through his barricades or jumped the artillery limbers, burst beyond the wagons, blew gaps everywhere in his thin, blue line. Custer's men were knocked backwards, sent tumbling, or slashed with swords as the Rebels leaped the barricades and bounded past the wagons. In only seconds his defensive line had been all but disintegrated.

A portion of the 5th Michigan—now mounted, with sabers whirling—countercharged and struck the Rebels just beyond the wagons, but they were much too little and far too late. Like a great, furious barroom brawl, the fighting rapidly devolved into a hundred separate engagements. Riders swirled in groups of two, ten or twenty, slashing, kicking, punching, firing their pistols at point blank range. Troopers on the ground ducked for cover and emptied their carbines into the freewheeling charge, darting between the wagons, frantically trying to reload. Men from both sides were cut off, shot down, taken prisoner. It was a wild, ungoverned melee.

Custer stood in his stirrups, jamming a few bullets back into his Colt as the Laurels swarmed around him like an irate swarm of bees. As a rampaging Rebel closed to within twelve feet with his sword raised high overhead, Custer shot him in the face and watched as he flew backwards off his horse. Then he fired twice more, knocking one man from his saddle, then missing the second, before being overrun by a dozen riders. He spurred his horse straight toward them, punched the closest Rebel in the face, then bolted through the remainder as their momentum carried them away.

The sheer power of the Confederate charge had jarred the Michigan defenders away from the wagons, and in the open fields they had to scramble to maintain any sort of defensive cohesion. The brigade fell back and seemed to congeal almost naturally along the slope below Pennington's Battery, where the guns had been spun around and were now spitting double charges of canister at the charging Confederates. The artillery quickly blasted the heat out of Rosser's charge, and the grey cavalry began to slowly fade back through the wagons.

Custer raced back to the improvised line across a blasted field of dead and wounded men. Horses—riderless now, many in a frenzy—ran wild, as a few small pools of combatants still swirled around the wagons, struggling with pistols and swords, the "pop! pop! pop!" of revolvers rising above the wagons. Once under cover of the battery, he dismounted and desperately began repairing his patchwork line. Custer grabbed men as they scurried back across the field, or pulled them from the woods, tossing them all into position. Gradually the blue line began to solidify.

Pennington's guns continued to blaze away from above, and Custer was just starting to feel a small measure of relief when Shanahan came bounding through the parked limbers and grabbed him by the arm. The lieutenant whirled and pointed furiously toward the east. "Behind us, General!" he screamed.

Custer turned and spotted them at once. Coming up the road from Louisa Court House—and already deploying in the fields and woods off to the south and east—was the vanguard of what appeared to be a substantial contingent of Confederate cavalry. Yes, it was Fitz Lee's entire division. The first brigade of Rebel horsemen was already in line off to the south, and before Custer could even shout a single order they commenced a wild charge at the full gallop, aimed directly at his exposed left flank.

A few of his men spotted the approaching cavalry before they struck and tried frantically to form a new line. But the advancing Rebels swept up and over them before Custer could even hope to change fronts to meet this new attack, sweeping up and over his line before washing out amongst those few

WINDMILL POINT

wagons his boys had managed to make off with, then thundering up the hill into Pennington's guns. There the artillerymen met them face-to-face with pistols, trail spikes, swords, and ram staffs, unhorsing several of the Rebels before finally beating back the rest. Custer reloaded his pistol and fired and fired and fired, the uncomfortable thought forming in the back of his mind that perhaps this morning he had bitten off far more than he could chew.

As the Confederate riders retreated downhill, Alexander Pennington had two of his pieces quickly brought around, rammed full with canister, then fired directly into the backs of the fleeing horsemen. When the smoke cleared the riders were gone, their horses, ripped to bloody tatters, lay like smoking lumps on the blackened earth.

Yet so fierce was the Rebel charge that they had swept entirely through his position, making off with Custer's own wagons. His headquarters matériel and personal effects were now in the hands of the enemy. Johnny Cisco and Eliza had been gobbled up in the frenzy, but there was no time to look for them now. A badly wounded trooper staggered up to Custer and requested permission to go to the rear.

"Yes, yes, of course," Custer cried, then turned and looked at the man for a moment. "Wait a second," he said. "Where the hell is the *rear*?" There was no front and there was no rear. There was only pandemonium. Custer reloaded his pistol, then walked calmly out in front of his men. "Right here!" he yelled, pointing to where he wanted a new line formed. "Form on me! Now!"

Staggering and exhausted—many already dazed by the ferocity of the Rebel onslaughts—his men began slowly falling into line, forming a new position along the base of the small knoll. Here there was no cover to speak of, so the men went into line on one knee, or on their stomachs, loading in frenzied preparation for the next Confederate advance. The artillery pieces above them were still active, and had free range in every direction, so, for the time being at least, the Rebels maintained their distance. But there was little doubt they would attack again soon. Fortunately, packed in below the guns as they were, if his ammunition held, Custer knew his position would be a tough one to break. That was the good news.

In the brief lull that ensued, George Armstrong Custer walked to the top of the knoll and stood with Pennington between the guns. He pulled out his field glasses, and had a long look in every direction. What he observed did not appear promising. Here, surely, was the bad news.

Custer watched as the horizon at every point on the compass slowly filled with the swirling dust and flapping battle flags of Confederate cavalry. He had come looking for a fight, but he had not come looking for *this*. Fitz Lee's entire division now filled the fields and wood lots to the east, while Rosser—now obviously reinforced by many fresh regiments—still faced him from the west. He was outmanned and outgunned by a margin of perhaps 5 to 1, and slowly the enemy's lines were closing as more horsemen poured from the roads into the fields and woods around him.

Custer realized then the mistake he had made. In the excitement of the moment he had assumed that dame fortune had delivered him from the mouth of Nunn's Creek Road far into Hampton's rear; the wagons were there unguarded, after all, and a lovely prize for his taking. But he had been wrong. He had not rushed his brigade into the rear of the Confederate column at all, but rather into what had now become its center, and the Rebels—angry and fully alarmed—were now closing like riled hornets from every quarter.

George Custer took a long, deep breath then let it out slowly. He had gotten his brigade into one hell of a mess. Rebel riders were now everywhere around him. The boy general was surrounded.

CHAPTER FORTY-TWO

JUNE 11TH—NOON

CUSTER

He was now on one knee in line with his men, breathing hard, near exhaustion. He flipped open the Colt and stuffed in the few rounds he had managed to scavenge off a dead officer nearby. The sun was high overhead in a clear blue sky, the day warming uncomfortably. George Custer wiped the sweat from his face.

He had just survived three of the most intense hours of fighting he had ever experienced, and the contest, he knew, was still far from over. Six times the Rebels had rushed his lines, and six times his Michigan brigade had managed to beat them off, but the toll had been heavy, and each time the issue had been very close. From all directions and every conceivable angle, they had come thundering on horseback, swords flashing and pistols blazing, jumping his lines and wreaking havoc amongst his guns and wagons. They had pounded every inch of his position until his lines—if they could even be called lines anymore—were curled back on one another in a tight circle. The cannons on the knoll above—although they were only a few yards apart—were firing in opposite directions. But it made no difference where they aimed or looked; the Rebels were everywhere.

Custer's boys had fought desperately all morning, loading and firing as fast as soldiers could load and fire, until many of the guns were jammed from filth or were simply too hot to handle. Yet no amount of exertion seemed to matter. Every attack they repulsed simply summoned another. Now many of his men were dead, wounded, or missing. Ammunition was running low. An hour ago the situation had been critical. Now it was desperate.

Custer flipped the pistol chamber closed, looked down the line, patted the trooper next to him on the back. "Nice job," he said, offering a smile.

The man nodded, but he looked worn. "The bastards just keep coming at us, General."

"It's good target practice," Custer joked.

"Long as we got bullets to fire, it is. But I ain't got but eight more rounds."

Custer looked away, said nothing.

All morning he had ridden along the thinning blue line, shooting, screaming, offering encouragement to his men. Twice he had been struck by spent balls, one of them knocking him flat on his back. There he lay for a few minutes staring into the blue sky, stunned. But soon he was back on his feet, pistol in hand, cursing loudly again. In the heat of the incredible, swirling fight, he had no other choice. Custer could only fight, and pray that Torbert or Sheridan would hear the sound of his struggle and rush to his assistance. He knew he could not continue to fend the Confederates off forever. Without help, his lines would not last much longer. He looked at his watch: 12:09.

Suddenly a fresh regiment of Rebels came bounding at his men again, horses snorting, pistols cracking. His men turned and began to return fire, but the riders were headed straight for Pennington's artillery, and they went flying through his lines. They stampeded up the short knoll, determined to make off with at least one section of the guns. Along the top of the hill there was yet another furious fight with the gunners, swords flashing in the sun, pistols and carbines popping as smoke filled the air. A number of the artillerymen were cut down, and a single gun left abandoned. This time the Rebels were able to grab hold of the cannon, and begin hauling it off toward their own lines. Custer became enraged.

Pennington leaped on his horse, then galloped down the hill to where Custer was watching. He pointed back toward his battery, above. "General!" he cried. "They've taken one of my guns!"

"No!" Custer responded. "I'll be damned if they'll get away with that! Let's go!"

Custer grabbed the nearest twenty or thirty men, and, with Alexander Pennington leading the way, they all let out a wild "hurrah!" and charged the Rebels, who were still manhandling the gun on the far side of the knoll. But Custer's small band was considerably outnumbered, and the Rebels stopped them with a well-directed volley before they'd gone ten paces. He realized then that it would require more than a few men and a wild cheer to retake the prize.

So he ran back, ordered up a full company from the 7th Michigan, most of his staff, and all the horse holders from the rear that he could locate. Formed into a rough mob, they started out after the gun again, and descended on the Confederates like true Wolverines, screaming as they ran, sabers swirling overhead. Others were on horseback, making headfirst for the Confederate riders. Custer, running right behind Pennington, knocked two men aside with swipes of his sword, then shot a third. A wild fight broke out around the captured piece: horses braying, pistols popping, swords cracking heads. When it was over, more Rebels than Yanks lay dead on the ground, and the rest of the Johnnies were running.

Custer got off one last good shot at the fleeing Rebels, then grabbed hold of the gun by the wheel. "Let's roll it back, boys!" he screamed.

They all heaved, and the artillery piece started moving backward. Custer stepped aside, watched with pleasure as the recovered piece began rolling back toward its rightful place on the knoll. He had never seen Pennington happier. Then Custer took a deep breath, and almost collapsed; he had never felt more weary in his life than he did at that moment.

But there was no time for rest. Custer looked around quickly to check on the men who had gone down. Then he spotted Mitchell Beloir, his color bearer, riding slowly toward him, blood covering his shirt. Custer's heart sank. He ran to the sergeant, grabbed his horse by the bridle and yanked him close. "You will be fine, Sergeant," he insisted, pulling the canteen from the man's side and offering him a drink.

Beloir leaned forward, eyes glassy. His hands were covered in blood. "No, General," he whispered. "They have killed me. Please, take the flag!"

"You will be fine!" Custer insisted again.

"No, General," the sergeant repeated. "Take the flag now, or the damned Rebs will get it. I cannot have that! You know I cannot have *that*!"

Custer took the flagstaff, ripped the colors from the pole. Then he stuffed the flag inside his shirt for safekeeping. There was no time for anything else. Beloir slipped, toppled from the horse and lay prostrate in the dirt at his feet.

"Surgeon!" Custer yelled. But there were no surgeons available. So Custer reached down, picked the man up, and threw him over his shoulder.

Two troopers came running. "We'll take him for you, General!" one of them cried.

"No!" Custer exclaimed. "I've got him now. Just cover us. Let's get the hell out of here."

WINDMILL POINT

"We got ya, General!"

He carried Beloir back inside the lines, up the knoll, then laid him down carefully near the guns. It was all he could do. He left instructions for someone to give him water, then rushed off once again. There was no time to rest, no time to worry, no time to think. The Rebels had already reformed and were charging again from two different directions.

"They're coming!" Custer shouted. He jumped on his horse and rode down to the base of the knoll. There he dismounted, yanked the pistol from his side again, and began firing, immediately taking down the lead rider with two well-placed shots. Spent cartridges littered the ground at his feet, and the crack of carbine fire soon rolled up and down the line like a string of firecrackers. Smoke billowed back and burned his eyes. Custer reloaded, fired again. Ten, twenty riders went down in a jumble, and this time the Rebels didn't get so close, their horses tumbling headfirst over one another some fifty yards out. The charge had been shredded in an avalanche of small arms fire, and then it faded away.

"Thank God," Custer said under his breath, feeling around in his side pocket for more ammunition, but now the pocket was empty.

As the dust from the Rebel riders filtered aloft, he turned and listened for the sound of approaching bugles or cavalry from the north, but heard nothing. *Where is Torbert?* he wondered. *Surely the rest of them heard the booming sound of this fight.* Custer yanked the watch from his pocket and had another look: 12:51. He had to have more men and ammunition if the brigade was going to survive, and he had to have them soon. One or two more furious charges by the enemy like the last few, and his thin line would simply melt away.

He went through all of his pockets, but he was entirely out of ammunition. Just inside his lines he found the body of a Rebel officer. He rifled the man's pockets and located a few extra rounds. Custer quickly reloaded, then dropped the remaining bullets into his side pocket. When he looked up he spotted Dana riding toward him, and his heart almost exploded.

"For God's sake, Dana!" Custer cried, leaping to his feet. "Tell Torbert to send me some men! I have saved Pennington's guns, but I've lost my teams and ambulances."

Amasa Dana was a captain in the 8th Illinois Cavalry, who now served as Torbert's assistant adjutant general. He was the first man Custer had seen all morning from outside his own brigade. Never had he been so happy to see anyone before in his life.

Dana looked him over, and an expression of shock crossed his face. "Are you alright, General?"

"Yes, yes, I'm fine," Custer replied. "But my brigade has been badly cut up. We're in one hell of a tight spot here, Dana. Where the hell is everybody else?"

"We've been sending out riders all morning long, but none has been able to get through," Dana explained. "I myself saw Williams and Bean try earlier, but they were run off by Rebel cavalry."

"Can you get back to Torbert?"

"Yes, I think so." Dana pointed back toward Pennington's battery. "I came through the woods just beyond the guns. There were no Rebels in the vicinity. At least not when I came through."

"Good."

Dana took a long look around for himself, saw Custer's almost circular battle line, the dead and wounded cluttering the bottom of the knoll, the Rebels circling like Comanches. He gave his cap a yank. "Well," he said, "I believe I've seen enough now. I'll get back and tell General Torbert at once. But frankly, it was my impression that Merritt had every intention of

WINDMILL POINT

breaking through to you with his entire brigade... orders or none. They were mounting when I left."

"Merritt?" Custer asked, referring to his chief rival in the cavalry corps. "Well, if Wesley Merritt is game enough to make the run to save us, you tell him I will surely owe him one."

Dana saluted. "I will do that, General."

"Thank you, Dana," Custer told him.

The captain smiled, trying, it appeared, to project a sense of assurance. "Is there anything else you would like me to tell General Torbert?"

"Yes," Custer said, rubbing the sweat, blood, and grime from his face with the back of his sleeve. "Hurry."

CHAPTER FORTY-THREE

JUNE 11TH—AFTERNOON

HAMPTON

Wade Hampton pulled the field glasses from his eyes, shook his head slowly, and frowned. For hours he had been forced to fight in both front and rear with a foe that significantly outnumbered him. He knew that that could not go on forever. Up on the Fredericksburg Road Butler's Brigade was holding its own against Sheridan's main column, but it appeared from Hampton's observations that almost three fresh brigades of Yankee cavalry were now deploying in the woods bordering the road. It was obvious that once they started forward, Butler would not be able to stop them.

Hampton had sent much of his force to the rear to cut off and then overwhelm Custer's impetuous strike at his wagons, and while for almost four hours his troops had mauled the boy general's brigade on the knoll beyond the tracks, they had not been able to destroy it. Hampton watched through his glasses as wave upon wave of Confederate riders swarmed Custer's position, only to eventually be repulsed. The boy general with the cartoonish uniform—easily identifiable to Hampton, even from a distance—had fought well. Out in front of his troops for much of the morning, Custer had fended off everything they had thrown at him, and now, for Hampton, the situation was becoming precarious. If Custer's brigade was not overwhelmed

WINDMILL POINT

soon, Hampton knew that Sheridan might break through Butler's weakened line up north, then come crashing down on both Rosser and Fitz Lee near the station in rapid succession. If he was not careful, what had begun that morning as an attempt to annihilate Sheridan's entire column, might rapidly turn into the rout and destruction of his own.

Outnumbered as the Southern troops were, their only possible chance of success lay in a coordinated and concentrated effort—exactly what he had originally planned. Yet now they were spread out all over the countryside, inviting the grim possibility that—should Custer hold on indefinitely as a thorn to their rear, and the Yankees come pouring down the road from the north—the distance between his individual units would only grow larger. That was nothing if not a prescription for disaster, and a possibility he had to avoid.

Hampton's plan for the morning assault was already a shambles, so it was time to think of something new—so much for good plans. He had sent his son off to Butler with orders to begin a withdrawal, but Butler replied that the numbers deployed against him were so great that he could no more withdraw than he could stay and fight. Butler knew he could not hold on forever, yet he dared not let go—he was, so to speak, holding the wolf by its ears.

So they agreed that Butler would withdraw by sections: a fighting retreat, and one of the most difficult things to manage in warfare. But there seemed no other choice. Once Butler fought his way back to the railroad, Hampton would endeavor to link all his separate brigades into a concentrated line where they could stand and fight as one.

He put the glasses to his eyes again, turned and scanned the area behind the tracks for a strong position he might fall back upon. He saw something interesting off to the west, on the south side of the railroad. Then, out of the corner of one eye, he spotted a column of blue riders where none should have been.

It was a disturbing sight. He called to his son and pointed. "Wade, do you see that column yonder?"

His son pulled a pair of field glasses from the case at his side, and had a look for himself. "Yes, sir. It is Federal cavalry."

Hampton sighed. "More Federal cavalry headed behind us?"

"Yes, sir. It appears that way."

"Who is it?" Hampton asked. "Can you tell?"

His son took another look through his glasses. "I see the flags of the 1st, 2nd, and 5th U.S. Cavalry, General. That would be Merritt's brigade."

They watched together as Merritt's column clashed briefly with a few of Rosser's troops, then turned and dashed off to Custer's relief on the knoll, a full cloud of dust roiling up over the tracks behind them. Now there were two crack brigades behind his lines, and if he could not move one, the chances of moving two were surely hopeless. Hampton grasped the implications immediately, then had to fight off an initial sense of panic. Wade Hampton took a deep breath and forced himself to relax.

"Okay," he said, turning toward his son again. "Go to Rosser and Fitz Lee and tell them I have ordered Butler's withdrawal from the Fredericksburg Road. We will all concentrate south of the tracks, so Lee must seek and hold Rosser's right flank. That is imperative. We cannot allow ourselves to be divided. I want them to wait until Butler has successfully fought his way back to the tracks. Then we will all move back together to that ridge beyond the station." He pointed. "Do you see the ridge yonder?"

His son followed his motion west. "Yes, sir. I see it."

"Good. And Wade..."

"Yes?"

"We have not destroyed Sheridan today. But we can still stop him."

His son smiled. "Yes, General."

WINDMILL POINT

Hampton looked up the Fredericksburg Road as his son rode off, and saw battle smoke rising furiously above the trees. The fight along Butler's front was intensifying. The steady boom of Federal artillery added a thumping chorus to the scene, and it was a tune Hampton did not care to hear. Here and there he saw small eddies of blue troops already snaking south through the wood lots near the road, a sure sign that Butler's front was beginning to crumble. Soldiers in blue were suddenly everywhere. The situation was rapidly deteriorating.

Suddenly the shrill howl of an artillery shell wailed high overhead, then exploded with a horrendous crack less than a hundred feet behind him. Then another whistled almost directly over his head and detonated even closer, shards of metal hissing and spinning in the grass nearby. His horse moved uneasily under him, and Hampton stroked the animal's side, trying to soothe and steady him. "Easy...easy, boy."

When he looked up he saw blue soldiers streaming through the woods all across his front like water gushing through a rotten rain barrel. On a hill near the roadway, one of his batteries—Hart's, it appeared from a distance—was now in danger of being overrun. The guns had been screening Butler's withdrawal, but now they appeared entirely exposed. If he had any hope of prevailing against Sheridan, Hampton knew he could not afford to lose even a single piece of artillery. There was no time to waste.

Wade Hampton gave his horse the spur and bounded downhill on the fly. He pulled up near the first available troops he encountered. They were the 5th South Carolina, just back from the front, and Hampton ordered them to dismount at once and go to the defense of the guns. The men were all weary from a long morning's fight, but dismounted and deployed as he asked without a single complaint or grumble. Then Hampton turned and dashed off in search of more help. On a hill nearby he found Major Tom Ferguson leading a small group of dismounted cavalry across the field.

He yanked his horse to a stop and pointed toward the guns. "What troops are these?" he asked. "I need men to defend that battery deployed yonder!"

The major saluted stiffly, took a quick look out toward the artillery, then pointed. "I have only these, General.... Every other company of mine is already engaged."

Hampton nodded. "Yes, fine then. Who is this?"

"They are Company F, 6th South Carolina, General... The Cadet Rangers."

Hampton glanced quickly at the small group of soldiers. They were nothing more than boys, recently arrived cadets from The Citadel in Charleston. He lowered his head for a moment, did not want to lead boys to their deaths, but he knew there was no time to lose. If they did not hold the guns, many more men would die that afternoon. "Where are their horses?" he asked.

"Not far behind, General."

"Bring them up quickly," Hampton ordered.

The horse holders were summoned, and soon the young men were mounted again.

"Deploy the cadets, Major!" Hampton ordered, his stomach twisting in a tight knot. But he would not simply order them forward. The folks in Charleston might never forgive him if he were to do that. So he politely asked the major to step aside. "I will lead the cadets myself, Major. I will ask nothing of them I will not do myself."

In a moment the cadets were aligned for battle, swords unsheathed at their sides, young eyes gleaming at him—some hopeful, some fearful.

"General Hampton," Ferguson asked. "Might I have the honor to at least ride at your side, sir?"

Hampton bowed. "Of course, Major. I would be honored."

WINDMILL POINT

Wade Hampton trotted out in front of the cadets, smiled at the line of boys, then pulled the saber from his side. He pointed toward the detachment of Federal cavalry on the Fredericksburg Road making hurriedly for Hart's battery.

"Gentlemen," he said, "today we will charge those Yankees, and secure the area so that our gunners might withdraw unmolested. Our artillery must not fall into the enemy's hands. Not today! Does everyone understand?"

The cadets stared at him gamely.

"Very well, then ... for South Carolina, gentlemen." He raised his sword, then whipped it violently forward. "*Charge!*"

The small group of riders bolted straight down the road as one, flags flapping, the Rebel yell echoing riotously in the air as they galloped. They struck the Federal cavalry head on, horse against horse, saber-to-saber, pistols blasting away. Hampton slashed one of the lead Yanks with his sword, then turned and knocked another out of his saddle with a single punch. The cadets heaved into the Yanks like veterans, and for four or five minutes a wild donnybrook swirled both around and through the battery of guns. The Yankees—if not outnumbered, then surely outfought—finally turned and headed back up the road. They had had enough. For the moment, at least, the guns were safe.

"Limber-up and get them out of here!" Hampton yelled, and in short order the crews had the guns on the move.

For the rest of the long afternoon Wade Hampton rode his lines tirelessly, moving regiments, redeploying artillery, filling gaps wherever necessary. Sheridan's men continued pouring down the road from Fredericksburg in strength. But Butler was at least able to dull their approach enough to keep them from overrunning his ragged and ever changing line as he fought his way back across the tracks. Then Hampton grudgingly withdrew to the ridges south of the station. No, he had not destroyed Sheridan, but he had at least saved his command to fight another day.

By nightfall, Wade had skillfully shifted his division into a strong blocking position on a good ridge adjacent the road to Gordonsville, two miles or so west of Trevilian Station. If Sheridan had it in his mind to march toward Gordonsville and then on into the Shenandoah Valley, he would have to first fight his way through Hampton's entire division.

Once deployed, they set about preparing the new position against a probable Federal assault come morning, piling fence rails and logs across the entire front. Hampton's division had suffered terribly. He had lost three regimental commanders in the day's fighting, a good many men, and he had just received word that Rosser had been badly wounded and removed from the field late in the afternoon. Hampton's cavalry had been hard hit, pushed back severely, but he had no intention of relinquishing the field. Not only would he not leave, but he was determined not even to budge.

After looking after the wounded, Wade Hampton established his headquarters behind the lines, and finally had a chance to sit down and rest for the first time all day. His son had a fire crackling, ham and bacon frying in a pan, and a pot of coffee sitting on a warm stone nearby. Hampton helped himself to a cup of coffee and sat on a log near the fire. They ate quietly, had little to say, exhaustion dulling their tongues.

Finally his son, dirty and clearly exhausted, looked up and across the fire at him. "What, may I ask, do you intend to do in the morning, Father?"

Wade Hampton took a short sip of coffee, swallowed a piece of bacon whole, then smiled. "Well, Wade," he said, "I propose to fight."

CHAPTER FORTY-FOUR

JUNE 11ᵀᴴ—EVENING

CUSTER

George Armstrong Custer walked slowly back through the dust near Trevilian Station, dragging one leg after the other, as bone weary as he had ever been in his life. Now the light was failing, the wounded crying for help, and for all of his tired troops—except for what little food the men carried with them—there would be nothing that night to eat. Some of the Yankee troops were already busy tearing up the railroad tracks, but for the time being, at least, his men were not involved.

Custer's Michigan brigade had fought like demons late into the long afternoon shadows until Sheridan's main column had finally arrived in strength. Only then did the Rebels eventually fade away, but they did not fade far, and everyone was confident that, come morning, the fighting would resume again. Now those few wounded who could be reached were being loaded into the ambulances or worked on by surgeons, while the dead had been left out in the fields for the buzzards.

Custer walked along the tracks past the Netherland Tavern, then back to the small knoll where they had made their stand earlier that day. He had pushed some pickets out that evening and discovered that Fitz Lee's division had moved south down the road a mile or so, while Merritt's brigade had reconnoitered west and finally located Hampton on a ridge overlooking the

Gordonsville Road. Merritt had gone into bivouac there, expecting to advance on the Rebels come morning, but Custer's brigade—worn and shot to pieces—remained more or less where it had struggled all day. Many of his men were curled up now, right where they had fought, asleep on their guns, exhausted.

On the hill by the artillery a small fire was burning, and Custer was drawn to the warmth just as a moth is drawn to the flame. Around the fire his staff and many of the artillerymen sat in weary silence, several bottles of confiscated applejack passing between them. The applejack smelled sweet and hot, but Custer had long ago forgone all forms of alcohol, at Libbie's behest. Several men nodded as he approached. Custer nodded back, and a spot was opened for him near Pennington. He slumped down tiredly, a few feet from the crackling logs. The heat felt good on his face.

"Hell of a fight today," Custer said finally. A few men nodded, but no one answered, and he decided to let the thing drop.

In the west the sky had darkened considerably, and the wind was picking up. The temperature had dropped and the smell of rain was distinct on the breeze. Men pulled their collars tight around their necks and edged closer to the fire. Custer leaned back on one elbow, thought of nothing, did little more than watch the flames flicker and glow. His mind was a blank. Tomorrow he would worry about the rest.

Suddenly there was a disturbance down along the line, much talking, some laughter, then Shanahan came bounding up through the guns and suddenly loomed above the fire. "General," he said excitedly, eyes oddly asparkle, "you'll never guess who just came in through the picket line."

Custer looked up, mind too weary to speculate. He blinked.

"Eliza! Eliza's back, General!"

WINDMILL POINT

Custer sat bolt upright. Alexander Pennington leaped to his feet as if shot from a gun. "What?" Custer cried. "Where?"

Shanahan pointed. "The boys are bringing her up now," he replied.

"Oh please let me sit by that warm far!" they heard her say, and Custer grabbed her up as she came past the last gun and merrily swirled her around.

"Eliza!" he howled, laughing wildly as he put her back gently on the ground.

She gave the boy general a big hug then took a step back. "Eliza ain't goin' off to no slavery with no Rebel soldiers," she said emphatically. "No! No!"

"What happened?" Pennington asked, grinning ear to ear as she stepped into the light by the fire.

"Well they's gobbled me an' Johnny up when they's come scrambling through the wagons," she said, eyes aglow. "Took us back to the Rebel camp, but they's just told me to stay close to some trees, and when they weren't looking no more, I slipped off and just kept a going."

"Splendid, Eliza!" Pennington said. "Splendid!"

She found a place by the fire and sat, held her hands up to the warmth. They all crowded around her. "Then when the guns stop banging," she continued, "I made my way through the woods back to the pickets."

"You're lucky you didn't get shot," Custer observed. "The damned Rebels aren't far off at all, Eliza. Pickets got to be very touchy tonight."

"You tell me, General George!" she said. "I was scairt of that, but when I seen a boy in blue I just called out, 'Billy, dis here's Eliza, da Queen of Sheba'—and he knew right off who I was alright. The rest was simple."

Custer laughed. "Well, I am glad to see you, Eliza," he said. "What about Johnny?"

She shook her head. "Don't know nothing about Johnny. He was alright, though, the last I seen him, that is."

"Johnny can watch out for himself," Pennington observed. "I think he'll be alright."

"Well," Custer said with a weak smile, "I'd like to say we have some food to offer you, but the Rebels ran off with everything."

"I know that," Eliza replied. "Seen the wagons in their camp. But that's okay," she continued, "I'll scrounge something up by breakfast. You wait and see."

Custer smiled, feeling better. "That would be great," he said. "Whatever you can manage; I'm just glad you got away."

Eliza remained by the fire for an hour or so, then slipped away into the darkness. She would make her way through the other divisions and scare up whatever she could. By dawn there would probably be a fine breakfast cooking nearby. So Custer curled up on his side and pulled his hat down over his eyes. He was very tired, but the sound of guns still rattled in his ears, and he fancied it would be difficult to sleep. Today he had made a mistake—perhaps, even, a bad mistake—but mistakes were simply a part of war. In the end he had been lucky, he knew, but then, he had always been lucky. So he didn't fret about the mistake. Tomorrow, he was confident, his luck would hold.

Just after midnight the rains came tumbling over the Blue Ridge, hard and steady, drenching everyone in the fields, blue and grey alike. The cold rain made for a long, miserable night, but it didn't bother Custer at all. Far more exhausted than even he knew, George Custer slept soundly under a blanket by the fire until the first scattered rays of light blossomed on the eastern slope of the mountain. Then he and what remained of his battered brigade stirred to fight again.

CHAPTER FORTY-FIVE

JUNE 11TH—LATE EVENING

ALEXANDER

Alexander crawled on his hands and knees through the Cold Harbor trenches, checking once more on the condition and positions of his guns. He was working his way through Cabell's battery, making sure all the pieces had been properly double-shotted in case Grant attacked again in the morning. While that possibility seemed to be becoming less and less likely with every passing sunrise, Alexander would leave nothing to chance. Some things in war could not be controlled, while others could. Alexander had decided long ago to consistently see to the ones he could, and do his best with those he couldn't. There, along Cabell's line, he found a gun whose wheels had been so shot up by the day's sharpshooting that he decided—even at that late hour—to have it pulled out of line and refitted. Who, after all, was to say which piece might fire the most important shot of the day?

So he sat in the back of the trench and watched as the artillerymen fixed ropes to the gun's trail, and began pulling it rearward to a position where it could be safely refitted. There the combined light of several lanterns quivered against the uneven sides of the works, casting an odd, flickering glow. Alexander was worn, tired, and sick of the trenches. "That's right," Alexander said. "Fetch the wheels from the rear of the caissons, and, if those aren't adequate, you will find more in the artillery reserve."

"Yes, General."

The day had been clear and hot, a glaring sun arching high and relentless as it crawled like a burning coal over the snaking labyrinth of trenches, gullies, and works that had become Cold Harbor. For most of that day there had been no relief from the heat, and the men simply baked away in the dirt like eggs on the skillet, hour upon unforgiving hour. Heat, tedium, dirt, and sudden death had become for both armies the common and daily itinerary. Alexander had fought for four long years, but only at Cold Harbor had death and boredom become synonymous. He pulled the canteen from his side, uncorked it carefully, and took a gulp.

Of Sheridan and Hampton nothing had been heard since the Confederate cavalry had departed days before, and across the way the entire Yankee army appeared content to remain in their trenches for all eternity. Nothing had changed, and nothing, it seemed to Alexander, was ever going to change again. Indeed, it seemed to him then that this barren God-forsaken landscape was what he would be required to endure until the end of all time. What, he wondered, had he done to deserve such a fate?

Then an odd thought struck him. Had there really ever been anything else? Had he really experienced a life *before* Cold Harbor, or were all those jumbled memories nothing more than self-serving fantasy, the insubstantial fluff of a war-weary mind? He tried hard to recall his wife's face then, but finally gave up trying. Edward Porter Alexander had been so long in the trenches that his brain seemed now entirely baked and virtually useless, but then of what use was a brain in such a place anyway? Yet he could recall her name, and he could recall his home, so surely that stood for something. Yes, they were real after all, although he despaired of ever seeing them again.

"These wheels, General?"

WINDMILL POINT

"Yes, those will do,"

So they worked at the wheels, prying and wrenching, and they finally came off with some elbow grease and a few hard tugs. The new wheels were fitted firmly into place, and the bracing removed from under the axles. That accomplished, the mouth of the gun was depressed for just a moment, and a flurry of spent bullets tumbled from the bore. Alexander sat bolt upright, amazed by the sheer number of balls that had come tumbling out.

"Count them!" he cried, astonished.

Since each gun was cleaned and double-shotted every evening, it was apparent that any balls that fell from the barrel would have to have been shot fresh on that day alone. Of course, no one was actually shooting at the mouth of the gun. The bullets inside the tube did not represent hits, but rather *misses*. In that sense, Alexander thought, the balls would clearly represent the volume of sharpshooting that had taken place throughout the day, a sort of macabre index of the level of violence that hummed just above their heads at Cold Harbor.

"How many?" Alexander asked as the last few were counted.

"Thirty-seven, General."

"Thirty-seven," Alexander repeated, almost in shock. "From one gun?"

"That's it, sir."

Alexander laughed. "Thirty-seven misses. Can you imagine how many shots had to be fired today for thirty-seven of them to accidentally wind up down the tube of that gun?"

"Don't care to, General."

Alexander smiled. "Nor do I. Well, wheel the gun back into position, gentlemen."

He strapped his canteen carefully around his neck, and started off on his hands and knees again. *Thirty-seven*, he thought to himself—*amazing*. It would never end, of course. Porter Alexander had come now to understand that much. He would crawl through the trenches, check the guns, live through the heat and stench, and lastly count the errant balls each night as they poured from the guns for all eternity. Nothing would ever change. Nothing at all. The Yankees would live on the horizon forever, and they would all die slowly, one at a time, with a bullet through the brain. But even that would change nothing. Dante had written it, of course. Now Alexander was living it.

CHAPTER FORTY-SIX

JUNE 12TH—FIRST LIGHT

GRANT

Grant watched the match flare brightly in the darkness, cupped the flame in his hands and bent forward to light his cigar. Then he leaned back in his chair and tried to get comfortable. He pushed his feet up under his desk then yanked them back again. Neither posture seemed to work. So he fidgeted awhile then took another puff on his cigar. He drummed his fingers along the edge of the desk. Then he reached for his coffee cup, picked it up, but there was no coffee to be found, so he put it back down again. He rubbed a hand back through his hair, tapped his toe on the ground. For Ulysses S. Grant, waiting did not come easily.

Rollins had told him earlier that Porter and Comstock were on their way, and were expected within the hour. It was the news Grant had been waiting for, of course. Yet instead of serving as a perfect tonic for his anxiety, it only served to heighten his sense of foreboding all the more. The army could not move if there were no suitable place for it to cross the river, and only Porter and Comstock had the answer to that riddle. Grant realized that now at last the long, anxious days of waiting were about to end—for better or worse.

Ever since he had sent the two aides off on their mission, Grant had seen to it that every conceivable order and preparation for the army's withdrawal from Cold Harbor had been properly addressed. This would be nothing like the horribly bungled assault of the 3rd. No, not that! So nothing had been overlooked. The routes, order of march, transportation and supplies, all the logistics and liaison with the navy, all that and much more had been worked out down to the finest detail. Now he need only give the order, and the great war-machine called the Army of the Potomac would begin the long march toward the James within the hour.

But that order could only be given if Porter and Comstock returned with a favorable report, that part of the enterprise being entirely out of his hands. So he'd left firm instructions with Rollins for them both to be brought to his tent the moment they arrived. Now, as they completed the last, short leg of their journey, Grant could do nothing but bumble around aimlessly in his tent, and fret. He noticed that his cigar had burned out, so he lit it again, then absently placed it on the table. He got up, poured himself a fresh cup of coffee, then immediately realized that he had forgotten where he'd placed the cigar.

For days he had received steady courier reports that Sheridan's column was moving slowly west, but had yet to encounter any resistance. It appeared his ploy had worked to perfection, for Wilson had kept a close eye on the Rebel cavalry nearby, and advised him days ago that two full divisions of Confederate cavalry had departed under the command of Wade Hampton. Lee had taken the bait, and now would be hard pressed to probe or expose Grant's withdrawal with the bulk of his cavalry long gone. Now Sheridan had only to defeat Hampton somewhere north of Richmond and the valley supply line into the Rebel capital would be severed. So far, so good. He drummed his fingers along the top of his desk... waiting.

At last Rollins poked his head through the tent flaps and nodded. "They're here."

WINDMILL POINT

Grant sat up stiffly. His heart quickened. "Yes, fine," he said, trying not to sound desperate. "I'll see them now."

"Very good, General."

They came in and sat directly across from him then, a thin film of Virginia dust still hugging their coats. Porter noticed it on his pants, tried to slap some away with his gloves. "Sorry, sir."

Grant shrugged, took a few long pulls on his cigar, put it down. "That's fine. Nothing but dirt and dust around here, anyway. Mud when it rains."

Comstock smiled. "That's true."

"So," Grant continued, already tired of the small talk, "it's good to see you two again." He nodded, waited....

"Yes, General," Porter replied. "Good to be back."

Grant stared at them anxiously, wanted to get to the point. "Tell me about your trip."

Porter smiled, looked sideways at Comstock. "Well, where should we begin?"

"The James," Grant interjected. "Tell me about the river. Can it be bridged? And where? And how far across?"

"Oh, yes. Absolutely, sir," Comstock answered. "We've found a spot where the river can be bridged."

Grant could feel a warm sense of relief flash through his body. Then quickly he became even more excited. "You've chosen a spot to cross over?"

"We have, General," Porter answered. "Actually, we looked at a number of potential locations, but we eliminated most all of those. We both agreed that the best location by far and away is Wilcox's Landing near Fort Powhatan."

"Yes, excellent!" Grant replied, simultaneously slapping the arm of his chair. "I had thought so myself."

Comstock leaned forward. "It has without question the best system of roads feeding in, and also meets all your other specifications."

Grant fished around absently on the table for his cigar, found it finally at the end of his desk. He picked it up, lit it again quickly, then just as quickly put it back down. "And the width of the river there? That won't be a problem? Barnard was worried...."

Porter screwed up his face. "The river is a good 2,100 feet wide there, General," he said. "It's wide but bridgeable. It's also the narrowest place east of City Point."

"I will notify General Barnard at once," Grant said.

"And General..." Comstock started.

"Yes, yes," Grant said. "Yes, what?"

Comstock hesitated. "Well, I just wanted to say that General Butler is now entirely familiar with your orders, and prepared to fully cooperate."

"You're sure?"

"Yes, absolutely."

Grant sat back and smiled.

For the better part of the next hour he grilled the two over every aspect of their trip, every detail, large or small. Once he was satisfied with all the particulars, Grant stood, took a short puff on his cigar, and stared at them for a moment. "Well then," he said finally, "we're ready to move."

Comstock crossed his legs, edged a bit closer on his chair. "Might I inquire, General," he asked, "when you intend to initiate the withdrawal?"

Grant cocked his head, caught almost by surprise by the question. "Immediately!" he said.

Porter's eyes widened ever so slightly. "You mean... today, sir?"

Grant shook his head. "No, not today. Tonight! We will move under the cover of darkness. That will be essential in order to steal the march on Lee. The orders are all prepared. I need only give the word."

Porter appeared mildly shocked. "So soon. I had no idea."

WINDMILL POINT

Grant blew a puff of smoke across the tent. "Time's wasting."

He dismissed them then, and as the two hurriedly gathered their notes together, he leaned back and considered all they had told him. As he did so, Grant could almost see the long pontoon bridge taking shape in his mind's eye, the planks reaching far across the James as a vast column of blue snaked over the river under a cloudless sky. It was a beautiful picture. In this vision the water was perfectly blue, the hills and woods bordering the river a deep, vivid green. The image was captivating, a picture of hope and deliverance. As he conceived it, the lengthy column of troops moved steadily across the enormous bridge then gradually disappeared into a thick fold of woods on the southern bank—up and out of the Chickahominy swamplands forever, and on to victory. If he closed his eyes, he could easily imagine them marching all the way to Petersburg undetected, the city falling, the war ending in only days. His heart ached at the thought.

Grant stood, the vision still fresh in his mind. Then he suddenly thought of something he had forgotten to ask. So he walked outside to where the two aides were mounting their horses. He smiled up at them again, pleased with their work. "Good job, gentlemen," he said, cigar smoke trailing from his lips.

Porter blushed, hardly used to praise from the commanding general. "Oh, yes... thank you, sir."

"Oh, by the way," Grant continued, "I was just thinking...."

"Yes, of course, sir."

"From Wilcox's Landing to... where? Does this place we're headed have a name?"

"Oh, of course. Sorry, General," Comstock answered. "Windmill Point, that's the name. We'll be leaving from Wilcox's Landing on the north bank and crossing over to Windmill Point on the south."

"Windmill Point," Grant repeated. He rubbed his face, thought again of the long column of blue disappearing into the lush green trees at Windmill Point. At that moment there was no place on earth he yearned to see more.

CHAPTER FORTY-SEVEN

JUNE 12TH—EARLY MORNING

CUSTER

George woke early, the cool night rains having soaked his uniform thoroughly enough to finally make him uncomfortable. Custer opened one eye, rolled from his back to his side, listened patiently for the sound of gunfire in the distance, but there was none. He heard only the horses stirring nearby—now antsy on the line—and the rain slowly dripping from the leaves and branches overhead. He looked up. The fire was out, gone over now to nothing more than a light crackling and a few white trails of smoke. Off to the west the long ridge lay silent and blue, stretching forever north like eternity itself, somber as the ages. All was quiet and still.

Custer sat up, had a look around. The men were still asleep, exhausted from a long day of some of the hardest fighting any of them had ever experienced. He was lucky, he remembered suddenly, to have gotten out of that one alive. He decided to let them all sleep.

Custer's stomach grumbled and he remembered with a start that he had not eaten since the morning before. Then he spotted Eliza working down by the tracks with a pot or two cooking on a fire, and the mere thought of food proved a considerable motivation. He stood slowly, stretched his legs, and twisted his knees until they finally felt loose enough to move freely. As he did, he felt the water slip down the backs of his legs into his boots, and he knew the next few hours would feel raw and uncomfortable. But at least the sky above was clear, and the day promised to turn warm and remain dry. Custer shivered once as a few cold raindrops slid along his neck, then he started off down the hill.

"Did you rustle up some food, I hope?" he asked, leaning over the fire.

Eliza looked up, smiled brightly. "Bacon, ham, and some fine cheese," she replied. "Bread too. And, of course, eggs."

"How'd you manage all that?"

She smiled. "I gots my ways, Gen'l," she answered with a wink. "Can't go giving out all my secrets, though."

Custer laughed. "Well, I'm just about starved. He looked around, found a stump and rolled it close to the fire. Then he had a seat, warmed himself, and enjoyed the smell of breakfast cooking as she sliced the ham and began frying it in the pan.

"Oh, yes," Custer said, nodding excitedly. "I'll eat every last bit of it." He turned, looked around. "I could sure use a piece of that bread you were talking about. And some coffee, too. How 'bout coffee, Liza?"

She pointed with a long spoon. "Right there. And cut yourself a piece of that bread an' fix it up with some of that strawberry preserve."

"Preserves? You're too much, Eliza," he said, jumping toward the food. He tore off a large chunk of bread and poured himself a hot cup of coffee. Then Custer stuck a finger in the jar and put it in his mouth. "Strawberry preserves. You know I love strawberry preserves. My, my, just like home."

She shook a bony finger at him. "Yeah, you go ahead now and eat good so you got enough strength in that skinny body so no moe Rebels come grab me up again. What was you thinking?"

Custer shrugged. "All's well that ends well."

WINDMILL POINT

"Easy for you to say, Gen'l."

Custer recalled the mess he had gotten them all into the day before, Rebels circling his battered brigade all morning and afternoon, his men shot to pieces. He rolled his eyes. "Not exactly, Liza" he said.

"Where them Rebels at now?" she wanted to know.

Custer nodded south, then west. "Down the road a piece, from what I hear."

"You gonna have a big fight today?"

Custer dipped a small stick into the preserves, carefully covered another piece of bread. "Don't know, Eliza. "Nothing happening now. Hard to say, really. When are those eggs going to be ready?"

"You never mind," she answered. "Soon enough. Plenty here for everyone."

They both looked up as a squad of troopers came up the road then turned out toward the tracks. A few more followed, and in short order they took up positions and began tearing up the rails.

"What they doing now?" Eliza asked.

"Tearing up the railroad. It's what we came to do. No railroad, no food, no bullets, no guns for the Rebs. That's how it works."

Eliza put her hands on her hips and watched as the men went about their business. The process had by then been standardized. First they broke all the joints along one side of the track, then they would move along methodically, prying up the ties and rails all on that side and hoisting all of it up several feet in the air. Then all of the rails were pulled and twisted until they were facing upside down and perpendicular to where they had originally been, spikes sticking straight up toward the sky. After that the ties would be placed in a large stack, the rails placed over top. Once that had been accomplished, the ties would be fired and, as they heated, the rails would slowly droop toward the ground—useless now. In a war where both armies had learned to move both men and supplies quickly by rail, each side had become adept at such destruction.

Custer ate a quiet breakfast as the wreckage along the rails grew and amplified, and he enjoyed the peaceful morning. There was no telling when it might suddenly and violently come crashing to an end, he knew, or, for that matter, what both commanders had in mind for the day's pleasure. He had yet to receive any orders from Torbert, so until they came looking for him with fresh instructions, he decided to do nothing more than finish his coffee, let his men rest, and eventually establish some sort of headquarters nearby.

With breakfast finally under his belt, Custer decided to stroll into the station for a look-see. No enemy troops were reported in the area, so he watched absently with one eye as more and more blue troopers descended upon the railroad and began pulling up the rails, while keeping the other eye open for a suitable location for a headquarters. Walking was a slow, uncomfortable affair, his wet trousers chafing his legs, but he took his time and tried to overlook the difficulties while enjoying the pleasant sunshine.

He moved from the tracks up a slight embankment and started down the Gordsonsville Road. As he entered the small station he noted nothing more than a store, a storage shed, and a few houses scattered about. Suddenly a slim, well-attired gentleman emerged from the store and hurried down the steps toward him. Custer stopped dead in his tracks.

"Are you a Federal officer, sir?" the man inquired.

"Yes, sir," Custer answered, impressed by the man's courtesy. "How might I be of assistance?"

"Well," the man continued, "I am Charles Trevilian, and I would very greatly appreciate a favor of sorts."

WINDMILL POINT

The man was polite enough, but appeared quite worked up. Custer folded his arms behind his back. "Just what sort of favor, sir?"

"Well, my young daughter is very sick, you see. All this activity of the past day or so has gotten her quite stirred up, and it's bad for her condition. I'm very worried for her. Very."

"What seems to be her problem?" Custer asked.

The man scowled miserably. "Doc says it's typhoid fever."

"I see."

"And now your soldiers have been all over my yard, and even in and out of my home. I don't care for myself or my property, but I do care for my daughter's health."

"Certainly," Custer replied. "Where is your home?"

Charles Trevilian pointed west to a fine plantation style residence just on the outskirts of town. "Right there."

It was a beautiful home, with a fine porch shaded by a large grove of trees. Custer suddenly imagined himself sitting comfortably in the shade of the porch with a glass of fresh lemonade in hand, and quickly concluded that it was a splendid location for a headquarters.

"Well, sir," Custer said, "the only way I can assure you of some peace and quiet is for me to establish my own headquarters on your porch. I'm not sure I care to do that, you see. But if I were to, the men would no longer be in any sort of a position to bother you in the slightest."

"Well, sir," Trevilian said, stepping forward earnestly, "would you possibly be so kind as to consider doing just that? I would consider it a personal favor of the highest order." Trevilian blinked, threw his hands in the air. "And here I don't even know your name, sir," he said apologetically. "In my anxiety and haste I've gone and asked a favor of a man whom I don't even know. I am sorry, sir, for my impudence."

"Not at all, sir," he replied. "Custer's my name. General George Armstrong Custer."

Charles Trevilian's eyes opened wide, and he took a step back. "My goodness," he said. "So you're the famous Yankee general. The 'Boy General' you are called, if my memory serves me. I must say, General, you are quite polite. I would not have expected it, no offense intended."

"And none taken, sir," Custer replied. "We are not all quite the fiends the Richmond papers make us out to be."

"Yes, yes," Trevilian said, "I can see that. Well," he went on, "as I was saying, General, I would be ever so honored if you would consider taking my front porch for your headquarters." He rubbed his hands together anxiously. "I'm sure we could rustle up some food and beverage for you as well."

Custer bowed slightly. "Well, if you put it that way, sir, then yes I will. For the health of your child, of course."

"Of course."

So after leaving word of his move to the fine shaded porch, Custer packed his gear, mounted his horse, and made his way to the Trevilian house. In the meanwhile Mr. Trevilian had moved a comfortable chair and fine desk from the parlor onto the porch for him, and they had even boiled a fresh pot of coffee and left it warming on a metal stand outside, replete with cups, sugar, and milk.

Dutifully, Custer walked the grounds and shooed away any unwanted trespassers in blue, and he was able to keep the clatter to an essential minimum. Then he met with his surgeon and asked him to pay a visit on Trevilian's child, and leave behind any medicines that might prove effective. That accomplished, George Custer returned to his comfortable chair on the shaded porch, put his feet up on the fine desk, and did nothing more than enjoy the day as it began to warm. As yet there were no gunshots, no orders, and thus no reason to be overly concerned. There would be time enough for all of that. Custer pulled his hat over his eyes and, in minutes, was asleep.

CHAPTER FORTY-EIGHT

JUNE 12TH—MID MORNING

LEE

R.E. Lee had made up his mind. He had decided to play the wild card, and since the most recent hand was already being dealt by General Grant, there was precious little time to lose. He'd decided he would match Grant's move in the Shenandoah Valley, then raise the ante considerably. Lee would send one entire corps—fully one third of his effective strength—to overwhelm the Federal army in the Valley, then have them work north through the Valley as a thorn in Washington's side. A freewheeling Confederate army in the Shenandoah Valley would surely cause alarm bells to sound in the Federal capital, and hopefully draw off much of Grant's strength from the Army of the Potomac in frantic response.

That exact ploy had played well in 1862 when Stonewall Jackson's Valley Army had out-marched and out-fought everything the Federal high command had thrown at him. Washington had been in a near panic for months, forcing Lincoln to keep an entire army on a short leash just to be on the safe side. But by June, 1864, two things had changed. Stonewall was dead, and Grant had stripped the Washington defenses of almost every available soldier for his spring campaign. So if Lee could come up with a competent commander who could handle an independent command, Washington just might lie vulnerable to a sudden raid. It was certainly worth the attempt.

Sadly, supplying the requisite manpower for the mission was far easier than was choosing the man who would have to lead it. Lee's top lieutenants seemed either worn out or overworked, and often those who excelled at following his orders stumbled inexplicably when it came to making decisions at arm's length on their own. So he had called for Jubal Early, "my angry old man," as Lee often referred to him. While Early certainly had his faults, he also had his positive side. Yes, Early was surly, cantankerous, angry, and often just plain mean, but he could also move men, and he knew how to fight. Recently he had taken over the 2nd Corps and had handled it well at Cold Harbor. And while Jubal Early was often more headstrong and opinionated than most of his other officers, Lee knew that strong opinions were for an independent commander a necessity, not a vice.

Lee crossed his legs, and handed Early a copy of his written orders. "Have I explained this mission thoroughly, General?" he asked, waiting patiently for Old Jube to respond.

Early nodded, leaned forward hesitantly. "Destroy Hunter's force, reclaim the Shenandoah, then move aggressively toward Washington."

"Yes, exactly." Lee was pleased.

Old Jube's eyebrow arched. "Just how *aggressive* do you want me to be, General Lee?"

Lee smiled; here was the crux of the issue. "Well, if the opportunity presents itself," he explained, "you might be able to do more than harass the Federal capital. You see, if Grant remains ignorant of our movements—which could easily happen, General, by using the Valley to screen your march—you may well be able to move on the Federal capital before help can arrive."

WINDMILL POINT

Early frowned. "Sir, with all due respect," Early replied, "I am given to understand that the fortifications surrounding Washington are formidable. Indeed, I am told they are perhaps the most sophisticated ever constructed in the world."

"You are entirely correct," Lee replied. "But all our spies tell us those fortifications have been stripped of troops by Grant to bolster his spring campaign. Now they are manned by nothing but some convalescents and militia, and there are not so many of those. You may find yourself facing nothing more than a corporal's guard when you get there."

"Well, that would certainly make a difference," Early agreed.

"Of course, General," Lee said. "But those are exactly the sorts of things you will have to determine for yourself. Whether to attack or not, what sort of force you are facing, the most sensible routes to use, and so on..."

"I see," Early replied, listening intently.

"You will be weeks on the march and a hundred miles away from here," Lee continued. "So you will have to use your own best judgment in all of these matters."

Jubal Early took a deep breath then let it out slowly. "I appreciate your confidence in me, General Lee."

"I have all the confidence in the world in you, General Early," Lee replied firmly.

Early shifted on his chair uneasily. "General," he started, "if I should discover the capital defenses to be but weakly manned —as you suggest they may be—would you have me assault? I mean... attack Washington? Attempt to actually *take* the city?"

"Absolutely!" Lee answered without hesitation, shifting forward on his seat. "Listen now, I can easily imagine that the reaction at the North would be one of complete panic should you just seriously *threaten* their capital, better yet to actually take and hold it for even an hour. Of course, we could never hold it for long; Grant will rush reinforcements. But to just storm into the city, perhaps sack a few of the government buildings...."

Early chuckled. "Well, sir, I would dare to hazard that the good people of the North would be, well... displeased by such demonstration of force on our part."

Lee laughed out loud. "Yes, *displeased*. Displeased with their own government, and certainly with their commanding general, Ulysses Grant, for allowing such a debacle to occur. Yes, displeased to say the least." Lee smiled again. "And let us not forget the fact that there will be elections in the North this fall. We might make it very difficult for Abraham Lincoln and the rest of the Republican Party to win reelection if Washington has come under fire, or is partly in ruins, or if the administration has been forced to *flee* the city for a day or even a few hours. The political repercussions of such a scenario would be dire indeed for Mr. Lincoln's administration. Indeed, we may be able to win our independence, not on the field of battle, General, but in the Northern ballot box this very fall, and end this bloodbath forever. So you see, sir, the stakes here are very high. Very high."

"Yes... I understand, General Lee. And I am honored that you have chosen me to command this mission."

"You have my full confidence, General Early," Lee repeated. "But you must also understand that for this mission to be successful, it must be done very quickly, and it must be kept as secret as possible. Your march from here to Washington will take weeks, while Grant has the luxury of reinforcing the capital garrison by water within hours. He has an enormous navy and a multitude of divisions at his disposal. But the Valley should provide you with good cover until you reach Maryland, and then I am banking on Grant's own misconceptions of our abilities to confuse him as to the true nature of your force and objective. By the time he realizes the truth, it may already be too late."

WINDMILL POINT

"Yes, I see," Early said. "This mission, then—at least as I comprehend it—may well represent a substantial opportunity for our cause."

"Oh, I agree absolutely," Lee concurred. "If handled properly, your mission could eventually turn the war in our favor. Yes sir, turn the war around to our favor. Politically, that is."

"What, may I ask, General, have you heard of Hampton and our cavalry?"

Lee hesitated for just a moment. "Well, nothing so far today... or yesterday, for that matter. The day before that, however, I received reports indicating they were closing rapidly on Sheridan's column." Lee rolled his shoulders. "For all I know, they may be engaged as we speak."

Jubal Early folded the orders over once, then stuffed them into his pocket. "When would you have me depart, General?"

"As soon as reasonably possible," Lee answered.

"It will require some time for planning and arrangements," Early pointed out.

"Of course," Lee agreed. "Let's say tomorrow morning, perhaps 3 a.m."

"That I can do."

Lee stood, and Early followed him outside. Old Jube saluted. "I will take Washington if humanly possible, General Lee," he insisted, clearly moved by his appointment.

Lee returned the salute. "Your best is all I can ask for, General. But take it, please, if you can!"

CHAPTER FORTY-NINE

JUNE 12TH—NOON

GRANT

U.S. Grant walked from his tent into the glaring light of the midday sun as the camera was being carefully readied. Numerous officers were milling about in the shade nearby, exchanging jokes, comparing uniforms. The circular had come from Meade's headquarters the day before, indicating that arrangements had been made for a crew from the famous photographer, Matthew Brady, to come by and take photographs of them all. It was something Grant did not especially look forward to—today of all days—but Mr. Brady's work was considered important, after all, and he didn't want to disappoint. Many of the corps commanders had already been photographed along with their staffs, and Grant did not want to appear obstinate or contrary.

Grant walked stiffly out of his tent and confronted the photographer. He was Egbert Guy Fox, and while Grant was in no mood to waste time, he knew he had to cooperate. Many of the officers fell silent. "Well, good morning, General," Fox said, smiling hopefully.

"Good morning, Egbert," Grant replied.

Fox glanced up at the sky and smiled. "A perfect day for a photograph."

WINDMILL POINT

Grant looked up into the clear sky above and could only hope that it would remain that way for their march that night. He had already given Wilson his orders, and soon the cavalry would be in motion. As soon as the sun went down, Grant's headquarters tents would be struck, and Wilson was then to drive off the Confederate pickets along the Chickahominy, hold the fording points, and then fan out and secure the area south of the river. It was only noon, but already Grant was growing impatient.

"Yes, yes," Grant replied finally, "you're right," suddenly recalling the photographer's remark; his mind had drifted again. He looked back up at the sky once more. "It *is* a nice day."

Egbert Fox smiled, went back to fidgeting with the camera.

The almost euphoric rush of emotion he had felt earlier that morning immediately after the meeting with Porter and Comstock had now given way to a sort of weary tension. Grant felt tired and irritable, in no mood for something as useless as a photograph. In a few hours the withdrawal would begin, and he had far more important things to attend to.

The photographer put his hands on his hips, then took a quick look around. "Well now, General," he asked, "where would you like to pose?"

Grant shrugged, did not feel like moving. "Why not right here?"

The photographer broke into a broad smile. "By your tent, sir? Yes, that would be fine. Excellent, in fact!"

Grant had on the same old, tired uniform he had been wearing for days. Baggy, rumpled, and spotted with a light sheen of powdery Virginia dust, he hardly appeared the mythic figure some in the newspapers had made him out to be, but so what? He sat his hat squarely on his head, as he always did, then leaned lightly against a tree. "How about here?"

The photographer had little choice, of course. "Yes. That's fine, General. Just give me a minute or so."

The strain of the last few days and weeks was beginning to show, Grant realized, and increasingly he had to remind himself to remain calm and patient. When he trimmed his beard in the morning he could see the lines streaking his face, and the droop around his eyes. He seemed to be aging by the day.

"Take your time," Grant said to Fox, but he didn't mean a word of it.

Fox smiled, still tinkering. "We're just about ready now!"

"Fine."

"Look this way now, General, if you would. Yes, that's got it. Right here now. Oh, perfect, General! And hold that please!"

Grant stared directly at the camera for a second or two, but his thoughts began to drift as the photographer continued to fiddle with this and toy with that. When the flash eventually caught him, he was no longer looking at the camera at all, but had shifted his gaze just slightly off to the left, his mind now focused on the Chickahominy, the James, and that patch of green on the far bank called Windmill Point. In truth, he had been a million miles away when the camera lens finally captured his image.

"Yes. I'm sure that one will be excellent, General Grant. Very fine, sir."

Grant looked back at the photographer. "Oh," he said, coming back suddenly to his senses. "Well then, thank you, Egbert."

Mr. Fox smiled, nodded slowly. "Deep in thought, I see."

"Are we done, sir?" Grant asked.

"Yes, of course, General, for the time being, at least. Perhaps a few more later? Thank you so much."

Grant nodded. "Thank you again, Egbert," he said. "My pleasure." Then he spun on his heel and returned to his tent.

WINDMILL POINT

General Ulysses Grant at his headquarters
in Cold Harbor, Virginia

CHAPTER FIFTY

JUNE 12TH—MID AFTERNOON

CUSTER

Custer dismounted, then walked to the crest of a small rise, turned west and stared directly down the road. No more than a half mile ahead he could see the Rebel position clearly. Dug in along the crest of a steep rise, it commanded not only the road, but all approaches.

"Major Kidd!" Custer shouted.

The major leaped from his horse, struggled up the rise and joined Custer. "Yes, General?"

Early that afternoon Custer had finally received orders from Torbert. Dutifully, he abandoned Mr. Trevilian's front porch, and went to rally his brigade. Sheridan had instructed Torbert's entire division to reconnoiter west along the Gordonsville Road, and Custer's weary brigade had been given the lead assignment for that reconnaissance. Still very much shot up and exhausted from the fighting of the day before, neither Custer nor his men were in any mood or condition for another scrap with the enemy.

Custer scowled at the hill in the distance, now fairly bristling with Rebel flags and guns. "Please send some men forward and determine just what the hell is out there ahead of us," he told Kidd.

WINDMILL POINT

"Yes, sir!" the major responded. Then Kidd whirled around. "Sergeant Avery!"

"Sir?"

"Please take a squadron of twenty men forward and determine the enemy's strength and position."

"Yes, sir!"

Dust flew and sabers clattered as the small group of riders started off on the fly. Custer watched them disappear around a bend in the road, rubbed his face, and wondered where Sheridan and the rest of the Federal column had disappeared to. Then he remounted, as the remainder of the 6th Michigan filed off the roadway into a small defile and formed in a rough line of battle. Custer took a look around, but did not care for the lay of the land. It was a grim place to fight, not at all suited to offensive maneuver. Moreover, his men seemed fatigued, slow, and unusually reluctant that afternoon. Nothing felt right. Directly above, the sun was high and very hot.

"Very good, Major," Custer said. "I am going to order the rest of the brigade to come up, but I must have some idea of what we are facing. Please let me know what Avery reports as soon as possible."

Sergeant Avery was back in a matter of minutes only and his report was gloomy: the Rebels were dug in behind a stiff wall of breastworks atop a high ridge. What's more, perhaps as many as a thousand additional enemy troops were moving into position on the Confederate right. The Rebel position appeared formidable, and was becoming more so by the minute.

Custer listened with folded arms. He did not want to advance his men into the teeth of all that, but he really had no choice. "Okay, then," he said with a sigh. "I want the 6th Michigan on the right, the 7th moving in tandem with them on the left. Both regiments are to dismount and advance on foot." He shook his head and spit angrily. "Our horses are useless in this damned scrub," he complained. Custer kicked at a tuft of grass. "What the *hell* is Sheridan thinking?"

In short order the battle line was formed, and the Michigan men began a slow, wary advance. Soon the sharp pop of carbine fire came filtering back through the trees, and Custer knew his line had struck the Confederate pickets. He sat his horse quietly, and listened as the rate of gunfire steadily mushroomed before reaching a constant drumming. In a few minutes Kidd was back, dirt and sweat smearing his face, shaking his head in disgust.

"It will take far more than *two* regiments to move them out of that position, General," he insisted emphatically.

"How much more?" Custer asked.

"Everything we've got and then some," the major answered, breathing hard. Kidd pointed an angry finger at the hill above them. "The Rebels are well dug in, with sweeping fields of fire all in front of their entrenchments. Their artillery is above them, shooting down at anything that moves. We are all clogged up below in the bushes about 500 yards out. Without considerable support I don't believe we're going anywhere further this afternoon."

Custer spit into the weeds at his feet again. "*Alright, then!*" he almost shouted, becoming more frustrated by the minute. "I'll put in our other two regiments and send word back to Torbert. Merritt should be up soon with everything he's got."

Kidd shook his head. "It will take a damn sight more than that, General."

Custer, surprised, just stared at him for a moment. Kidd was not one to back away from a fight. "How much more are you talking, Major?"

Kidd wiped the sweat from his chin. "Most every division we've got, as I see it." He shook his head. "To advance directly up that hill into all that... Well, sir...."

Custer frowned, shoved his hands down into his pockets. "Just go ahead and do the best you can for now," he said, "but don't do anything foolish. I'll see what Torbert has in mind."

"Yes, General," Kidd replied, but he did not appear enthusiastic.

As Kidd disappeared into the thick woods again, Custer turned and rode back toward Trevilian Station, hoping to find either Torbert or Sheridan on the road. He soon ran into the van of Merritt's brigade coming up, then Merritt himself, riding toward the front with the 2nd U.S. Cavalry. Spotting Custer, Wesley Merritt directed his men forward, then stopped alongside the road to talk.

Custer spurred his horse, and came up next to him. "Have you observed the Rebel position?" Custer asked.

"Enough of it," Merritt admitted.

"What are we to do?"

Merritt rolled his shoulders. "Sheridan wants the road to Gordsonsville cleared. Our orders are to move on and tear up as much track as we can."

Custer pointed emphatically down the road. "That's Hampton's entire division deployed ahead," he declared. "They are on a steep hill behind stout works with artillery covering them from above. Tell me, General, how are our two brigades supposed to move them from there?"

"I don't know," Merritt admitted. "I just have my orders. But Devin will be up soon, too, and that will give us three full brigades. Is it just Hampton we are facing up there?"

"That's all we have identified, but who knows what the hell is behind that hill or out there in all those trees."

"Where the hell is Fitz Lee's division?" Merritt wanted to know.

Custer tossed his hands in the air. "Beats me. Last night we found him pulled off towards Louisa Court House. Don't know where he is now." Custer nodded west. "Maybe he's up there with Hampton already. Maybe not."

Merritt frowned. "Well, I'm going to go in alongside you. We'll link up with your right flank. Then Devin will deploy on my right."

"Fine," Custer replied.

Merritt sat his horse, thought for a moment. "Then we'll all go in hard at once," he suggested. "That should move Hampton off his hill."

"Yes, perhaps, if it's just Hampton," Custer pointed out. "But suppose Lee is up there with him? We'll be cut to shreds."

Wesley Merritt shrugged. "We've both got our orders. What choice do we have but to obey them?'

"Hell!" Custer snorted.

Merritt rolled his shoulders. "Look here, if Lee is up there we'll just get word back to Torbert. Sheridan still has Gregg's entire division in reserve. But we won't know what we're facing until we hit them."

"Okay, fine," Custer said. "Once you and Devin are deployed, go ahead and advance. I'll move forward on the sound of your attack."

"That's good," Merritt answered, then turned and rode off.

Custer returned to his brigade, dismounted, and moved forward gingerly through the scrub and briars to where Kidd's regiment was bogged down in the woods. Bullets were thumping into tree trunks, and clipping branches overhead at an alarming rate. Leaves were spinning downward in the air, and a heavy blanket of smoke lay thick and dense under a canopy of branches. It was a tight, hot, angry piece of business, and Custer didn't like it at all. Especially not looking up at all those Confederate guns.

His men were exchanging heavy gunfire with the Rebels above, but Custer could easily see that any sort of advance was impossible without help on both of his flanks. The hill ahead

WINDMILL POINT

was simply too steep, and the firepower they were facing far too heavy. Any sort of direct attack appeared virtually suicidal, and after yesterday's dicey flirtation with annihilation, Custer was in no mood to tempt the fates again.

Within the hour both Merritt and Devin had dismounted their brigades and were deployed on his right, well north of the tracks. Moments later the heavy thunder of their combined assault came booming through the woods, and just minutes after that much of Merritt's brigade became visible moving up the slopes of the ridge on Custer's right.

With that, Custer ordered his entire brigade forward. The bugles blared, the flags lurched forward, and his men leaped from behind their trees and rocks and started gamely up the hill. They did not get far. At once the ridgeline above them exploded in almost a ball of fire, and his men were literally blown backwards into the trees, as if they had stumbled into the headwinds of a hurricane. Men tumbled to the ground all along the face of the hill, screaming and writhing in pain. Blood splattered the rocks and grass. So fierce and well directed was the Confederate fire that Custer had no choice but to order his men back to the relative shelter of the trees. But he did not even have to issue the order. His men, their instinct for survival well honed after years of combat, had already made that decision for themselves.

Dragging their wounded behind, the Michigan brigade stumbled and tumbled back down the face of the hill, far quicker than they had gone up, and resumed their places behind the rocks and trees. From there they covered Merritt's advance as best they could, but for the remainder of that long afternoon, Merritt's regulars fared no better advancing against Hampton's position than had Custer's volunteers. For two full hours they gave it their best, and for two full hours they were bitterly repulsed. Six times Custer watched them go up, and six times they came tumbling back down, leaving many of their comrades behind, wounded or dead, on the flank of the hill.

Afternoon slowly turned into evening, and evening into another, bloody, mess. Now there were but a few hours of daylight left. A large, red sun was beginning to set behind the Blue Ridge, spraying a crimson glow throughout the darkening woods. Perhaps, Custer thought, Mother Nature would finally put a stop to what common sense apparently could not.

CHAPTER FIFTY-ONE

JUNE 12TH—EARLY EVENING

HAMPTON

Wade Hampton walked purposefully down the back side of the hill in the splashing glow of a red, setting sun, put his hands on his hips, and tried with all his might to conceal his anger. He was not by nature a violent man. He could easily count on one hand the number of fights he had been involved in even as a youth, and he fancied the elaborate duels honored by many of his countrymen to be nothing more than immaturity run amok. But now, as Hampton stood on the back of the ridge, he was as close to fighting mad as he had ever been in his life. All afternoon he had been waiting for Fitz Lee's division to ride to his support, yet all afternoon he had waited in vain. Many of Hampton's officers were convinced the delay was purposeful, and that Lee's absence was calculated, their comments evolving slowly over the course of a long and bloody afternoon from bewilderment to outright disgust.

For hours now Hampton's division had been holding alone against everything Sheridan could throw at them, and despite all his messages and pleas, it had taken Lee and his division almost a full day to travel a circuitous route of at best five miles to join them. Yes, they were operating in unfamiliar country, but it was *Confederate* country, and no doubt there were hundreds of nearby residents who would gladly have directed

Lee to Hampton's position had they only been asked. But that had not happened, and now there was little doubt in Hampton's mind that Lee—who could not have failed to hear the sound of battle ringing violently for hours—was deliberately late. Whether his delay was the result of petulance, ignorance, or ambition Hampton could not accurately gauge, but he was positive now that Lee's tardiness was intentional. Could Fitz Lee be trusted? Wade Hampton had doubts.

But right now Hampton had a battle on his hands, his situation was becoming desperate, and he needed all the help he could get. So he knew he would have to swallow his anger for the time being and make the best of a very difficult situation. Hampton needed fresh troops in order to survive, and survival naturally trumped anger.

For most of the afternoon Butler's men had been bearing the brunt of the Federal assault, and while they had held Sheridan at bay, the Yankee attack had been both hard and relentless. The Federal cavalrymen, with their seven-shot repeaters, were hurling a devastating volume of fire into his lines, and even with the advantage of good ground and solid entrenchments, he could not hold forever against such overwhelming firepower. Late in the afternoon, his men had come close to running out of ammunition, and it was obvious that his lines were growing increasingly thin and fatigued.

Fortunately, at the last moment, Butler's train of wagons had pulled up behind the hill with fresh ammunition, and Lee's long column had not been far behind. Now Hampton had more than enough ammunition to hold his line, and an additional division with which to hopefully tilt the contest in his favor. So, for the time being, at least, he would have to put aside both his pride and his anger, and get on with the task at hand. He would deal with Fitz Lee later.

From the very top of the ridge Hampton could look out and observe the entire length of the Federal line as they deployed

WINDMILL POINT

for charge after charge against him. He watched each advance carefully, and soon noted that the Federals seemed so intent on running him off his hill that they were apparently indifferent to the possibility that he might go over to the offensive himself, abandon the heights, and come storming down after *them*. Indeed, so carelessly placed were their lines, the thought seemed not to have even occurred to them at all.

From prisoners taken, he knew that Merritt's brigade formed the right of the Yankee assaulting line, and he could clearly see that Merritt's right flank was completely in the air. That fact would have been meaningless, of course, had not Lee finally appeared with his fresh division, but now Lee was on hand, and Hampton sensed a golden opportunity out there in the woods, ripe for the taking. He clasped his hands behind his back.

"Well, General," Hampton said, offering his hand to Fitz Lee, and forcing himself to smile as warmly as he could manage, "nice to see you today."

Lee bowed slightly, smiled sheepishly. "Yes, General Hampton. We are glad, of course, to be here. How might we be of assistance?"

Hampton got straight to the point. "Why don't you leave your horse behind, General, and walk with me to the top of the hill. I'll show you a little something that I believe you will find of interest."

"How, sir, can I refuse such an offer?" Lee said, trying to sound cooperative.

They walked together across the top of the ridge to where Butler's line was working furiously, pouring down fire on the Yanks in the trees below. Bullets snapped in the logs along the front and whizzed in the air overhead. Neither man paid them any mind. The two stopped just above where the Cadet Rangers were fighting tenaciously from behind a barricade of logs and dirt. Hampton watched them approvingly for a moment, then turned and pointed north.

"If we can get a brigade up that way," he said, "you can see for yourself that the Yankees are entirely strung out and almost begging to be flanked. There is absolutely *nothing* out beyond Merritt's right, and I believe a well-timed attack could roll up their entire line—a sort of Chancellorsville in miniature, General."

Lee put his field glasses to his eyes and stared out at the Federal line for a few minutes. "Oh, my, yes," he said finally. "I see what you mean. There is quite an opportunity here. Is there a direct route out to the Yankee's flank?"

"Not direct," Hampton replied, "but there is a route. I've had scouts out for a few hours now, and I've received favorable reports." He pointed again. "You see that lumber road that runs north? Well, it goes up through the woods, across a few ravines, then winds its way out across Hickory Creek. It may not be an easy trek, but I can assure you the trip—if made before nightfall —will be worth it."

Lee nodded his head slowly, agreeing. He tucked his field glasses away. "We must move at once," he said.

"Yes, exactly" Hampton agreed. "I suggest we send Lomax's Brigade out that way for the flanking movement, while Wickham deploys along Butler's left, joining with the 4th South Carolina. That should hold the line and give Lomax time enough to get into position."

"I will issue the orders immediately, General Hampton," Lee said, and for once he moved with dispatch.

So they sent Lomax's entire brigade, along with a section of horse artillery, out the woods road just as the sun was starting to dip below the Blue Ridge. The troopers stumbled and fumbled their way across ravine and creek, but finally swung their horses into position just before nightfall, no more than a few hundred yards north of Merritt's right flank. The artillery

WINDMILL POINT

quickly unlimbered and quietly rolled their guns into almost point blank range of the Yankees. Then, without the slightest hesitation, the guns cut loose a fearsome volley, almost directly into the faces of the Federal cavalrymen. With that, Lomax's charge went sweeping out of the trees, catching the Yanks by complete surprise, and all hell broke loose.

From high atop the Confederate position Hampton watched the whole thing unfold as if in a picture book, the Federal line bending back in shock, then crumbling inward. Men screamed, fell, ran. Flags toppled to the ground, carbines banged, and sabers flashed in the amber glow of the setting sun.

Then, with the trap fully sprung, Hampton unleashed his second wave. As Lomax's flanking movement swept across the Confederate front, Hampton sent Wickham's and Butler's men charging downhill, one unit at a time, just as Lomax's brigade came rolling abreast of them. In that manner the entire Confederate battle line went storming downhill with a wild Rebel yell to join in the fray, now striking the Federal line from two directions at once.

In the darkness of the woods Hampton could discern the progression of his lines by long strings of bright rifle flashes, like glittering beads dancing on a chain. He watched, almost transfixed, as they swept everything before them. The Federal brigades crumbled from left to right, one after the other, stampeded by Lomax's whirling assault. The result was pandemonium. Within minutes the Yankees were all on the run, stumbling through the trees in chaos, racing back down the Gordonsville Road toward Trevilian Station. Only darkness served to finally bring an end to the Confederate effort, dropping its dark curtain on the last act of the drama, but not before the Yankees had been utterly routed from the field. For Wade Hampton—watching as he had been from high above—it had been the stuff of dreams.

CHAPTER FIFTY-TWO

JUNE 12TH—EVENING

GRANT

Ulysses Grant waited patiently as they brought his horse around; now, at least, the seemingly endless wait was over.

All around him the tents were coming down, and the headquarters wagons were being carefully packed for the trip south to Long Bridge on the Chickahominy. It promised to be a long, tedious ride, but at that moment Ulysses Grant could not have wished for more. A tedious trek beat by far and away another dreadful day in the trenches at Cold Harbor, a place he hoped he had now seen for the last time.

That night his staff had gathered round at dinner, and in due course the conversation had turned to the casualties both sides had suffered so far that spring. It was generally agreed that the Army of the Potomac had sustained roughly 54,000 in dead, wounded, and missing since early May, but it was also agreed that many of those losses would eventually be made good. Many of the casualty reports were exaggerated, Grant knew, for often after a battle men somehow seemed to return from the dead with peculiar regularity. In all the confusion of war soldiers often became disoriented or displaced, and in the days that followed generally made their way back to their rightful units. So Grant was assured by his staff that the damage was in all probability nowhere near as dire as the reports suggested, and it was presumed that the Rebels had suffered to an equal degree. Whether any of that was an accurate appraisal of the situation, or simply wishful thinking, only time would tell.

Equally as problematic, from the perspective of future planning, was the number of fresh replacements promised by Washington. Those reports also tended to be grossly inaccurate, and almost always on the short side. For some reason units reported to be carrying as many as, say, 1,000 men would arrive in camp only 500 strong, while some failed to post at all. So the replacements never really made up for the men who were mustered out, whole regiments seeming to vanish somewhere on the road between Washington and the Army of the Potomac. President Lincoln hit the nail on the head when he said, "We get a large body of reinforcements together, and start them to the front; but after deducting the sick, the deserters, the stragglers, and the discharged, the numbers seriously diminish by the time they reach their destination. It's like trying to shovel fleas across a barnyard; you don't get 'em all there."

So Grant would have to fight with what he had—whatever that number ultimately proved to be—and trust that his strategy alone would be sufficient to force Lee out into the open. But that was all in the future. Tonight he had an army to move.

"Here you are, General," the orderly said, bringing his horse around.

"Thank you," Grant answered, tossing his cigar aside.

Thankfully, the sky that evening remained clear and striking. The moon was shining brightly, a few stars beginning to twinkle around the darkest edges, and the likelihood of rain appeared slim. Moving an army of over 100,000 men through dust and darkness was difficult enough without the added misery of bad weather. The men might well complain of dust, but it was still far better than mud.

Grant swung up into the saddle, and prepared to ride, but some of his staff held back momentarily for one last look around the campsite. Grant waited, but did not share their enthusiasm for recollection. He leaned back in his saddle and took in the rich fragrance of swamp magnolia that hung low on the western breeze, but frankly it was an aroma he hoped he would never have the pleasure of encountering again. Cold Harbor was not a place he wanted to remember. He had a war to fight, and he fancied recollections of the disaster the army had experienced there of no earthly use. The sooner he could forget the place, the better. Now the long days and nights of planning were over. There was nothing remaining to be done, as far as Grant was concerned, but to strike the tents, take to the road, and then say a prayer for their deliverance.

Once his staff finally fell in behind, Grant spurred his horse gently, and led them all down the dark road into the gathering gloom of night. He did not feel particularly good about things, but then neither did he feel particularly bad. He most certainly did not look back.

CHAPTER FIFTY-THREE

JUNE 12TH—LATE EVENING

CUSTER

Custer watched solemnly as the wounded were lifted, one by one, from the roadside and hurriedly loaded into the ambulances for the long trip back. They were, of course, only those few whom the troops had managed to drag or carry off as they'd fled from the Confederate assault that had struck their ranks like a hurricane near sundown. Some of the wounded were still stumbling in. Many more had been left behind in the weeds, scrub, and darkness, to suffer overnight. For them nothing could be done. Hopefully, come morning they would be found and cared for by either the locals or the Rebel surgeons, but no one could say for sure.

After the Confederate assault sent them all flying back to the station, nothing but confusion prevailed. Who could really say just what was in store for the wounded, or for any of the weary Federal troops for that matter? The Rebels had caught them by complete surprise, and now the woods were littered with Custer's injured friends and comrades.

Sheridan had ordered an immediate withdrawal back across the North Anna, so there would be no additional time to collect the wounded. If they were not discovered and cared for by the locals, they would be left to either die or fend for themselves in this barren and unfriendly territory. Many others had been brought in and were lying on the ground near the railroad station, crying for help, for water, or for their God to come and take them. Thoughts of victory had simply evaporated. Now blood, dust, fear, and flies ruled the night at Trevilian Station. Some men were in such pain they begged for someone to come shoot them. The surgeons had their hands full, more so the chaplains.

Custer dipped a ladle into a bucket of water, kneeled down on one knee, and handed it over to one of the wounded soldiers.

"Thank... you,... sir," the man sputtered, but Custer required no thanks. He had always taken pride in looking after his men, and leaving any number of them behind to the mercies of the Rebels infuriated him. But that portion of the field where they lay was now in control of the Confederates, and within the hour the Federal column would be in retreat. So there was nothing he could do.

Most of the wounded had received little, if any, medical care and, with Sheridan planning to move out as soon as possible, they would not, for hours, perhaps even days. For them it would be a slow, dusty, agonizing trek. Many, Custer knew, would not survive it. Worse still, for the most seriously wounded, as the wagons began creaking along the path back, death would seem a welcome joy compared to the bumping, jerky, crowded ambulances, where every mile would feel like an eternity of undeserved suffering.

Custer shook his head, tried to put the thought out of his mind. He continued walking amongst the long rows of battered men, looking for some of his own troopers, trying to at least do... something.

It wasn't long before the wounded overflowed the space available for them in the ambulances, so Sheridan ordered out a detail to confiscate every wagon, carriage, or buggy in the vicinity. But soon even those were packed to the limit with screaming men, and it proved a grim and bloody business. It

WINDMILL POINT

was one thing to lead men in battle, George Custer had learned, quite another to listen to their pitiful, tortured groans and pleas, especially when there was nothing at all that could be done for them.

Custer grabbed hold of a surgeon's aide by the shirtsleeve. "Have you any of my Michigan boys here?" he asked.

The young man looked at him as if he were crazy. "I have no time, General," he replied, "to ask where they are from. There are so many...."

Custer frowned and moved on. He should have known better. The attacks, he thought, had never been sensibly coordinated. As a result, they had been left open to counter attack, and Hampton had proved no fool. Most of the wounded, he noticed, appeared to be from Merritt's brigade, and he was glad for once to have held his own men back. The whole thing had been a fiasco.

Custer walked out of one hospital tent and headed for another. Along the side of the road the wounded were still being carried in from the field and laid out in rows on the grass. Since yesterday, three field hospitals had been set up, but now all three would have to be abandoned to the enemy. Leaving wounded friends behind was never a pleasant task, and always a sure sign of defeat, no matter how cleverly the officers tried to disguise it. Moreover it always had a demoralizing effect on the troops; to leave their injured comrades to the enemy seemed almost a moral failing. Even if those left behind were lucky enough to survive, their reward would be nothing more than prison. For most that meant Andersonville, and Andersonville, everyone knew, was simply another word for death.

In the third row in the second hospital he finally located one of his boys, a private shot through the thigh the day before. Custer found and filled his canteen, then kneeled by the boy's side. The boy could not walk, and they were scared to move him, despite all his pleas to take him along. The soldier dreaded being left behind, but would surely bleed to death if left to bump around in an ambulance.

"Please, General?" the boy asked, tears running down his face.

"You'll be fine," Custer replied. "You'll heal up like new, and then I'll see to it that you are exchanged as soon as possible."

But the boy knew that Grant had already stopped the practice of exchanging prisoners, and that if he were to heal it would be Andersonville for him. He reached into the blanket, pulled out his bible. "Would you see my ma gets this?" he asked.

"Of course," Custer answered, understanding that the boy had already accepted his fate—surely a far braver act than hoisting a pistol. He took the bible, stuffed it in his shirt ... moved on.

Outside, the night sky was glowing with the flames of a thousand campfires, all ordered by Sheridan. He had the fires built large, then layered with plenty of extra wood so they would burn well into morning. Sheridan wanted to fool the Confederates into believing the entire Federal force had remained for the night, while in fact they were sneaking off and stealing a march of at least a few hours. So the fires would be tended until the last of the rearguard pulled out and the Federal column was well on its way back across the river. That, at least, was the plan.

Of course, a night march under such conditions would be grueling. Almost all of the men had had little if any rest for almost two days, and not much in the way of food. Some were collapsing now as they came in, and to expect them to ride for hours through the darkness would be asking a great deal, but that's exactly what would be asked. If they were going to get a jump on the Confederates they would have to depart soon, and disguise the withdrawal as much as possible. Those who could not ride would be left behind to test the fates come morning.

WINDMILL POINT

It was surely a dismal ending to what at first blush had seemed a promising campaign. Everyone understood by now that their goal had been to link up with General Hunter in the Shenandoah Valley, destroy the railroad that ran into Richmond, then return with Hunter's entire command to the Army of the Potomac. While they had succeeded in tearing up a few miles of track, it was common knowledge that the Rebels would have it repaired and the entire line operable again in just a few days. So the Yankee efforts, the fighting, and now their wounded and dead, had been for nothing. Not a single objective of the raid had been met as far as Custer could see, and all they had to show for it now was a long train of wounded, shrieking men. The dead, of course, had nothing to say, yet in many ways they spoke the loudest.

Worn and dejected, Custer finally rejoined his brigade out near the tavern and took a seat by a fire. He made sure that what little food was available was evenly distributed, but there was not much to be had, and there would be even less time to enjoy it. The joviality that had marked their excursion out from Cold Harbor was now long gone. There would be no dancing or clowning on the ride back. Many were just glad to be alive.

Just prior to midnight, the column began its trek back to the Army of the Potomac, the 1st Maine cavalry taking the lead. They left in silence. A New Jersey regiment took up a rearguard position, and was not expected to depart the station until near dawn. The plan was for them to continue feeding the campfires until the last, then steal away as discreetly as possible. Maybe it would fool the Rebels, maybe not.

It was not long before Custer received orders to ready his brigade, then fall in and join the line as it began inching its way north toward the river. Dust was already thick in the air, water scarce, breathing difficult. Weary men mounted once again, and the wagons bearing the wounded began to bump and jolt and creak their way down the rutted turnpike, causing many of the boys to cry out in pain.

The leaping flames from the fires seemed to writhe like incarnate spirits just beyond the trees nearby, dreadful and grotesque, as though the cavalry had somehow stumbled headfirst upon a portion of Lucifer's gruesome playground. Added to that appalling image were the hunger, exhaustion, and pitiful cries of the wounded. To Custer's mind the scene soon took on a morbid, almost demonic quality, unholy by nature, like the end of days, and he tried to push the thought aside, but it was not easily moved.

Just how he had escaped the fate so many others had suffered was certainly a mystery: in the end perhaps nothing more than another example of his own extraordinary good luck. George Armstrong Custer had gotten his entire command surrounded, had fought out front once again like a wildcat, and yet had somehow managed to escape all the carnage unharmed —barely, yes, but unharmed nevertheless. But, then, Custer had always gotten along on daring and good fortune and, despite his brigade's recent battering, his daring remained inexhaustible. But luck was a much different thing. Luck, Custer realized, was far more slippery, a mystery beyond his ken or reckoning, something much more akin to the queen of diamonds. Luck, he knew, might ride joyfully with him for a long string of days, only then to turn away and abandon him the next.

CHAPTER FIFTY-FOUR

JUNE 12TH—MIDNIGHT

WHITE

Wyman slipped back into the dark trench one last time and methodically checked each man over again. Orders had come down just within the last hour for the Sharpshooters to quietly pack all their gear and be ready to move out immediately. Special attention was to be paid to anything—canteens, bayonets, cups—that might clank or make even the slightest noise as they moved. Everything was to be tied down or carefully packed away, and all of it double-checked before leaving.

Wyman White grabbed hold of Tommy Gorman's haversack and gave it a tug. "Is this tied tight now, Tom?" Wyman whispered.

"Yes, Sergeant."

"Nooo it ain't," Wyman said. "Lookee here, Tom."

"Oh, I see now."

"Shhh! No, you don't see too good at all, Tom," Wyman snapped. He yanked the strap on Tom Gorman's haversack and fixed it tight himself. Satisfied the sack was now fastened appropriately, he nodded. "Now you'll do, Tom," he whispered. "Listen to me, I don't want you to say another word to anyone until I say it's okay." Wyman nodded at him sternly.

Tom nodded back, seeming to understand.

"Fine," Wyman said, then stepped to the next man. It was Joe Thompson.

"What you guess is up, Sarge?" Joe asked, raking a hand through his beard nervously.

"Don't know, Joe," Wyman told him, looking the corporal over closely. "But I think the whole corps's on the move. I can hear men shifting around down the line, but quiet as mice, I must say. Yes, sir, quiet as mice."

Joe took a deep breath, and Wyman could feel his fear right through the darkness like electricity. "You mean... attack?" Joe asked.

Wyman shook his head. "No, I don't think so," he replied. "If it was an attack we'd just be laying all our gear down behind us, not tying it up tight as a drum to take along, Joe. Don't that make sense? I think we're leaving."

Thompson grabbed Wyman's arm. "Leaving? ... Really? You think so?"

"Yes, I do.... Hey, get back in line, Tom!" Wyman hissed.

"What? Oh, sorry, Sergeant," Tommy answered.

"What do you know for sure, Sarge?" Joe went on, staring at Wyman hopefully.

Wyman waited for Tom Gorman to get back to his place, then continued. "Well, you see, Joe, General Grant has, of course, confided his entire plan to me as is his usual way, but I am not at liberty to share it with you just yet."

Joe Thompson blinked, frowned. "Well, I'm just asking. Ain't no need to get so smart, as I see it, Sergeant White."

Wyman smiled. "Have you checked all your men, Joe?"

"I have."

"And yourself, Joe? Did you check yourself?"

"Oh."

Wyman pulled him close, went over everything carefully again. "Okay, Joe, take a few steps so's I can hear you walk."

Thompson did as ordered and made no noise.

Wyman nodded, feeling satisfied. Then he called the squad together. "Listen here," he whispered as they gathered round, kneeling in the bottom of the trench, "We're all gonna go out together tonight, slow, easy, and quiet. Real quiet. If you got anything that makes even the slightest noise, you're gonna have to sit back down and get it straight. Them's the orders. So fix it now if you can, or leave it behind."

"Where we's headed, Sarge?" a voice in the darkness asked.

"Don't know, fellas," Wyman answered, "but I think it's away from here. That would be my guess, anyway."

"Outta here to where?" Tom Gorman asked.

"Does it really matter?" Wyman answered. "Anywhere's better than here, as I see it."

"You got a point, Sarge," Joe Thompson agreed.

Wyman leaned forward on one knee, spoke very softly. "Has everyone got plenty of ammunition? At least sixty rounds, boys?"

They all nodded that they did.

"Never know when we'll have to fight," Wyman pointed out. Then he thought for a moment. "And your weapons are clean, right?"

Once again they all nodded "yes."

"Okay, then," Wyman said. "You got anything, Joe?"

"Whadaya mean?"

"To say, Joe," Wyman answered. "You got anything to say?"

"Yeah, let's get the hell out of here."

Wyman smiled. "Well, that's about right."

Once he was sure they were all ready, he had them sit back down along the edge of the trench and wait. They did not have to sit for long. Within the half hour a lieutenant came scuttling into the trench, bent low, holding his sword tight against his side. "Who's in charge here?" he whispered.

Wyman leaned forward, cupped his hand around his mouth. "Right here."

"Okay, Sergeant," the lieutenant said. "You're next. Let's move it."

"Where to?" Wyman asked.

The lieutenant pointed back toward the rear. "Just go that way," he said. "Do you see those troops moving there now?"

Wyman squinted into the blackness, saw only the vaguest outline of forms, something like shadows or apparitions moving in the distance. "Yes, sir."

"Well, that's the rest of your brigade. Fall in and follow along."

"Okay, boys," Wyman said. "Real quiet, but quick. Let's go."

Joe Thompson led them off and Wyman stayed behind until he was sure every last man was out of the trench and on his way. Then he bent low and hurried along after them, moving at a good clip, yet silent as a deer bounding through a winter wood. When he hit the end of the trench he stayed low for about fifty yards, then turned and headed off toward the faintest sound of men moving through the night. Light on his feet, elusory as a phantom, in just seconds Wyman White had disappeared into the trees, leaving nothing but darkness behind.

CHAPTER FIFTY-FIVE

JUNE 13TH—DAWN

ALEXANDER

Edward Porter Alexander woke with a start as hurried footsteps approached across the campsite. Alexander opened his eyes as the tent flap flipped wide. He looked up. It was his cook, Charley.

"General!" Charley said, trying to catch his breath. "The... Yankees... gone!"

Alexander smiled, sat up on the edge of his cot. "Which Yanks, Charley?" he asked, knowing that many Federal units had been coming and going for days.

"All 'em, General!"

Alexander rubbed his face, found his canteen and took a drink. "What 'all em'?" he said, suddenly curious. "You mean the Yanks on our front, all of them?"

"No, sir. I mean all 'em."

Alexander smiled, shook his head. "You mean the whole Yankee army, Charley? The whole doggone Federal army has just up and left?" He smiled again, rubbed his face, shook his head. "I rather doubt that."

"That's it. All 'em."

Alexander frowned. "Well, that's impossible, Charley," he replied. "Maybe some of them have left, or more likely shifted around. They all couldn't have left."

"They all's gone, General. Come see for yourself."

Alexander knew that Charley could not be right, that the entire Yank army could not have simply up and left during the night without the Confederate pickets knowing about it and giving word. That was impossible. In places the opposing lines were no more than fifty or sixty yards apart. Indeed, they were so close that at times the men in the trenches could hear one another's conversations, had even come to know their adversaries by name. So there was no way the entire Federal army could withdraw from the Cold Harbor trenches without Lee's army knowing about it instantaneously. But Alexander also knew that Charley was reliable, and that he obviously thought he was onto something important.

Alexander reached for his trousers. "Well, now," he said, "let me come have a look, Charley, and we'll go see what this fuss is all about. Ask them to saddle my horse."

"Yes, General."

He put on his pants, quickly tied his shoes, and walked out to the campfire. From his bivouac behind the front there was no clear view of the Yankee lines, so he quickly grabbed a cup of coffee, then went to his horse.

"Come along, Charley," he said. "Let's go see just what you've discovered."

They hadn't ridden far before Alexander realized that something indeed had changed. Where just last evening men had had to hurriedly crawl or duck-walk to avoid bullets, they now stood and milled about in small groups and congregations, no more sign of fear or apprehension in their movements than might be seen at a country square dance. His heart began to race. Could it be true? Might Charley be right after all? No, it was impossible.

Alexander rode on, came upon Colonel Henry Cabell near his battery of guns just behind the front line. Cabell was

WINDMILL POINT

standing with his hat off, laughing with a small group of officers. They all saluted as Alexander approached.

Alexander returned the salute, glanced east, could see nothing clearly. "What is going on, Colonel?" he asked.

"The Yankees have high-tailed it, General."

Alexander simply stared at him. "What do you mean, Henry?"

Cabell smiled. "I know what you're thinking, General Alexander. I thought just the same when the first report came in from the pickets. I just laughed, thought it had to be some sort of joke or tomfoolery, you know."

"Are you telling me the *entire* Federal army has withdrawn?" Alexander asked, unable to credit the report.

"Yes, sir," Cabell affirmed. "That's exactly what I'm saying."

"Where are they?"

The colonel shrugged. "No one knows, General. We've pushed pickets out over two miles now, but they've all come back empty handed. They found nothing."

"*What?*"

"That's what I'm saying, General. Nothing."

"Does General Lee know this?"

"Of course, sir. We sent back reports right away."

Alexander shook his head, stared off to the east. "I cannot believe this. It's... well, it's just impossible."

"I know it is, General, but it has happened nevertheless," Cabell replied. "Why don't you ride over and take a look for yourself. It's quite a scene over there. A bunch of us have already been over to see for ourselves."

Alexander took a deep breath. "Come on, Charley," he said, then spurred his horse.

They rode the short distance between the lines, then up and through the first Federal entrenchment. Alexander stopped, stood in his stirrups, saw nothing but empty works, garbage strewn everywhere, dirt and blasted trees for miles. There was not a single Federal soldier, officer, gun or tent to be seen. He could not believe his eyes.

"Well, I'll be damned," he said.

"Gone, General," Charley said.

"Where can they be?"

"Don't know," Charley answered. "No one knows, General. They's just *gone*."

Alexander smiled weakly, tossed his hands into the air. "A whole army cannot simply disappear, Charley. That cannot happen."

Charley said nothing, simply stared off toward the miles of deserted trenches, abandoned works, and empty roads that hugged the horizon, proof positive of what had occurred.

"And yet that is exactly what appears to have happened," Alexander admitted finally, trying somehow to fathom the whole thing. Porter Alexander brushed the hat back on his head, sighed. "Amazing, Charley," he said. "This is just... amazing."

The entire Federal army, well over 100,000 men, along with all its artillery, wagons, ambulances, horses, and baggage had seemingly vanished without a trace into thin air.

CHAPTER FIFTY-SIX

JUNE 13TH—EARLY MORNING

LEE

Lee had heard, for some peculiar reason, the commotion of the courier approaching long before he rode into camp, the horse's hooves resonating in his ear—distinct, almost providential—while still far down the Cold Harbor Road. Perhaps it had been a sign, a brief glimmer of God's design, a good omen for the Army of Northern Virginia. Of course, Lee knew fully well that the Creator's will was generally inscrutable, but who was to say?

Robert E. Lee had been up earlier than usual that morning and distinctly noted that daybreak had materialized with an unusual sense of peace and stillness. Used to the rumble of guns for so long, their absence dawned on him with a certain charm, just as the abrupt loss of an old injury or nagging pain suddenly delights the conscious mind. So perhaps it was simply the unexpected peace that made him focus so clearly on the rider as he approached. Or maybe it was the lack of activity at the front, or perhaps it was a case of that most unusual sort of anticipation that at times accompanies momentous events. But whatever the reason, he seemed to sense more than understand that something important was afoot, long before the facts had been laid bare.

Lee had thoroughly planned his responses to Grant's next move—whatever that might be—having conceived of every possibility far in advance. In that sense he had never been more prepared, yet, oddly enough, never before had he been taken so thoroughly by surprise. Indeed, when word came of Grant's departure he was almost shocked. Not only had Grant's mammoth army departed, it seemed to have literally dematerialized, and it had done so apparently in only a matter of hours, from a position only yards away from his forward pickets, as if some kindly wizard had simply snapped his fingers in order to—*poof!*—grant a wish.

Lee's initial reaction to the report had been the same as that of all of his staff and senior officers: incredulity. Surely, they all thought, there had to have been some mistake or oversight to account for it; roads not thoroughly checked, or areas along the front not properly investigated. So he ordered the pickets to push out a good mile or two all along his entire six-mile front, then report back once Grant's position had been pinpointed. That had been hours ago. Now all the reports were in and they were remarkably identical; no contact had been established at any point. Like ice left too long under an August sun, the Army of the Potomac seemed to have literally evaporated into the Chickahominy swamp.

No matter. Lee had long ago deduced Grant's options, and south of the Chickahominy River there were really only two. The Federal army could attempt to cross over to the south side of the James—a very difficult and risky proposition—or simply attempt another short, stabbing maneuver in yet another attempt to turn the Confederate right flank and barge its way into Richmond. Lee had naturally prepared for both, but assumed the latter to be the most probable. It was surely the simplest maneuver, and most in keeping with—at least from what he had so far been able to deduce—Grant's accustomed headfirst strategy.

WINDMILL POINT

Yet either of those maneuvers by the Yankees would require Lee's Army of Northern Virginia to move rapidly below the Chickahominy and deploy in a blocking position across the roads leading west into Richmond. From there, once the precise location and direction of Grant's army had been ascertained, Lee would be free to determine his next move. Until then he would simply have to defend against the obvious, and consider the hypothetical possibilities once he had more precise information. He realized, as well, that it would take Grant a considerable amount of time and energy to move his gigantic army across the James. So if Lee could redeploy rapidly, Richmond would remain protected and the Confederate Army reasonably safe.

"Colonel Taylor..." Lee called.

"Yes, General?"

"I'm afraid this army will have to move at once."

Taylor came close to his desk. "Of course, General."

"These are my orders," Lee continued, folding his hands together in his lap, giving Taylor time to write. "I want Hoke's division to march immediately for Drewry's Bluff. We have a pontoon bridge there, already in place. From that position Hoke will be able to rapidly deploy on either side of the James, depending upon what our scouts tell us of General Grant's direction and intentions."

"Yes, sir," Taylor affirmed. "General Hoke is to remain on this side of the river, but be ready to move in either direction."

"Exactly," Lee replied. "Then I want both Hill's and Longstreet's corps to break camp immediately and go into line between White Oak Swamp and Malvern Hill, covering all the roads leading into Richmond; Hill on the left, Longstreet on the right."

"Fine, sir," Taylor said. "General, may I ask ...?"

"Yes, go on...." Lee responded.

"Well, sir, just what *do* you expect?"

Lee rubbed his face for a moment. "Well, sir, without accurate knowledge of Grant's exact location and direction we cannot be sure. But, Colonel, I do suspect he will turn up the Long Bridge Road and make a run at Richmond, just as we have anticipated all along. But we must not become complacent. No, sir! General Grant may well have something entirely different up his sleeve, and we cannot afford to be caught napping. That is why we must push out and discern his whereabouts. I must know what is going on. Please see to that, Colonel."

"I will," Taylor replied. "And, General..."

"Yes."

Taylor grinned at him, pulled out a telegram from a small stack of papers in his hand. "This just came in from Fitz Lee, sir. I thought you would like to know."

Lee's heart began to beat harder. He took the message, began to read:

> Sheridan was defeated yesterday afternoon at Trevilian Depot by our two divisions, and retreated during the night, abandoning his dead and wounded, in the direction he came. I am moving along the railroad toward Hanover Junction, which place I will reach tomorrow morning.
>
> Hampton is moving between me and the North Anna, and expects to intersect my line of march at Beaver Dam. We hope to intercept the enemy as he crosses the Fredericksburg Railroad.

Lee read the message thoroughly one more time, then leaned back and smiled at Taylor. "Now *this* is good news, Colonel. My, yes," he said, trying not to get carried away. "This is exciting news, Colonel. Please send my compliments to General Hampton at once. And, of course, General Fitz Lee, as well."

WINDMILL POINT

"I will, General."

Lee watched as Taylor scurried out of the tent, felt his heart almost flutter with joy as a great wash of satisfaction swept through his body. He closed his eyes. *It's working*, he thought. *Yes, everything is falling into place. We have thwarted Grant's designs north of Richmond—thanks to generals Lee and Hampton—and now that Grant is once again on the move, we will have an opportunity to foil him here near Richmond as well. Soon the great Federal war machine will be out of both time and options, and, if bloodied once more, quite possibly shorn of the will to fight. Then perhaps the great Northern "cause" will finally implode for the sheer lack of desire, the war will come to a grinding halt, and the South will at long last be victorious.* He opened his eyes again. *Yes, yes*, he thought. *With God's blessing, it is all falling into place.*

CHAPTER FIFTY-SEVEN

JUNE 13TH—AFTERNOON

ALEXANDER

Alexander watched intently as the guns were hurriedly unlimbered, the horses led off, and the artillery pieces rushed into position. All around him men were digging with pots, shovels, cups, and bayonets, gouging out a new set of entrenchments and piling up cover for the gunners. The work was proceeding smoothly. The men, Alexander thought, seemed to sense that the end might truly be in sight.

Porter Alexander had selected the gun emplacements with considerable care, and he was satisfied that each offered broad fields of fire, for the ground around Riddell's Shop was even flatter and less wooded than it had been at Cold Harbor. While the army was now shy a full corps—Early having departed for the Shenandoah Valley earlier that morning—the position was still tight, well defended, and formidable.

They had broken camp and quickly departed the Cold Harbor entrenchments around 8 o'clock that morning. By 3 o'clock in the afternoon they had begun construction of a new line south of White Oak Swamp, stretching clear down to Malvern Hill, and covering all the roads west into Richmond. If Grant were indeed moving in that direction, he would not have to look far to find them.

WINDMILL POINT

Alexander was quite familiar with the area around Riddell's Shop. It was virtually the same ground that they had fought over two years before, when George McClellan had been in command of the Potomac army and had suddenly withdrawn from the gates of Richmond on a route south toward the James. Indeed, Alexander had stood behind the Confederate lines the day Longstreet's corps had broken through the Federal rearguard at Glendale, and, for a moment at least, had come close to putting the Federal army to rout, and perhaps ending the war that very evening. It was strange, he thought, that today the lines conformed so remarkably to just what they had been on that day two years before. In a way it was almost disconcerting to think that nothing had really changed. Yet Alexander knew only too well that—just as they had near Riddell's Shop two years before—the next few hours might well prove ultimately critical for their cause.

Dust spiraled into the air while men cursed and sweated and strained, as they labored the last of the guns into position. The infantry was pouring down the road and deploying into the trenches, eager to give Grant's army one last taste of Southern lead. Then, with luck, they might all go home for good.

Late in the afternoon, pickets were pushed out well beyond Riddell's Shop, and they soon struck a strong line of Federal skirmishers. At once the crack of rifle fire rattled in the woods to the east, and in no time it was discovered that the Yankee pickets were the advance of Warren's entire corps. Word of that was quickly relayed to General Lee in the rear, for little had been known of the Federal army's whereabouts. Alexander listened absently to the sporadic nature of the engagement between the lines, and noted that—at least along Longstreet's front—the contest appeared somewhat half-hearted. This was not yet the next great push, he surmised, but it was in all probability the preliminaries to something big.

Further north along Hill's front the fighting escalated considerably for a while, the rumble of artillery joining heavy volleys of musketry to produce a steady thunder for a few hours. That continued on into the early evening, but finally sputtered out to almost nothing. While no serious Federal assault appeared imminent, it did appear as though the Yankees had crossed the Chickahominy with designs of taking Richmond via the roads south of the river. All evening Alexander could see Yankee cavalry through his field glasses, operating in the open fields about a mile out. Warren's corps surely appeared to be the vanguard of something big, but until more of the Yankee corps had been spotted and identified it would be premature to draw any firm conclusions.

That evening the fighting settled down to almost nothing. The pickets merely pecked at one another. Occasionally the rumble of artillery rose again from up north, but nothing came of it. The air was warm, dry, and pleasant. With nothing to fuss about, Alexander had Charley cook up a good meal, and by nightfall they had pitched their tents and gone into bivouac, no more than ten to fifteen miles from where they had broken camp earlier that morning.

Just after dinner, General Lee rode by with his adjutant, Colonel Taylor, and Alexander wandered out from his tent a few yards to intercept them.

"Good evening, General," Alexander offered, smiling broadly.

Lee returned the smile. "Well, yes, good to see you, General Alexander." Lee gazed out toward the new line where the men were still digging and piling dirt. "I trust your guns are all in place by now."

"Yes, General. We've taken care of all that."

"I should have known," Lee said. "Tell me, what have you seen of the enemy so far this afternoon?"

WINDMILL POINT

"Very little, sir," Alexander replied. "Just the van of General Grant's army, is all. There have been a few hot clashes between the pickets, but that is all."

"I have been advised by General Hill that we have General Warren's corps on our front," Lee continued. "Is that your understanding, General?"

"Correct, sir. Warren's is all that we've identified," Alexander replied, "although I have spotted quite a bit of cavalry activity as well. I believe the cavalry is Wilson's."

"Yes, that is correct," Lee agreed. Then he stared at Alexander closely. "What do you make of all this, General Alexander?"

Alexander folded his arms across his chest and thought for a moment. "Well, sir," he replied, "I believe it is just what you have told us to expect all along. It appears General Grant is attempting to make another turning movement on our right."

Lee nodded. "Yes, I agree, sir," he said. "Yet we have only actually spotted *one* Federal corps. There are four others, and we seem to have no idea where they may be. That concerns me. And I think it odd that he would lead with Warren."

"Well, General," Alexander replied, "if General Grant *is* coming this way, I'm sure those four other corps will find *us* very soon. Then perhaps we will wish we didn't know where they were."

Lee grinned. "You raise a good point, sir," he said. "Perhaps we should be pleased that they are all not marching down out throats as we speak. Still ..."

Alexander laughed. "When they do come, General, we will be ready."

Lee nodded. "Oh, I know that, General. Believe me, I know that. This army has never been more ready to fight, and I have every confidence that we will inflict as much damage to Grant's army here on this new ground as we did at Cold Harbor. Indeed, sir, it is my honest hope that he try us here. If Grant attacks us here, I firmly believe that we will secure our independence on these fields. Perhaps it is fate, General. What we could not do in '62 just up the road at Glendale we will finally have the opportunity to accomplish now. That, sir, is a distinct possibility. I just wish I knew where those other four corps were."

"I'm confident they will show up soon, General," Alexander told him. "It has not been Grant's habit to remain apart from us for too long. Like a persistent suitor, he keeps calling and calling with great regularity."

Lee nodded, but was gazing far off toward the horizon. "Yes, I'm confident you are right, General. And please do keep me informed. You know I always value your judgment."

"Well, thank you, General," Alexander said. "I am flattered by your confidence. I will try not to let you down."

"You have never let me down, General Alexander. Now, good day, sir."

Alexander watched them both ride slowly down the line, stopping to chat with officers from time to time, and he felt a great wave of both confidence and affection for Lee. As Lee rode along, the troops stood and cheered as he approached, and even after all the months and years of war, it was obvious that they would do anything for him. Without Lee they were nothing. With him, the Army of Northern Virginia felt unbeatable.

Alexander turned and walked back to his camp, took a seat by the fire, and slowly poured the last of the coffee from the pot into his cup. General Lee was probably right. The next few days might very well determine the ultimate outcome of the war, but for the time being, at least, nothing of consequence seemed afoot.

CHAPTER FIFTY-EIGHT

JUNE 13TH—EVENING

LEE

R.E. Lee watched the light from the lantern flicker on a soft breeze, casting playful shadows on his tent's interior. He let his mind go blank, then tried his best to rethink everything, as Taylor nearby struggled diligently through a small mountain of paperwork.

While it was true that events were playing out much as he had anticipated they would, it was also disconcerting that most of the Federal army remained out of both touch and sight. It was still possible—although entirely unlikely, as Lee saw it—that Warren's corps was functioning simply as a rearguard, and that Grant's true intention was a withdrawal south toward Harrison's Landing on the James, just as McClellan had done in '62; in short, an inglorious retreat. But that seemed so far beyond Grant's usual bulldog nature that the prospect of a Federal retreat was for Lee hard to take seriously.

No, he thought. Either Grant would come to fight him south of the Chickahominy in his present position, or seek to cross the James, join with Butler's forces at the Bermuda Hundred, and move on Petersburg from the south. The first possibility still seemed the most likely to Lee's mind, but the second was hardly outside the realm of possibility. And the second, if successful, would constitute nothing short of a disaster for the

Confederate cause, for Lee had warned his lieutenants long before that the Army of Northern Virginia could never prevail in a siege, and that the only way to avoid such a siege was to stop Grant short of the James.

Taylor looked up from the last of his papers. "Do you have anything more for me this evening, General?" he asked, looking tired and drawn, hinting perhaps that he would like to retire for at least one morning before dawn.

"Yes, but just one," Lee replied. "I want you to tell General Hill to attack the Yankees across his front come morning."

"Attack?" Taylor asked, as if he had not heard him correctly.

"Yes, Colonel. If the Yankees will not be kind enough to show themselves to us, then perhaps we can *make* them reappear with a concentrated effort. You see, if Grant still has ideas of moving on Richmond north of the James, then I would think that the bulk of his army cannot be far behind Warren. So if we hit Warren hard in the morning, then my guess is that at least some of those missing corps will come to his assistance, and that we will know then where the bulk of the Potomac army is located."

Taylor smiled. "Ahh, I understand, General."

"Yes," Lee said. "We cannot afford to just sit and wait for them to do whatever it is that they have in mind. If we can create some urgency, then we might also be able to create some confusion, and wherever there is confusion, opportunity lurks. If they come up disorganized, for instance, we might be able to drive one Federal corps back on top of another, and so on. We must always be looking for an opportunity, Colonel. *Any* opportunity."

"Do you really believe that Grant will attempt to cross the James, sir?" Taylor asked. "That seems a very precarious maneuver to me."

"Quite possibly. If he joins with Butler, you see, their combined force would outnumber us so substantially that I do

WINDMILL POINT

not know how we could ever hope to defeat them. Moreover, if we become bogged down in a siege at, say, Petersburg or Richmond, I have maintained all along that against such odds we could never prevail. Our army has always done splendidly in the open and on the offensive, or perhaps on the defensive in a blocking position as we did in the Wilderness. But, a siege... never. We simply do not have the manpower or resources. So we must remain very, very alert, Colonel, and do everything we can to develop Grant's intentions."

"Yes, General. But are we not in a good position here to react to *either* of those strategic possibilities?" Taylor wondered. "We are, after all, no more than a half day's march from the pontoon bridge at Drewry's Bluff. From there it is easy marching to Petersburg."

"You are entirely correct, Colonel Taylor," Lee agreed. "Here we have a better defensive position than we had at Cold Harbor. And we also have the advantage of good interior lines, so we can quickly shift troops in any direction. So if Grant comes after us here we will certainly punish him. Or, if he moves away from us, perhaps we will be able to catch one or two of his corps in transit, divided by the river, and crush them here, north of the James. Those are wonderful possibilities. But both of those possibilities remain no more than fond aspirations until we have some clear information as to where the Federal army is located. Oh... one more thing...."

"Yes, of course."

"I should send a message to His Excellency, the President," Lee said. "I know the hour is late, but would you be so kind as to take it down?"

Taylor located his pen, found a piece of paper, and then waited patiently for Lee to compose his thoughts.

"Okay now, send this:

"At daybreak this morning it was discovered that the army of General Grant had left our front. Our skirmishers were advanced between one and two miles, but, failing to discover the enemy, were withdrawn, and the army was moved to conform to the route taken by him."

As Taylor finished writing, Lee requested, "Read that back to me, please."

Taylor read the short note, and Lee, satisfied that it covered the day's events, directed him to send it by telegraph to Richmond.

"Will there be anything else, General?" Taylor asked.

"Just make it clear to General Hill that he must hit Warren *hard* in the morning. We must give the Federals something to fret about, or they will not come running. General Hill needs to understand that."

"I will make it very clear, General Lee," Taylor promised.

Lee smiled. "Are you a chess player, Colonel?"

"Only in passing, General." Taylor broke into a quick grin. "Which is to say, not much of one."

"You are too humble, Colonel. With your quick mind, I'm rather sure you would be an excellent player. But at any rate, the war is now entering that phase that, in the game of chess, is referred to as the endgame: those last few, crucial moves wherein victory or defeat hang in the balance. Yes, Colonel, we have now come down to our own endgame of sorts, where each move or lack thereof will tilt the war one way or the other. There can be no mistakes now. Whichever side makes that mistake, or is fooled by the other in these next few, critical days, will lose this war for sure. Then it will be over: checkmate. Hill *must* understand that.... We must all understand that."

CHAPTER FIFTY-NINE

JUNE 14TH—NOON

HAMPTON

Wade Hampton understood now why at times will and tenacity alone were not enough to overcome the more pressing requirements of body and soul. For the past two hours his men's horses had been breaking down at an alarming rate, and many of his troopers were literally tumbling from their saddles asleep, left behind in the roadway just where they'd fallen. Hampton wanted to press on, but had to admit that that now appeared impossible. Neither his men nor their mounts could go on. So, just outside of Garrett's Store he finally called the long column to a halt, and issued orders for everyone to dismount as they came up.

Earlier that morning, Hampton had stopped along the Gordonsville Road at Frederickshall Station and telegraphed a report to Lee's headquarters. It was Hampton's intention to follow close on the Yankees' heels, skirting the bank of the North Anna River while shadowing Sheridan's right flank, then moving over to the attack whenever the first opportunity presented itself. But the Federal column had veered north toward Todd's Tavern, and Hampton knew it would not be wise to wander too far afield from Fitz Lee's trailing division. So, for the time being at least, it appeared he would have to wait and bide his time.

Wade Hampton had always been one to push himself hard, presuming, of course, that his men would strive to keep up with his rigorous pace. But there was no question now that his command was fatigued to a point almost beyond exhaustion. After six days in the saddle, they had simply ridden and fought themselves to a frazzle. Hampton himself had hardly slept for four days, and most of that time, it seemed, had been spent either riding or fighting. None of them had changed their clothes, washed, or eaten much to speak of since departing Cold Harbor, and those deficiencies had at long last taken a severe toll. The men were coated in dirt, many of them too dull now from lack of sleep to make sense of simple orders. Those horses that were still on their feet were weakening by the hour. It had finally become apparent that if he insisted on pushing much further, he would soon have nothing left to push.

So Hampton dismounted and watched the men as they labored past in the dust and insufferable heat. Then he spotted his son riding behind Butler's staff.

"Wade!" he croaked, his throat dry as the dust he'd been eating for hours. His son rode over slowly and drew to a stop. Hampton looked up, squinted. The sun was directly overhead, intense and painful to the eye. The dry, hot air hovering over the Gordsonsville Road felt like a furnace. He wiped the sweat from his face with the back of his sleeve.

"Yes, sir?" his son asked wearily.

"We will rest here for the better part of the day," Hampton said. "I would like to press on and catch Sheridan, but I fear we really have no choice. The men appear worn."

"I agree, Father. The men are quite weary and jaded. I can assure you of that. They all need rest and food. I hate to admit it, sir, but I feel the same."

"I understand," Hampton said. Then he smiled, tried to sound reassuring. "I'm just as tired, Wade. Listen, I want you to send out some parties to try and locate food—enough rations

WINDMILL POINT

for at least a day. Our men are starving. But we must be gentle with the people, very gentle. That must be understood." Hampton glanced across the road, then pointed. "Do you see that field yonder, Wade?"

Young Wade turned, appearing groggy, and tried hard to stare through the shimmering waves of heat and dust that hung over the road. "It appears to be a full field of clover."

"Yes, indeed," Hampton agreed. "Let's turn the horses out. That will do them well for the time being. And there was a stream not too far back, as I recall. The horses must all be brought over and watered."

"I will see to it, sir."

"Also tell the foragers to be on the lookout for oats. Without plenty of food these horses won't move another mile, and if they don't move, we won't either."

"I will issue the orders, Father."

"Very good, Wade," Hampton replied. Then he looked at his son closely. "You should get some rest yourself."

His son forced a smile. "No need to worry about that," he replied.

Hampton watched as the worn column limped its way into the small village, dust so thickly cloaking the riders that men could not see twenty feet in front of them. It had been a dry, suffocating, and exhausting trek. He stood along the side of the road and pointed toward several groves of trees, and the men gladly made their way to the shade. They did not so much dismount as fall from their horses into the grass. Many were asleep before they'd hit the ground.

It would take at least a day to feed and rest all the men—thus they would lose a full twenty-four hours in their pursuit of Sheridan—but there was nothing else to consider. They had all reached the limit of their endurance, and only a fool would push them further.

As the last of the column arrived and departed for the trees, he wrote another short report to General Lee explaining the reason for his delay, and sent it back by courier to be telegraphed from Fredrickshall Station. Then he watched as the foraging teams departed, all under strict orders to treat the people with decency.

That accomplished, Wade Hampton wandered out behind the store and found a rain barrel in the shade, still brimming with cool, clear water. What a find! Never before had anything appeared quite so inviting. He dunked his canteen into the barrel, let it fill halfway, then yanked it out, turned it upside down, and drained every last drop. Then he did it again, letting small splashes of water drip over his chin and down his shirt.

His thirst now momentarily quenched, Hampton tossed his hat aside, stripped off his shirt, and began splashing water across his face, arms and chest. It felt wonderful, and in minutes his skin actually became visible again. He pulled an old handkerchief from his baggage, toweled himself dry, and, with that, felt almost human for the first time in days. A few minutes later he located a fine stand of large, old maples behind the store and laid claim to the trunk of the largest. There in the shade the light breeze felt almost intoxicating. Within moments his son was back by his side, hat off, sweating profusely.

"I don't recall that it was ever this hot in South Carolina, Father."

"Go wash off in that rain barrel over there," Hampton told him, and as his son walked away, he began to feel the first signs of his own exhaustion creeping up his legs.

Wade Hampton sat for a while, sipped water from his canteen, and yanked a piece of hardtack from his bag. He ate a few bites then put what remained down. Young Wade returned and sat by his side in the cool grass.

"My goodness, Father," he said, pulling his legs up under his chin, "it feels almost pleasant back here."

WINDMILL POINT

"Yes, Wade," Hampton replied wearily. "Yes, it does."

In the refreshing coolness below the trees he began to feel his body relax, and with that the weariness soon washed through his muscles and consumed him. With no reason to resist any longer, Wade Hampton gave in to the inviting possibility of sleep. He yawned, pulled his hat down over his face, and stretched out comfortably in the shade. He had every intention of chasing Sheridan down and destroying him, but that would have to wait for a while. Just a while. The light breeze and cool grass felt wonderful on his skin. His eyes grew heavy. Hampton put his hands behind his head, crossed his legs, and felt sleep—like a great, tender darkness—descend upon him. He would worry about Sheridan tomorrow.

CHAPTER SIXTY

JUNE 14TH—AFTERNOON

LEE

Lee sat on his horse, just off the Longbridge Road in a field bursting with flowers and wild mustard, seeing none of it, aware only of his own confusion. Lee was trying to fathom what had gone wrong. Early that morning—when he had not heard the sound of guns rumbling on Hill's front—he had sent off message after message demanding an explanation as to why Warren had not been attacked, only to be advised in return that Warren's corps had disappeared overnight. With no one to assault, Hill had naturally sat immobile. Robert E. Lee was not used to being beaten to the punch by Federal commanders, and now it appeared to have happened two days in a row. He was not sure exactly what it meant, but pleased he was not. Where was Warren? Where was Grant?

So Lee had issued orders for every available scout to push out as far as necessary in the hopes of pin-pointing the location of Grant's army, but so far little, if anything, had come of it. Suddenly it seemed he was fighting nothing more substantial than ghosts and whispers. Where was Grant? Was Warren's corps the vanguard or the rearguard of the Federal army? Good questions. But there were no answers, and now Robert E. Lee was becoming frustrated.

WINDMILL POINT

Adding to his confusion was a steady stream of requests from General Beauregard in Petersburg demanding reinforcements to man the barricades around that city. Beauregard was convinced that Grant was on his way to lay siege to the town, yet without clear evidence that Grant was crossing the James, Lee could not abandon his defensive line north of the river. To do so would provide Grant the opportunity of achieving through little more than Confederate befuddlement, what he had not been able to achieve all spring: the occupation of Richmond. No, Lee was not about to hand away what one-quarter of his army had died that spring to prevent. Now, on top of the messages, Beauregard had sent along a staff officer to try and coerce Lee into doing what he had no intention of doing, and he was in no mood to deal with Major Paul, Beauregard's imperious surrogate.

"Good afternoon, General," Paul said, saluting stiffly.

"Yes, good afternoon," Lee replied curtly, returning the salute.

"General," Paul continued, "General Beauregard asks that I make it as clear as possible to you, sir, that the situation he is facing in Petersburg is rapidly deteriorating. Grant's army is on the way, and General Beauregard has little if any manpower to fend him off. The general requests reinforcements immediately, sir."

"Deteriorating in just what sense, sir?" Lee responded coolly.

"Well, General," Paul went on, "General Beauregard is convinced Grant's army is crossing the James with an eye toward moving on Petersburg. As you know, General Lee, we have nothing but boys and old men to defend the works. General Beauregard insists that you send him at least one full corps as soon as possible."

"*Insists?*"

"Yes, General."

"A full *corps*?"

"Those are my instructions, General: a full corps."

"Sir," Lee continued, his anger blossoming, "do you have any evidence that Grant has actually *crossed* the James? I mean, Major, Grant's army only disappeared from our front yesterday morning. To think them across the James already is beyond imagination."

"No, sir, I do not. Not, at least, in the detail you are suggesting. But the reports...."

Lee took a deep breath, tried to swallow his anger. "What *reports*?" he hissed. "If you have no evidence, then what are these *reports* you refer to, Major?"

"Sir," the major continued, seemingly unperturbed by Lee's rising hostility, "General Beauregard is insisting..."

"Enough!" Lee almost shouted. "I cannot strip this position of troops without clear evidence that Grant is crossing the river in strength!" He pointed east. "Just this morning Warren's entire corps was deployed across our front, Major....Here!"

"Sir, I repeat, General Beauregard..."

Lee held up a hand, would listen no more. "Go tell General Beauregard that I will do what I can, Major, but that I will *not* move from this position until I am entirely satisfied it is safe to do so. I will *not* hand Richmond over to the Federal army!"

Major Paul, crestfallen, turned away. "Yes, sir."

"Good day, Major," Lee said, and with that the courier rode off.

Lee took a few deep breaths, letting the anger in his chest subside. He was, of course, as mad at himself as he was at Beauregard's courier, furious with the situation he suddenly found himself in. What was he to do? He had been forced to send the bulk of his cavalry off to counter Grant's move in the Shenandoah Valley. Now, when he needed them most, his cavalry was a full day's ride away, and broken down from exhaustion. Without Hampton's cavalry he could not locate

WINDMILL POINT

Grant, and with no clear understanding of the enemy's current location and direction, his hands were simply tied. Now his scouts were out trying to find the Federal army, but everywhere they were bumping up against Wilson's cavalry and coming back empty handed. It was as if a giant curtain had been dropped from the heavens to obscure the Yankees' movements. The worst part of it all, of course, was that Beauregard might well be right.

Lee turned it over again and again in his mind, and by late afternoon finally came to a decision. If there was no more Federal activity across his front by nightfall, he would send Hoke's division back across the river to Petersburg, and put the rest of his army in motion toward Drewry's Bluff come morning. But it was far more guess than decision, and nothing about it felt right.

CHAPTER SIXTY-ONE

JUNE 14TH—EVENING

WHITE

Wyman slipped his shoes off, unbuttoned his shirt, and tested the dark water of the swirling James River with his toes. It felt cool and inviting, so he tossed his pants aside and promptly waded in up to his chest. After the better part of twenty-four hours on the march down the dusty roads of the Virginia backwoods, it was a pleasure of the rarest variety. And while a bath was surely a fine experience, Wyman could not even recall the last time he'd been able to stretch out and swim. So he closed his eyes and floated on his back, for a moment at least, as free of the dust and misery of war as any bird soaring through the clouds above.

The Sharpshooters had slipped away from Cold Harbor with the rest of the Army of the Potomac late on the evening of the 12th, marched across the pontoon bridge at Longbridge on the Chickahominy late the following morning, and by midnight of the 13th had arrived at Wilcox's Landing on the James. There they camped, to be moved slightly south the next morning, to a point on the river where a full fleet of boats waited to ferry them across to the south shore. That had all been accomplished without a single shot being fired as far as Wyman knew, and with a precision the army rarely achieved. On the south bank of the river there were no Rebels to be seen, so the regiment went happily into bivouac, taking full advantage of what appeared to

WINDMILL POINT

be a short break in the marching and fighting, to eat, bathe, and rest.

Wyman's regiment had been one of the first to make it across the river. The rest of his corps was still being ferried across as he slipped into the water, and far upriver he could just make out the engineers scurrying about on what appeared to be the beginnings of an immense pontoon bridge that would ultimately stretch clear across the James. But those things were of little interest when compared to the cool water, and the enormous sense of freedom that had suddenly overwhelmed him. After days in the trenches at Cold Harbor, the ability to simply move freely and float, play, and dive as he pleased, felt almost like an unnatural indulgence.

Soon others joined him in the water, and in the blink of an eye the mood of the regiment quickly changed over from a sort of morbid weariness to amusement. Strange what a little peace, quiet, and water could accomplish.

"Yo, Sergeant White!"

Wyman looked up, spit the water from his mouth, and spotted Joe Thompson running along the shore. He was waving a bar of soap overhead while at the same time trying to undress as fast as was humanely possible. Joe yanked his shirt off, then reached for a boot and—twisting and flapping—fell flat on his face in the mud. The sight, Wyman thought, was comical to the extreme.

Joe finally managed to right himself and then discard his trousers—hopping from foot to foot like a drunken circus performer—then yanked each boot in turn from his feet. That accomplished, he gave a mighty yelp and sprinted into the water with a splash. Thrashing wildly across the river, Joe finally made his way out to Wyman, half exhausted, but just as pleased with himself as could be.

"This is just wonderful, ain't it, Sarge?!" Joe cried, beaming from ear to ear.

"Who ever taught you to undress?" Wyman asked.

"Wha-da-ya mean?"

"I mean it is common knowledge, Joe," Wyman explained, "that it is a far superior procedure to remove your boots *before* removing your trousers."

"Oh, that."

"Yes, that."

Joe dunked his head underwater, then came back up with a grin. "I will admit," he said, "that when I am prompted to excitement I tend to forsake convention."

"Yes, I have noticed that," Wyman agreed.

Joe Thompson combed his hair back with his fingers, took a gulp of cool water, spit most of it out. "Do you recall that gal, Ruby Forrester," he asked, "with whom I became intimately acquainted up near Fredericksburg last year, Sarge?"

Wyman smiled, knew what was coming next. "In a manner," he said. "Are you going to regale me with yet another of your stories?"

"I am."

"Well then, go ahead."

"Well, sir," Joe said, setting both feet firmly on the river bottom as if his story would require a substantial platform to recount, "I will tell you truly, Wyman. That gal took me down along the Rappahannock for a nice picnic one Sunday afternoon, and before we'd even opened the basket she just stood right up in front of me and dropped her dress clear down to her ankles—didn't have a *stitch* on underneath! *Good* God Almighty! I will tell you, Sergeant White, my clothes done flew off that day faster than anything you'd ever seen, and without one bit of strategizing on my part. And me and Ruby did just fine for it. Yes, sir, just fine. 'Corporal Joe Thompson reporting for duty, Mam!' I told her, tossing my boots into the bushes. I tell you truthfully, Sarge, I ain't necessarily a thinking sorta man, and I sure don't spend much time wondering about how I'm gonna get my boots off next, yet here I am alive and well."

" 'Cept for the mud still all over your forehead, Joe," Wyman pointed out.

Joe frowned. "Don't care about no mud."

"Well, then," Wyman replied, "I reckon you have a point there, Joe. Whatever works for you, I guess."

Joe grinned, splashed around in the water. "This here is just wonderful, ain't it?"

"It is that," Wyman agreed, then turned and floated off on his back again. He drifted awhile, enjoying nothing more than the coolness of the water and the lazy flow of the current. The drift brought him in close to the bank, and when he glanced up he spotted what appeared to be a tree chock full of cherries leaning out over the river. Loving cherries, Wyman decided to investigate.

He scrambled back up the bank and found the tree amongst a tangle of undergrowth overlooking the water. Sure enough, it was a tree brimming with wild blackheart cherries. Wyman shimmied up the lower portion of the trunk, then grabbed hold of the first stout branch he came upon and pulled himself up into the heart of the tree. There he sat on the first firm branch he encountered and promptly enjoyed a small feast of cherries, all wonderfully plump and perfectly ripe for the picking. Pleased after just a few minutes of work, he began snapping off branches and dropping them down to the boys below. Many of them had spotted him feasting above, but did not possess either the nerve or skill to duplicate his effort. Wyman didn't mind; there was more than enough for everyone.

Later he climbed back down, took another short swim, then made for the regiment's bivouac. They were camped along a small stream that fed into the James, and it was as pleasant a site as he could recall. The boys all seemed relaxed and happy for the first time in months.

That night they fried fresh pork and hoecakes purchased from a nearby plantation, and bedded down under a cool, clear sky. With more water nearby than they possibly could drink, ample food, and no Rebels to bother them, Wyman White could not have asked for more.

As the sky darkened, Wyman sat by the fire and listened to Joe Thompson recount many of his favorite tall tales, and he laughed right along with everyone else until weariness finally overcame him. Tomorrow, he knew, the long drum roll would sound for them again. Then they would break camp and begin the dusty march toward Petersburg, and soon, no doubt, another pitched battle with the Rebels. But that was all tomorrow. Tonight the gentle crackle of the fire, the men's laughter, and the black, starry sky would do just fine.

CHAPTER SIXTY-TWO

JUNE 15TH—MORNING

ALEXANDER

Edward Porter Alexander had all his men roused well before the sun was up, with fires burning and breakfast cooking. Overhead the sky remained clear and black. The stars were just beginning to fade as the horses were brought around and harnessed. The drivers were smiling, teamsters whistling. There was a definite sense of excitement about the coming day. Orders had come down from General Lee the night before to be up and on the road to Drewry's Bluff by first light, and the men needed no special prodding to comply.

The sweet aroma of fried bacon, coffee, and wood smoke still clung close to the earth all around, though the pans were now long put away. Alexander had all of his batteries limbered-up and in the grass alongside the road, patiently waiting to take their places in the column. The infantry was already on the move, trudging slowly down the pike toward the pontoon bridge near the bluff, and the scattered dust from its march filtered back into the grass and settled like a smoky film on the waiting men, limbers, and guns.

While Alexander was hardly privy to General Lee's thoughts and intentions, it was not hard to determine what the army was about. The Yanks, it appeared, were in all probability headed for the James, then on toward Petersburg, and Alexander's newest set of orders was in reaction to that movement. Alexander was not concerned. The march to Petersburg for the Confederate forces was only some 25 miles, and, if pressed, could be achieved by most of the army in a single, long day. Whether they punished Grant's army one last time near Riddle's Shop or in the works surrounding Petersburg was of no matter to him, only that the enemy be soon located and punished.

As they sat in the grassy meadow along the road, a courier from General Lee came bounding up in an obvious hurry, horse in a great lather. It was easy to see he had ridden hard, and it appeared he carried important news. Alexander wandered close and cocked his ear. Yankee cavalry had just been spotted operating in strength on their front near Malvern Hill, and the courier carried orders for all divisions to temporarily suspend the march south. Expecting the next order to put them back on the road momentarily—and probably in a great rush—Alexander did not even unhitch the horses, and the infantrymen simply fell off into the tall grass alongside the road to wait.

There they waited. And waited. The sun rose, hot and steady, in the eastern sky, but no fresh orders arrived. Bees buzzed about in the tall grass and flowers nearby, as men glanced down the road, waiting for the next courier to arrive, but no courier appeared all morning. The troops sweated in place, waiting for orders that would put them back on the road again, but those orders never came.

Around noon the skillets came out again, and they started frying some bacon to eat along with biscuits and hardtack for lunch. Alexander could not figure what was going on, but he kept the battery horses harnessed, to be on the safe side—although there was ample grazing for them nearby—confident that any orders that came along would call for them to move off in a hurry.

WINDMILL POINT

Just after the bacon was tossed into the frying pans another courier finally came down the road in search of General Lee. He had a message from the cavalry officer down near Malvern Hill who had initially spotted the Yankee activity that morning. The courier stopped, showed the note to several officers standing nearby, and Alexander overheard that the demonstration they had seen earlier had proved to be nothing more than a Yankee reconnaissance. By noon the Yanks had disappeared back down the peninsula, and no other troops could be located behind them.

Alexander jogged back down to his guns. "Hustle up with that bacon now," he told Charley. "We will have orders to be on the road before we can eat it if we don't hurry. You know I hate wasting good food."

"What was all dat fuss about, General?" Charley asked, working the bacon back and forth with his knife.

"Nothing much it seems," Alexander replied. "Just some Yankee cavalry out nosing around."

"I'll have this bacon cooked up lickety-split."

"That's fine, Charley," Alexander told him. "I'll go tell the battery commanders to be ready to move on a moment's notice."

But nothing happened. Lunch came and went. The sun continued its trek overhead, but fresh orders never arrived. The hours passed slowly. Porter Alexander sat with his men in the grass. Some slept while others played cards. Still others read, or worked on letters home, waiting for something to happen. The bees continued their incessant humming, as flies buzzed the horse's tails and ears. There was no place to go and little to do. Like a clipper ship caught in the doldrums, the Army of Northern Virginia bobbed along the edges of the Longbridge Road, seemingly dead in the water.

CHAPTER SIXTY-THREE

JUNE 15TH—AFTERNOON

GRANT

Grant dropped his hat, tossed his cigar aside, and, for the moment, simply allowed the scene to wash over him. The vast movement across the James had been ongoing for some few hours now, staggering in its scope, momentous in its implications, transcendent in its meaning. He tried to take it all in at once, but that task was simply beyond him.

On the enormous pontoon bridge below, troops now filed in a steady procession across the James, as if from one end of the earth to the other, in an unbroken ribbon of blue. For as far as the eye could see, division after division marched on, while along the north bank bands played, men cheered, and regimental flags by the hundreds snapped in the breeze. Just behind him an unending sea of blue soldiers flowed in from the adjoining roads, taking up specified positions along the riverbank, all prepared to join in the crossing.

Grant crossed his hands behind his back, tried to absorb it all. He felt so alive, so incredibly light and free, that for a moment he thought he might literally disappear into the spectacle. Above his head the sky was perfectly clear; below, the water shimmered like a sapphire, and across the river the far shore awaited, green and inviting, almost precisely as he had envisioned it. Down the rutted road to the bridge men marched,

WINDMILL POINT

wagons bumped, and cannons roiled up whole clouds of red dust as drums beat a steady, martial rhythm. Across the river's blue surface a fleet of boats ferried troops from two designated points, as naval gunboats patrolled the waters both above and below the bridge. Guns, sabers, buckles, ship's anchors, all glittered in the bright sun, suffusing the entire spectacle in a bright, almost incandescent glow. More than merely a stunning scene, however, or even a grand symphony of movement, this was everything Ulysses Grant had hoped and prayed it would be. This was deliverance.

The great movement that had commenced on the evening of the 12th was now coming to its final fruition on the banks of the James. Wilson's cavalry had begun the whole thing, followed closely by Warren's corps, which had pushed out the Longbridge road toward Richmond and demonstrated in front of the Rebels for the better part of a day. Then Grant sent Smith's entire corps marching back to White House and from there by naval transports to Butler at the Bermuda Hundred. Hancock followed Warren across the Chickahominy, while Burnside's corps marched for Charles City Court House by way of Jones Bridge, with Wright close on his heels. It had all worked almost to perfection, and now Warren was in the process of disengaging and withdrawing back down the peninsula. The rearguard would be the last to cross over, but if things kept going as smoothly as they had, even that would not be long in waiting.

Grant himself had arrived at Wilcox's Landing late on the 13th, and yesterday had taken a steamer upriver to confer with Butler. From there he sent a telegram to Washington advising of his progress, before returning to greet the rest of his army as it came up.

Around 4 o'clock on the previous afternoon the work on the great bridge had commenced. General Barnard had hundreds of engineers on hand and many more infantrymen pressed into service. Their work was a marvel to observe. The bridge stretched over 2,100 feet in length and utilized over 100 pontoons, which were in turn lashed to boats that had been anchored for that purpose in the channel by the navy. It featured a draw in the center for the passage of naval vessels, and Grant fancied its erection nothing short of a miracle of engineering and human industry. Men scurried over its length like busy bees for hours until finally it was completed around 11 o'clock that evening. The longest bridge of boats ever built since the days of Xerxes, and all completed in less than seven hours. Indeed, it was the completion of the bridge—so well done, and in such short order—that had finally convinced Grant that his plan was going to work.

At once the troops started crossing over, and since then it had been nothing but a long and unbroken stream of activity: men, caissons, wagons, horses, artillery pieces, ambulances, all moving in an uninterrupted flow to the opposite shore. Already, the march toward Petersburg had begun, and Grant expected both Hancock and Smith to strike the city's fortifications late in the afternoon. That morning he had Wilson send out a brigade of cavalry to take a last peek at Lee's lines, and, according to Wilson's reports, the Confederate forces were still in a defensive posture near Riddell's Shop. So Grant knew that he had stolen the march on Lee, and soon he might even steal the war.

Now, Ulysses Grant stood on the northern bank of the James taking it all in, the architect, in a sense, of this extraordinary panorama. Beyond satisfaction, he had become lost in the moment, transfixed in a way that he had never experienced before. All men and women, he thought, at least once in their lives, should have the good fortune of feeling exactly as he did at that moment.

Surely no one who observed the army crossing the river that afternoon felt more satisfied or relieved than Grant, but in the end that success, he knew, had precious little to do with him.

WINDMILL POINT

No, it was not for himself that he had vowed to succeed, but rather for Lincoln, the country, and, in the end, that strange concept they all called... democracy. Abraham Lincoln had placed the mantle of liberty on his shoulders when he had accepted command of the army, and it was that heavy, almost unbearable burden that he intended to carry out of the dismal mud and trenches of Cold Harbor, across General Barnard's bridge, and deliver safely to Windmill Point.

Of course, that mantle was in fact nothing more than an abstraction, a vague conviction of the importance of democracy, an idea still very much in its infancy, yet an idea the world had long awaited and desperately needed. And like every infant, self-government would require both care and nurture before it could stand on its own two feet. For Grant that meant men who would willfully rise from the debacle of Cold Harbor and march once more with spirit and purpose. They did not march for him; that much he already knew. They marched instead for their own convictions, an army of free men animated by nothing more than their own ideas of right and wrong.

So, as he watched them cross over the long bridge, Grant understood only too well that what he was watching was far more than just another column of soldiers. Rather, it was history on the march, liberty struggling to emerge from an unforgiving past right before his eyes, complete with its own anthems, drums, and banners. This much was clear: the long blue column neither began nor ended on the James. It stretched far out over the green hills, backward into the past, well beyond the American Revolution, embracing such thinkers as Locke and Voltaire, reaching back still further and enfolding every man or woman who had ever dared dream of a better day. The great, democratic experiment had begun on the North American continent, and they all marched now to ensure that it would continue and prosper, even spread, perhaps, beyond those American shores.

Surely more lives had been consumed in freedom's long, desperate struggle than could ever be counted. Now in a moment of crisis it seemed that that great endeavor had turned to him. To that summons Grant had responded with the most sophisticated and well-planned series of maneuvers he had ever conceived, and that plan had now succeeded in delivering the Potomac army to the banks of the James, and perhaps to the very brink of victory. He had set about that mission with every fiber of his being, and realized now—as he surveyed the scene below—that the day had finally come when he could look history straight in the eye and know that he had been up to the task. That had been no small achievement in itself, yet as the long train of men and equipment rumbled by below him, Grant felt far more humbled than accomplished.

"General!... General Grant!"

Grant spun around. "Yes?"

"A message from Washington, sir."

Grant frowned. "Is it from Halleck?"

"No, sir. From the President."

He walked slowly toward the orderly, took the message, and for just a moment did not want to read. There was no one in the world he respected more than Abraham Lincoln, and the thought that the President might have been dispirited by his bloody campaign and the disaster at Cold Harbor had been preying on him for days. Yesterday he had telegraphed a brief report to Washington, but there were those in Washington who always twisted his words to their own purposes. Grant felt his heart quicken, unfolded the note, read...

> I begin to see it. You will succeed. God bless you all.
> A. Lincoln

WINDMILL POINT

Grant folded the note carefully, slipped it into his pocket, let the air out of his lungs slowly. Yes, this was one message he thought he would keep.

"Orderly!" he called.

"Sir?"

"Please bring my horse."

"Yes, General."

So, it was done. In the distance Grant could hear the sound of artillery rumbling—Warren still playing the decoy—and knew from it that Lee remained unsure of the Federal Army's intentions. From all reports it appeared that Grant had been able to finally fool his opponent, and gain the James without Lee's knowledge. If that were true, Grant knew that Petersburg would be virtually undefended, and soon he would force the Confederate army out into the open, where overwhelming Federal numbers would surely prevail. Grant's maneuvering might well have won the war, still there was no gloating or even a sense of victory in it; he felt far more relieved than triumphant.

Now it was time to move on. Grant's intention that afternoon was simply to cross the river and establish his headquarters at City Point, from where he could coordinate the overall assault on Petersburg. He smiled to think that as Warren withdrew from the peninsula, already Hancock and Smith were going into action. While the tail of the long rattler was still shaking near Riddell's Shop, the head was preparing to strike at Petersburg.

Grant could order up one of the naval launches, of course, to ferry him across the river, but that would never do. No, he had decided that he would ride down amongst the troops and cross over the James, one more soldier in that long line of blue: the shopkeepers, farmers, teachers, and lawyers—his army, his men. He would ride slowly across Barnard's extraordinary bridge, joking with the soldiers, reveling in their cheers. That would be his joy, his reward.

Then he would emerge at the far end of the bridge, stop, and look back for just a second, the one small indulgence he'd promised himself. It was the private moment that he had been waiting for, and one that he knew he would never forget: to see it all from that far shore, knowing then that he had not only saved his army, but in doing so had in all probability maneuvered Lee into defeat. The view would be clear and indelible, he fancied, an enduring image of absolute determination, seared into his memory from a spot on that green hill waiting just now across the river. The name was Windmill Point, of course, but for Ulysses S. Grant its true name was Redemption.

CHAPTER SIXTY-FOUR

JUNE 15TH—EVENING

ALEXANDER

Alexander sat leisurely atop a parked limber, gazing east. He looked long and hard through his field glasses, carefully scanning the area where Warren's corps had previously been deployed for any sign of activity, but there was none at all. No, there was nothing out there now but trees and open spaces, and all the reports that he had heard suggested that the Yankees had withdrawn down the peninsula toward Westover. Since departing the night before, nothing further had been heard of Warren, and the brigade of Wilson's cavalry that had been spotted earlier that morning proved to be nothing more than a reconnaissance. Now the Federal cavalry was long gone, and the situation was becoming somewhat perplexing. If the Yanks were preparing for an assault, they were certainly going about it in an unusual manner.

"General Alexander!"

Alexander turned quickly, spotting Henry Cabell walking toward him between the long lines of parked limbers. He waved. "Yes, Henry!"

Cabell stopped, placed his hands on his hips and shook his head mournfully. "General, may I ask, were you able to spot anything out yonder?"

"No, nothing, Colonel."

"I didn't think so," Cabell replied. "I've been looking myself all afternoon. The Yankees have flown, General."

"Yes, it would appear that way at the present," Alexander admitted.

"Just how long do you reckon we're going to sit here with the guns limbered-up and the horses in their harnesses, sir? We've been here all day."

"Yes, I know," Alexander said. "I've been expecting orders all afternoon."

"I'm sure General Lee has his reasons," Cabell said.

"Yes, I'm sure he does," Alexander agreed. "I have not seen him all afternoon, however, so I cannot say. I wish I knew what the situation was, but I don't."

Cabell stepped closer, lowered his voice. "How long would you have me keep the horses harnessed like this, sir? I fear they are becoming weary, and they could sure use some of that fine clover I see over yonder."

Alexander put his field glasses back into their case. "Not much longer, Henry," he said. "You have a point, and it doesn't appear as though anything much is going to happen today. Why don't we just go ahead and turn the horses out. That way when we are finally ready to move they'll be fresh to the task."

The order went down the line, and late in the afternoon the horses were finally turned out into the nearby fields. Not long after that, all the infantrymen who had been waiting along the road got up and returned to the same bivouacs that they had used the night before. Cooking fires were kindled, dinners tossed into pans, and tents pitched again. Not a shot had been fired, nor any Yankee infantry spotted all day across their front. Alexander expected fresh orders at any moment, but who could say what was going on? But no one fretted or second-guessed for even a moment. They all knew Robert E. Lee would make it right.

CHAPTER SIXTY-FIVE

THREE DAYS LATER—FIRST LIGHT

LEE

Robert E. Lee lay quietly on his back, staring at the dark canvas overhead, trying hard to make his mind focus. In the distance he noted the vague aromas of coffee and cigar smoke, the murmur of low voices just beyond his ear. It was very early morning, June 18th—so quiet, still, and dark—and while he felt unusually tired, he knew he had to force himself to think clearly. This was the end game, after all, and there could be no mistakes. Not now. Not today. But for days he'd been receiving conflicting reports, and he'd been left desperately trying to sort out just what Grant was really about.

On the 16th he had shifted his headquarters to Drewry's Bluff, overlooking the James, and since then Lee had been getting a steady stream of messages from Beauregard insisting that—if not immediately reinforced—Petersburg would soon disappear under Grant's enormous thumb. Smith's corps of the Federal army had been clearly identified as the assailant, but Lee knew that Smith had only been off on loan from Butler to the Army of the Potomac in the first place, and had recently returned by means of a circuitous water route. So Smith really meant nothing. Indeed, Smith's corps might be nothing more than a ruse, a carrot on a stick, meant to entice him away from the Richmond defenses.

For two days Lee had been pacing, fretting... worrying. Where was Grant? Was Warren's brief appearance on their front a withdrawal disguised to look like an attack, or an attack now cleverly designed to resemble a withdrawal? Without precise information, he was left to guess, yet Lee knew that he could not afford to guess wrong. He longed for those times—not so terribly long ago—when the dashing Stuart had ridden around the entire Federal army and returned with all the information he needed. Then, knowing virtually everything of the Yankee dispositions, Lee could pull the rug right out from under their feet. But now Stuart was dead, Lee himself had sent Hampton off with the cavalry to counter Sheridan, and all he had left to fill the void was conjecture.

He had received the first message from Beauregard during the early hours of the 16th. By then, Lee had already put Hoke's division into motion toward Petersburg, followed shortly thereafter by much of Longstreet's corps, sent across the river to face off with Butler at the Bermuda Hundred. Then for the better part of two days he and Beauregard had sparred back and forth over the telegraph, Beauregard constantly demanding support, Lee constantly demanding evidence that Grant was across the James in force. Lee still considered it far too soon for Grant to have effectively crossed the river—if, indeed, that was even his intention—and, consequently, any wholesale response on his part entirely premature.

Of course, this did not sit well with General Beauregard, and earlier that evening Lee had met with the first of three staff officers sent up from Petersburg to convince Lee that his views on the subject were wrong. The first, Colonel Chisolm, had briefed Lee around 1 o'clock that morning. Lee had not been impressed, but agreed to send Kershaw's division on to Beauregard the following morning. The second messenger was rebuffed by his staff, but the third—a Major Giles Cooke—would not be turned away.

WINDMILL POINT

So now Lee lay partially awake, trying to force his mind to work through his exhaustion, as he stared at the dark canvas overhead, trying to think.

"General Lee," Cooke whispered in his ear, "I regret deeply, sir, this intrusion, but I firmly believe you will want to consider the evidence I have gathered together. As the situation is becoming ever more critical by the hour, sir, I was forced to insist upon an audience. But I promise you, General, I will be brief and to the point."

Lee did not move or look at the man, just tried to make his mind remain steady and clear. "You did exactly right, Major," he said finally. "Now, just what have you brought me?"

"*General*," Cooke went on excitedly, "I secured statements from a number of Federal prisoners clearly indicating Grant's entire army is now before Petersburg; every single corps, sir. I have also taken the liberty of removing the corps insignia from many of these men to demonstrate their presence visually for you, sir."

Lee lay still for a while, swallowed hard, then thought for a moment. "Read a few of your statements to me, Major," he said.

Cooke dug through a large leather satchel, pulled out a raft of papers. "Yes, General, here we are... Corporal Albert Butler Benjamin, 2nd New Jersey, 1st brigade, 1st division, 6th corps... Ahh, that would be General Wright's corps, sir."

"Yes, I know," Lee said, the knot in his stomach twisting slightly.

"Oh, yes, of course...."

So Lee lay still and listened patiently as Cooke rattled off statement after statement, and soon it became evident that Beauregard was correct. How exactly Grant had been able to move so many men, wagons, and supplies so quickly over two rivers remained a mystery, but it was a mystery that no longer mattered. The facts were now painfully clear. Grant had gained the James, had crossed his army, and now Petersburg was under siege. The very thing he had warned repeatedly that the Confederacy could never overcome had now occurred, and the realist in him knew exactly what it meant. Lee sat up.

"Would you care to see the corps insignia we have collected, General?" Cooke asked.

"No, Major," Lee replied calmly. "That will not be necessary. You have done a fine job and are to be commended. Please return now, and tell General Beauregard that I am ordering this army to move to his support immediately."

"Yes, sir."

Lee watched as the young major gathered his papers and stuffed them back into the satchel. He then returned the salute as Cooke scurried away through the flap of the tent. Lee would, of course, concentrate the army on Petersburg as soon as possible in order to hold off Grant for whatever time they could manage. There was still in all of this, he thought hopefully, at least a chance....

Lee stood, took a few sips of coffee from a fresh cup Taylor had set at his side, and tried to think it through. The railroads... yes, he needed to telegraph the railroads to see if it might be possible to move the troops somehow by rail. Taylor could see to that. And he had to let Jubal Early know what had happened. Early, after all, was hurrying up the Shenandoah Valley toward Washington and just might.... Well, Lee was no longer in a mood for that sort of optimistic speculation.

He walked slowly out of his tent, called for Traveler, fiddled idly with his gloves. The morning was cool and moist, rather like the fall, he thought. He missed the fall, Lee recalled with sudden vividness, the changing leaves and the cool air slipping down from the north, the blankets, sweaters, and smoky fires. He missed many things, now that he thought of it, too many left unattended for far too long. But that was war.

Soon the tents would be struck, he would shift his headquarters to Petersburg, and from there try to direct the defense of the siege that would in all probability spell the end of the Confederacy. He wondered: did the cause of Southern independence really ever have a chance, or had the whole thing been doomed from the start? Would they think it his fault? Would it matter?

The orderly came with Traveler. Lee pulled his gloves on tightly over his fingers, fiddled with them some more, then took the reins. Off to the east, the first white tinge of light was just announcing its presence along the horizon, vague and milky. Who could say what it meant, what anything meant anymore?

He had not been fooled, out-maneuvered, or out-generaled, he knew. He could at least take some comfort in that. He had simply been swamped in a sea of men and resources that the South could not hope to match. The result, of course, had been the same, and there would be no award for second place. Lee knew perfectly well that the great game of war recognized only winners. But he would fight to the bitter end, of that he had no doubt, or, for that matter, much choice. History, Lee knew, did not deal favorably with the leaders of failed rebellions. Lee put his foot in the stirrup, swung himself up slowly into the saddle. Just behind, his staff was already mounting up.

Did the men know, he wondered? Did they understand that the long odds had just become infinitely longer? Probably not. They would fight on as long as he fought on, all of their fates and futures intricately bound in the mutual web of defiance and revolution that they had all spun together so hopefully three years before.

So they would fight together, possibly die together, and who among them could say how it would finally end? There was always a chance, the slim possibility that Grant might still commit a serious blunder. Lee had that at least to think about, to mull over, to hope for. But he would see it clearly straight to the end, just as he saw the brutal truth so clearly now. There would be no excuses, no self-serving lies or alibis. No, the endgame had now come and gone, the last crafty moves north of the James finally completed, and Robert E. Lee knew this one fact as clearly as he had ever known anything before in his life: the chess match was over, and he had lost.

EPILOGUE

While brilliantly planned by Ulysses Grant, the Army of the Potomac's investment of Petersburg was unfortunately bungled by his approaching corps commanders, and the opportunity to take the city by rapid storm—and thus the possibility of ending the war within a period of weeks or even days—lost to their sluggishness. Hancock's Corps would be delayed for hours on the morning of June 5th, due simply to the fact that General Benjamin Butler—a personal friend of Grant's, but of questionable military ability—would fail to deliver an agreed upon shipment of rations.

William "Baldy" Smith, meanwhile, approached the Petersburg defenses—manned by at best some 2,400 troops, along with a few old men and boys—in command of close to 16,000 men. Spotting almost no infantry opposing him, Smith would nevertheless spend most of the afternoon and evening of the 15th reconnoitering the Confederate position—no doubt a reaction to the disaster his corps had experienced at Cold Harbor—and ultimately squander the time and manpower advantage Grant's skillful passage of the James had gained. The objective was now Petersburg, but Cold Harbor was still very much on everyone's mind.

Hancock's corps arrived during the evening hours, but Hancock and Smith passed on a nighttime attack, in favor of waiting for dawn, allowing Hoke's division to march rapidly and reinforce the Petersburg defenses overnight. Despite the remarkable march and river crossing, the boldness and initiative often displayed by officers of the Army of the Potomac in previous battles and campaigns now appeared utterly lacking.

Ulysses Grant would prove to be entirely correct in terms of his tactical evaluation of the situation he faced, but sadly mistaken when it came to gauging the lasting effect the previous month's bloodbath had made on his army, and in particular the physical, moral, and spiritual catastrophe his troops had endured at Cold Harbor. The fighting spirit of the Federal army seemed to have been just as bloodied during Grant's overland campaign as had the ranks of its adversary, and it would never return to its previous ardor. As author Ernest Furguson points out, "A Cold Harbor syndrome, a reluctance to charge enemy breastworks, a memory of comrades left dying in the sun, hung over Grant's soldiers, especially his generals." And so the brief opportunity to end the war rapidly at Petersburg was lost.

North of Richmond, the Confederate cavalryman, Wade Hampton, came very close, however, to making good on his promise of chasing down and destroying Sheridan's horsemen. Dogging the Federal column all the way back from Trevilian Station, Hampton finally fell upon Sheridan's rearguard—Gregg's isolated division—at Samaria Church, not far from Charles City Courthouse. There on June 24th—now reinforced by another fresh South Carolina cavalry division—Hampton routed Gregg from the field, and came close to cutting Sheridan's retreat off from the James, where the Union general hoped to crossover and rejoin the Army of the Potomac. Grant, learning of the calamity, quickly sent infantry marching to Sheridan's support, and the Federal cavalrymen were finally able to gain the cover of Wilcox's Landing from where they were ferried quickly to safety.

Meanwhile in the Shenandoah Valley, Jubal Early easily defeated David Hunter's Federal army at Lynchburg, and regained control of the vital breadbasket of the Confederacy.

WINDMILL POINT

Then Early continued as ordered up the Shenandoah and crossed the Potomac River into Maryland. Just as Lee had suspected, Early's raid on Washington would be initially misinterpreted by Grant as nothing more than a ploy to divert his attention. Crossing the Potomac, Early was able to march almost uncontested directly toward the lightly defended Federal capital. Brushing aside a valiant effort to stop him on the banks of the Monocacy River near Frederick, Maryland, Early arrived in front of the Federal defenses before Grant's reinforcements could make a mad dash by water to stop him.

The opportunity to enter the Federal capital, cause mayhem, and perhaps set the Lincoln administration to flight waited. Early's small force could never have held the city, of course, but his cavalry could have entered Washington, put the torch to Federal buildings, and caused the Lincoln administration irreparable political harm. But even as John Gordon, one of Early's division commanders, sat his horse on the vacated Washington battlements peering down at the government buildings in the capital, a wary Early balked, then backed away from the city. With that would go one of the most extraordinary opportunities the Confederacy would ever have had to seriously damage Lincoln's chances for reelection in the coming fall election, and Early was left with little more than the necessity of beating a hasty retreat back to the Shenandoah Valley.

While the opportunity to end the war rapidly at Petersburg had been fiddled away by slow-moving Federal officers, the overwhelming strategic advantage seized by the Potomac army's crossing of the James would never be lost. Once firmly established on the south bank of the river, Grant held the Confederacy by the figurative jugular and, barring a collapse of Northern political and popular will, the only real question remaining was one of time.

Rather than a quick seizure as initially contemplated by Grant, the assault on Petersburg thus devolved into a siege, and a situation that Lee had already correctly predicted invariably meant defeat for the South. Fighting valiantly nevertheless, the ill-fed, exhausted, and grossly outnumbered Army of Northern Virginia hung on for another ten months of bitter, bloody fighting before—stretched finally to the breaking point—their long lines of trenches and fortifications collapsed under continuous Federal pressure.

Lee then sought to escape and flee with his army, trekking west in search of rations and an open rail line south. Ultimately running out of both time and possibilities, the Army of Northern Virginia would be surrounded at Appomattox Court House in April, 1865, where Lee, abstaining from further bloodshed, finally surrendered.

But that surrender was nothing more than the almost inevitable consequence of the events of June, 1864. Prior to then, the issue still hung very much in the balance until Grant engineered his remarkable withdrawal from Cold Harbor and crossed the James, effectively reducing the contest to nothing more than a question of resources. While hard fighting would continue for months, for all practical purposes the war had been decided on June 15th, 1864, while Edward Porter Alexander sat idly near Riddell's Shop with his fellow artillerymen, waiting for orders that never came, just as Ulysses Grant crossed the long pontoon bridge to Windmill Point. Indeed, years later that same Edward Porter Alexander became one of the conflict's first serious historians, and Alexander would later both admit and lament of Grant's crossing: "That was the time & the place, the date & the hour, when the last hope of the Confederacy died down & flickered out."

THE END

AFTERWORD

THOSE IN GREY

Walter H. Taylor: Was born June, 13th, 1838, in Norfolk, Virginia, and later attended the Virginia Military Institute. With the outbreak of Civil War, Taylor was appointed second lieutenant in the Virginia Volunteers, but on May 2nd, 1861, he was promoted to Robert E. Lee's staff with the rank of captain. He served in that capacity until the end of the war, and rose to the rank of colonel. Taylor was considered Lee's "right hand man," and was indispensable in running the Army of Northern Virginia. After the war Taylor became a prosperous businessman in hardware, and later banking. He died in 1916 and is buried in Elmwood Cemetery, Norfolk, Virginia.

Wade Hampton: Was born in 1818 in Charleston, South Carolina, to a family of considerable wealth. Hampton graduated from the South Carolina College (today's University of South Carolina) in 1836. At the advent of the Civil War, Hampton was considered one of the South's largest landowners and wealthiest citizens. He served in the South Carolina legislature, but his ideas regarding slavery ran counter to the pro-slavery advocates of the day. Wade Hampton believed that slavery was an inefficient means of labor and that the "curious institution" actually injured Southern business rather than helped. He was against secession—seeing war as foolish and unwinnable—but later raised the Hampton Legion once South Carolina seceded from the Union. He was wounded at First

Manassas, but returned to command a brigade of infantry under Stonewall Jackson during McClellan's Peninsula Campaign. He then eventually rose to the command of the Confederate cavalry after J.E.B. Stuart's death and served in that capacity until the end of the war. Hampton was eventually promoted to the rank of lieutenant general for his stellar performance while handling the cavalry wing. After the war Hampton served as governor of South Carolina, and later as commissioner of the Pacific Railway. He died in 1902, and was buried in Columbia, South Carolina.

Edward Porter Alexander: Was born on May 26th, 1835, in Washington, Georgia. He graduated third in the West Point class of 1857, and served on an expedition to Utah to quell a Mormon revolt. Alexander later returned to West Point as assistant professor of engineering. When Georgia seceded, he resigned his commission and joined the Confederate Army as a captain of engineers. Alexander served at First Manassas and was soon promoted to chief of ordinance for the Army of Northern Virginia. In addition to his oversight of the ordinance department, he was also involved in intelligence gathering and analysis, along with the signal corps. Porter Alexander was selected by General Lee as one of the Confederacy's first aeronauts, and he performed a critical role in that capacity during McClellan's Peninsula Campaign. He was eventually promoted to the rank of brigadier general in 1864, and was wounded outside of Petersburg, Virginia. Alexander returned to the army, however, prior to the final surrender at Appomattox Court House. After the war he worked as a professor of engineering, railroad executive, and planter. He also handled a variety of government appointments, most notably in Central America. In Alexander's later years he researched and wrote an examination of the war entitled *Military Memoirs of a*

WINDMILL POINT

Confederate: A Critical Narrative. Alexander died in 1910, and was buried in Augusta, Georgia.

Jubal Anderson Early: Was born in Franklin County, Virginia, in 1816, and graduated in the class of 1837 from West Point. Prior to the Civil War, Early practiced law, and was a member of the state house of delegates. He argued against secession, but entered the Confederate Army when Virginia voted to leave the Union. Early saw action in numerous campaigns from First Manassas through Gettysburg, and was promoted to lieutenant general in May, 1864. After his famous raid on Washington, Early was given command of the Valley Army in the Shenandoah, and was eventually defeated by Phil Sheridan at Cedar Creek. After the war "Old Jube" fled to Mexico, then Canada, but later returned to his native Lynchburg, Virginia, where he resumed the practice of law. He became the first president of the Southern Historical Society, wrote his own memoirs of the war, and later supervised the Louisiana Lottery. He died in 1894 at the age of 78, and is buried in Lynchburg, Virginia.

Robert E. Lee: Was born on a plantation in Westmoreland County, Virginia, in 1807, the son of the Revolutionary War hero "Light-Horse Harry" Lee. Due to his father's financial problems, Robert was raised in a small home in Alexandria by his mother, while his father sought extended medical treatment in the Caribbean islands. His mother was able to secure an appointment to West Point for him, however, and he graduated with the class of 1829. After graduation from West Point, Lee handled a variety of army positions, eventually including commandant of the military academy and later the suppression of John Brown's raid on Harper's Ferry in 1859. He married Mary Ann Randolph Custis in 1831, and fathered seven children. Through his marriage he came to own the plantation house and lands named "Arlington" overlooking Washington, D.C., which during the final years of the Civil War would be forever transformed into Arlington National Cemetery. At the outset of the war, Lee was offered command of the Union forces, but refused and promptly resigned his commission. He then offered his sword to the State of Virginia, and was later promoted to command of the Army of Northern Virginia in June, 1862. Lee's audacity and record of success soon catapulted him to legendary status across the globe. More than any other man, Lee's efforts held the Confederacy together until his army simply became swamped and surrounded by Federal forces. In April, 1865, he surrendered at Appomattox Court House, and returned to Richmond under parole. He later accepted the presidency of Washington College where he served until his death. Lee died in 1870, and was buried in Lexington, Virginia, on the grounds of Washington College.

THOSE IN BLUE

Wyman S. White: Was born August 11th, 1841, in Fitzwilliam, New Hampshire, a descendant of William White, who had arrived in America on the *Mayflower*. Educated in the public schools through high school, before the Civil War Wyman was involved in farm and shop work before first qualifying for, then enlisting in, the 2nd U.S. Sharpshooters in November, 1861. White would see action in almost all the Eastern campaigns, was promoted to sergeant, and saw action in the siege of Petersburg until ill health forced his discharge in March, 1865, one month before Lee's surrender. Reduced from 180 to only 125 pounds by stomach ailments, Wyman returned home by train, but was so ill he would require a full hour to walk the last mile from Fitzwilliam Depot to his parent's home on the outskirts of town, where he literally collapsed into his mother's arms. Nursed slowly back to health by his family, White would require almost eight full months to regain his strength. After the war he married and enjoyed a productive life as a stonecutter, farmer, police officer, and assistant tax assessor. Always known as "an upright good living man," Wyman White died in 1923 at the age of 81. He is buried in Fitzwilliam Cemetery, Fitzwilliam, New Hampshire.

John G. Barnard: Was born May 19th, 1815, in Sheffield, Massachusetts. He graduated second in the West Point class of 1833, and had a distinguished career in the Corps of Engineers where he served for forty-eight years. Before the Civil War,

Barnard worked in the construction of coastal fortifications and improvements in New York City's harbor. With the outbreak of war, Barnard supervised the construction of the Washington defenses, where he commanded until Grant's overland campaign of 1864. For his distinguished service he was promoted to major general. After the war Barnard redesigned the coastal defense system, established the parallel jetty system at the mouth of the Mississippi River, and wrote a number of scientific treatises. He died in 1882, and is buried in Sheffield, Massachusetts.

George A. Custer: Was born December 5th, 1839, in New Rumley, Ohio, and graduated last in the West Point class of 1861. He was immediately ordered to report to duty at Manassas, Virginia, where he began a remarkable military career. Brave, rash, energetic, dashing, and, above all, lucky, Custer experienced an almost meteoric rise through the ranks of the Army of the Potomac. In June, 1863, he was jumped from the rank of captain to brigadier general, and served with extraordinary skill and dash in all the cavalry battles of the war. At Cedar Creek Custer led the charge that broke Jubal Early's flank, and at Five Forks he virtually saved the day, and it was Custer's Michigan cavalry that cut off Robert E. Lee's escape route at Appomattox Court House, ultimately forcing Lee's surrender. After the Civil War, Custer continued his career in the Western territories, fighting the Sioux and Cheyenne. In 1876 he took part in an expedition into the Black Hills that ultimately led to the battle of the Little Big Horn. There, Custer rashly divided his small force into three battalions and led an unsupported attack against an enormous Indian village, culminating in the slaughter of his entire command. "Custer's Last Stand" bears an eerie resemblance to the error Custer had made years earlier at Trevilian Station: dashing headfirst once again into the midst of an undetermined foe only to become cut off and entirely surrounded. George Armstrong Custer died on the bluffs of the Little Big Horn on June 25th, 1876. What were believed to be his remains were later removed and buried at the U.S. Military Academy, West Point, New York.

Ulysses Simpson Grant: Was born in Point Pleasant, Ohio, in 1822, and graduated from West Point with the class of 1843. In the war with Mexico, Grant served with distinction, but afterwards suffered in the post war army due to being separated from his wife and children. As a result, he was forced to resign his commission in 1854 due to problems with alcohol, rumors of which would dog his later career. The next few years for Grant represented a significant downward spiral—from farmer, to salesman, to customhouse clerk, to leather goods clerk—that ended with the beginning of the Civil War and an unparalleled rise from obscurity. By the spring of 1864 Grant had achieved the rank of lieutenant general and had been given command of all Union forces, and in 1868 he was elected president of the United States. The last years of Grant's life were wracked with illness and misfortune, and he tumbled into bankruptcy when the brokerage firm of Grant & Ward became insolvent. With the assistance of Mark Twain, in the last months of his life Grant successfully completed *The Personal Memoirs of U.S. Grant,* which proved to be an enormous literary and financial success for his family. He died of throat cancer in 1885 in Mount McGregor, New York, at the age of 63, one of the most remarkable stories of both failure and success in American history. Ulysses Grant was buried in New York City.

ABOUT THE AUTHOR

JIM STEMPEL

Jim Stempel lives with his family in Western Maryland overlooking the Blue Ridge. His wife, Sandie, is on staff at nearby McDaniel College where she teaches astronomy and physics. His three children—a daughter and two sons—have moved on to professional careers. An avid athlete for most of his life, Jim is also the author of seven books ranging from satire, psychology, spirituality, to scholarly works of historical nonfiction. He is a graduate of the Citadel, Charleston, S.C.

Jim is considered an authority on the Eastern campaigns of the American Civil War. His recent book, *The Nature of War: Origins and Evolution of Violent Conflict* has been well received by an international audience for its willingness to delve into the basic motivations of human warfare and the true prospects for peace those motivations suggest. His novel *Albemarle* was nominated for the James Fenimore Cooper Prize in Historical Fiction.

IF YOU ENJOYED THIS BOOK
Visit

PENMORE PRESS
www.penmorepress.com

All Penmore Press books are available directly through our website, amazon.com, Barnes and Noble and Nook, Sony Reader, Apple iTunes, Kobo books and via leading bookshops across the United States, Canada, the UK, Australia and Europe.

The Lockwoods

of Clonakilty

by

Mark Bois

Lieutenant James Lockwood of the Inniskilling Regiment has returned to family, home and hearth after being wounded, almost fatally, at the Battle of Waterloo, where his regiment was decisive in securing Wellington's victory and bringing the Napoleonic Wars to an end. But home is not the refuge and haven he hoped to find. Irish uprisings polarize the citizens, and violence against English landholders – including James' father and brother – is bringing down wrath and retribution from England. More than one member of the household sympathizes with the desire for Irish independence, and Cassie, the Lockwood's spirited daughter, plays an active part in the rebellion.

Estranged from his English family for the "crime" of marrying a Irish Catholic woman, James Lockwood must take difficult and desperate steps to preserve his family. If his injuries don't kill him, or his addiction to laudanum, he just might live long enough to confront his nemesis. For Captain Charles Barr, maddened by syphilis and no longer restrained by the bounds of honor, sets out to utterly destroy the Lockwood family, from James' patriarchal father to the youngest child, and nothing but death with stop him – his own, or James Lockwood's.

PENMORE PRESS
www.penmorepress.com

HEAVEN CRIES
BY
STEPHAN SILVA

When Artemio Battaglia joins the *Regia Aeronautica* to become a fighter pilot at the beginning of World War II, he's inspired by the romanticized patriotism of the Fascists. His idealism is challenged when he witnesses atrocities committed against indigenous populations in North Africa, shattered after the officials he informs do nothing to stop the murderers. Their response is to transfer him to the most dangerous front in the war.

A disillusioned Artemio returns to Piacenza only to find his city occupied by ruthless German soldiers. He enlists in the war again, this time as a member of the Red Brigades. With a renewed sense of purpose, Artemio repeatedly places himself in peril, sabotaging German supply lines and giving aid to the Allies. But when his comrades capture a downed Italian pilot and schedule a hasty execution, Artemio recoils at the senseless violence. Once again he is called to act in accordance with his conscience and embarks on a bold plan to set things right.

Based on the experiences of the author's great uncle, *Heaven Cries* is a story of a young man who confronts the brutalities of war armed only with a courageous heart and an unshakable faith in moral decency.

When the Jungle Is Silent

by

James Boschert

Set in Borneo during a little known war known as "the Confrontation," this story tells of the British soldiers who fought in one of the densest jungles in the world.

Jason, a young soldier of the Light Infantry who is good with guns, is stationed in Penang, an idyllic island off the coast of Malaysia. He is living aimlessly in paradise until he meets Megan, a bright and intelligent young American from the Peace Corps. Megan challenges his complacent existence and a romance develops, but then the regiment is sent off to Borneo.

After a dismal shipping upriver, the regiment arrives in Kuching, the capital of Sarawak. Jason is moved up to Padawan, close to local populations of Ibans and Dyak headhunters, and right in the path of the Indonesian offensive. Fighting erupts along the border of Sarawak and a small fort is turned into a muddy hell from which Jason is an unlikely survivor.

An SAS Sergeant and his trackers have been drawn to the vicinity by the battle, but who will find Jason first: rescuers or hostiles? Jason is forced to wake up to the cruel harshness of real soldiering while he endeavors stay one step ahead of the Indonesians who are combing the Jungle. And the jungle itself, although neutral, is deadly enough.

PENMORE PRESS
www.penmorepress.com

Penmore Press
Challenging, Intriguing, Adventurous, Historical and Imaginative

www.penmorepress.com

www.ingramcontent.com/pod-product-compliance
Lightning Source LLC
Chambersburg PA
CBHW071553080526
44588CB00010B/895